W9-DEO-749

DELINQUENCY IN GIRLS

DELINQUENCY IN GIRLS

by

John Cowie

*Director of the East Ham and Roehampton
Child Psychiatric Units;
Consultant Psychiatrist to Starhurst School
for Maladjusted Boys, Dorking;
Chaworth Approved School for Girls, Ottershaw;
Princess Mary's Village Homes, Addlestone,
and Little Heath Remand Home, Newham.*

Valerie Cowie

*Assistant Director of the
Medical Research Council's Psychiatric Genetics Research Unit,
the Maudsley Hospital;
Consultant Psychiatrist, Fountain Hospital Group and
Honorary Physician, Bethlem Royal and Maudsley Hospitals.*

Eliot Slater

*Director of the Medical Research Council's
Psychiatric Genetics Research Unit, the Maudsley Hospital;
Honorary Physician, Bethlem Royal and Maudsley Hospitals.*

HUMANITIES PRESS

Contents

Figures

Foreword

by

Leon Radzinowicz

THE number of women and girls involved in crime has always been, and still is, very much smaller than the number of men and boys. Only one girl is convicted of an indictable offence for every seven boys.[1] When criminal statistics first came under analysis over a hundred years ago this difference in the 'penchant au crime' was a feature that sprang at once into prominence. Only a small part of it seems explicable in terms of more leniency in prosecutions: the police caution more than four times as many boys as girls, though we do not know whether a smaller proportion of girl offenders are brought to their notice in the first instance.[2] Not until we look at proceedings on the basis of care, protection and control do we find girls outnumbering boys.[3]

The discovery of the difference was followed by attempts to explain it, or even to explain it away. The hunt for hypotheses goes on, with little progress achieved. But the moral and social problems of the delinquent girl remain. These may be more complex than in the case of the boy, more closely interwoven with her emotional development and her sex. They also call for consideration of more appropriate ways to deal with her. The books on women in prison by Dr Smith and Mrs Xenia Field, and the more recent one by Mrs Kelley, together with the Report of the Committee on Estimates, show how crude, anachronistic and inadequate many of our correctional arrangements for women offenders still remain.[4]

[1] The figures for 1966 were:
   under 14: boys—21,648; girls—2,469
   14 and under 17: boys—32,948; girls—5,068.
[2] The figures of oral cautions for the same year were:
   under 14: boys—11,222; girls—2,385
   14 and under 17: boys—6,459; girls—1,942.
[3] Even here there are more boys under the age of 14. The figures were:
   under 14: boys—657; girls—588
   14 and under 17: boys—377; girls—1,611.
[4] Ann D. Smith, *Women in Prison: A Study on Penal Methods* (1962); Xenia Field, *Under Lock and Key* (1963); Joanna E. Kelley, *When the Gates Shut* (1967); *Eleventh Report from the Estimates Committee*, Session 1966–67, Prisons, Borstals and Detention Centres (599), HMSO, 1967, pp. xiii and xiv.

The authors of the present work have concentrated on the hard core of younger delinquent girls who are committed to approved schools. Their book does not describe research carried out under the auspices of the Institute, but we welcome it to our series: first because it is our purpose to encourage interesting enquiries from other quarters and second because this whole topic has been so persistently neglected. For that very reason we felt that it would appeal to a wider circle of readers than the more technical criminological subjects dealt with in some of our other volumes.

INSTITUTE OF CRIMINOLOGY,
UNIVERSITY OF CAMBRIDGE,
May 1968.

Preface

IN 1758 Robert Dingley, F.R.S., published a pamphlet entitled 'Proposals for Establishing a Public Place of Reception for Penitent Prostitutes'. Five months later Magdalen House opened its doors for the first time, admitting seven young women who were the forerunners of over 20,000 women and girls who have found their way into the Magdalen Hospital since its inception. A new chapter began in May 1944, when the Magdalen became the Classifying School for Approved School girls for the South of England. The term 'Approved School' will shortly be abolished, and the new title of 'Community Homes' is proposed. No matter the name given to establishments set up for the welfare of our wayward, deprived, emotionally disturbed and underprivileged children, the philosophy embodied in the original Constitution of the Magdalen Charity Foundation survives and, two centuries later, is worthy of repetition: 'Always observing in this and every other Circumstance the utmost Care and Delicacy, Humanity and Tenderness; so that the Establishment, instead of being apprehended to be a House of Correction, may be gladly embraced as a safe, desirable and happy Retreat from their wretched and distressful Circumstances.'

In 1958, the authors of this book decided to study all the girls admitted to the Magdalen Classifying School in that year, and observe their subsequent careers for four or five years. The problems of the interaction of nature and nurture are of primary importance in studies of this kind. It is necessary to evaluate in each case the relative parts played, on the one hand by inborn factors as shown by familial concentration of abnormal personalities and by constitutional defects in the girls themselves, and on the other hand by environmental factors.

The reader may be surprised to find in this book no reference to the problems of drug-taking among adolescents. In 1958 only the very first indications of the present day epidemic were beginning to show. Cases of toxic effects from glue sniffing had begun to appear, the habit having been spread by R.A.F. National Servicemen who sniffed the solvents used in aircraft repair work. About the same time misuse of amphetamines was beginning. However in 1958, in the group of girls studied in this book there were only two who had taken an 'orgy'-size dose of amphetamine. Both girls had toxic hallucinations and became temporarily

ix

deluded. Follow-up studies confirmed that neither of them lapsed into drug taking. In addition, a number of younger girls had been plied at some time by young men with drugs, whose effects were potentiated with spirits, in order to lower their resistance to sexual importuning. The myth that 'drugs' have effects as aphrodisiacs and sexual stumilants in our experience supplies most of the motivation underlying initial experimentation by the young adolescent. In short, though there were some among the girls of the 1958 series who had had occasional experiences with drugs, there was not one who had formed a drug habit or who had become addicted.

Our first thanks must go to the girls themselves for their willing co-operation during the Classifying stage of their care and later when follow-up information was being sought.

We are also grateful to W. J. Langford, Esq., C.B.E., M.Sc., J.P., Chairman of the Committee who gave permission, on behalf of the Governors of the Magdalen and with the approval of the Home Office, to V.A.C. to visit regularly and to have access to the Records of Information and other records concerning the girls.

After the Classification stage, some of the girls prematurely failed to benefit from their training, and other individual pro-grammes had to be devised for their continued welfare. The follow-up studies of this small group would have been impossible but for the willing help and advice of members of the Home Office Inspectorate. The authors would like to say, however, that the views expressed in this book are their sole responsibility and that any similarities with official Home Office opinions are coincidental.

Our general thanks are due to the Headmistresses and Staff of all Approved Schools concerned in this study, to the Probation Officers, After Care Officers, Members of Children's Departments, and to our medical colleagues who supplied us with relevant information about the girls whilst they were in their care.

We also thank Miss R. E. Miller, Headmistress of the Magdalen Hospital and all her Staff; Miss E. M. Downing, Secretary to the Headmistress; Dr C. Sommer, Medical Officer; Miss D. C. Chaplin and Mrs Neville Smith, Educational Psychologists; Miss Mary Hurford and Miss J. M. Maxwell for secretarial help; and Miss V. G. Seal for reading the proofs. JOHN COWIE
May 1968 VALERIE COWIE
ELIOT SLATER

I

Early Studies of Delinquency in Girls

THE literature on the subject of delinquency in girls is not more than a small fraction of that relating to crime and delinquency in the male. This is for many reasons. In the first place the delinquent girl is much less frequent than her male counterpart, and in the second place she is criminologically much less interesting. Her offences take predominantly the form of sexual misbehaviour, of a kind to call for her care and protection rather than punishment, and of their nature not liable to be made the subject of official action after the age of 17, or 18 under certain circumstances. These modes of behaviour are frequently and properly classified as 'waywardness' rather than delinquency. The indictable offences for which the adolescent girl is likely to be held responsible are in the great majority of cases such simple forms of stealing as shop-lifting. Delinquency in the male at an equivalent age is very much more varied, dangerous and dramatic.

It is accordingly possible to review the relatively small number of works in the English language which offer a descriptive account of delinquent girls, in a relatively short space. It is not possible to cover the large field of psychometric work, with a great variety of tests of attitudes and personality traits. The main interest in what follows will be on the psychiatric side; and to cover the development of ideas which has occurred, the material can be presented in sequence of time.

Women from penal institutions

An early study on a large scale is that of *Mabel Fernald, Mary Hayes and Almena Dawley* (1920), and concerns 587 (the total varies in some tables) women, two thirds of them prostitutes, from a variety of penal institutions in New York State. Their ages at time of present conviction ranged from 14 to 75 years, with only 15 girls aged 14 to 17 years. The contribution which this work makes to the study of adolescent delinquency is accordingly a very restricted one. Nevertheless a number of points of interest arise. It is, for instance, noteworthy that only 40 women out of the entire group had been convicted in a court of law before their sixteenth birthday. On this basis the contribution made to adult criminality by the persistence of delinquent habits from adolescence would appear to be a small one; and the finding stands in contrast to what is often held to be the case in males.

The work provides a detailed statistical analysis of criminological, civil and social data. Mental and educational tests were carried out, but there is little information about the psychiatric state of the women; 4 per cent had at some time been patients in hospitals for the insane. Early home conditions had been very unfavourable: 43 per cent had come from economically poor or very poor homes; moral standards were estimated as poor or very poor in 33 per cent; parental supervision as poor or very poor in 62 per cent. The authors show comparative data from a report on juvenile courts; girls were found to come from economically very poor homes much more frequently than boys (69 per cent : 38 per cent). There was a significant correlation between the age at first conviction and the estimate of home conditions. Some data were available about genetical factors; but unfortunately the tabulation is in the form of per cent of the sample who had a 'defective strain' in a father or mother or member of the fraternity: alcoholism 22 per cent, criminal record 16 per cent, epilepsy 3 per cent, feeblemindedness 4 per cent, insanity 3 per cent.

The educational background was also unfavourable; 11 per cent of the sample were illiterate, as compared with a somewhat unreliable census figure of 6 per cent. Educational tests were carried out for reading, spelling, handwriting, arithmetic. The median scores reached were very low, varying about the 5th grade. Although these women had mostly left school unduly young, the school grade reached was low for the number of years spent in school. The occupational history showed poor ability, great irregularity, a low wage. The distribution of intelligence (Stanford-Binet) was shifted to the left, with a mean mental age of 11·8, which the authors compare with an age of 13·4 years for Army recruits.

In their conclusions, the authors state their disagreement with Goring, in the importance he attached to constitutional rather than environmental factors; and they point out that, in their material such a constitutional factor as intelligence seemed to play a much less significant role than the indices of social and economic factors.

Sexually delinquent girls

A detailed, comprehensive and extremely competent study of 500 sexually delinquent girls and women was made by *Anne Bingham* (1923), a woman psychiatrist attached to the New York Probation and Protective Association. There is a fair amount of statistical detail, and also a large number of illustrative case histories. The case material did not consist of consecutive cases, but rather of those which had been adequately worked up over a period of five years. The age range of these women is not stated, but their median age was seventeen and a quarter.

The incidence of psychiatric abnormality was high. Only 28 per cent were regarded as normal; 24 per cent were feeble-minded and 13 per cent mentally subnormal; 26 per cent were diagnosed as constitutional psychopathic inferiors. The group also included 29 mentally ill women, including 10 suffering from dementia praecox and 10 suffering from manic-depressive illness. The average mental age was 10·4 and the average intelligence quotient was 65. Five per cent of these women were illiterate, and educational standards were very low. Their physical standards of health were also poor, with poor general development and nutrition, anæmia, defective vision, spinal curvature, heart lesions, etc. present in proportions from 24 per cent down to 6 per cent. Their past occupational record was also poor, with no good showing in type of work, quality of performance or steadiness of application. Sexual delinquencies had begun at an average age of 16, range 5 to 36. On the other hand these women do not seem to have been sexually initiated very young as a general rule; in only 23 were the first sexual 'delinquencies' in the age range 5 to 11.

The home background of these women seems to have been very unfavourable in a high proportion of cases. More than three quarters came from immigrant families living in poverty. The family would put tremendous pressure on the girl to start earning early, but show no interest in how she spent her leisure hours. Faulty habit formation in early life was regarded as a very frequent factor, with both punishment and indulgence haphazard, with low ethical standards in the family, and habituation to dishonesty.

Faulty habit formation repeatedly appears as an important factor in misbehaviour, and may be traced back easily enough to defective home training or none at all. Traits, which if detected early might have been modified or directed along constructive lines, become exaggerated and pathological when neglected or unskilfully handled and may really determine social disaster. It is evident that in the building up of inhibitions training in self-control is a most important factor, but one needs little acquaintance with the family life of these girls to become fully convinced that intelligent discipline is practically a negligible quantity in their lives. From infancy on, not only are they yelled at, jerked about and hit, but even these would-be deterrents from wrong-doing are not consistently employed. An act may be severely dealt with at one time which at another may be allowed to pass without notice, or punishment out of all proportion to the delinquency may be impulsively inflicted and the effect entirely offset by an equally impulsively given threat.

Bingham emphasizes that delinquency is basically physiological, an essentially individual reaction to an emotional situation. While heredity, circumstances of development and of environment, physical and mental condition when abnormal, play a role it is a contributing one. The fundamental factor is the personality. Certain personality traits have a crucial effect, and first in significance is a low order of self-control, the product of absent or ineffectual home training. Next in significance come a low ethical sense and a reduced critical faculty regarding personal behaviour. Others of no mean potency are exaggerated suggestibility and sensitiveness, timidity, craving for approbation, shrinking from ridicule.

Delinquent boys and girls

The work by *Cyril Burt* on *The Young Delinquent*, first published in 1925, was repeatedly revised and ran into a number of editions; we refer to the fourth edition, reprinted in 1948. The group he studied consisted of 123 boys and 74 girls, and they were compared with a control group of 400 non-delinquent children; ages ranged in the girls from 7 to 18 years. The aspects of delinquency enquired into included hereditary conditions, the home with its possible poverty, defective family relationships and defective discipline, conditions outside the home at leisure and at work, physical development, physical defect and disease, mental deficiency and educational retardation, supernormal and special abilities, temperamental conditions, habit formation, sentiments and complexes, neuroses. We shall be referring to Burt's findings in later chapters, where they can be brought in for comparison with our own. Burt's work is almost unequalled in its comprehensiveness, and his wide-ranging and penetrating discussion of all the problems he uncovers has made his book a classic. However, it is not well suited for comparison with contemporary studies. Burt worked with coefficients of association, which were related to the ratio obtained by dividing the frequency of a condition in the delinquent sample by its frequency in the non-delinquent sample; and in tabulating his findings he presents numerical estimates of the degree to which a given condition was a 'major' or a 'minor' factor'. No subsequent writer has analysed his material in this way.

The principal conclusions reached are perhaps of more historical than current significance, since the sample he investigated some forty years ago came from a much more underprivileged social class than the average of delinquent girls of recent times. Thus he found that over one half of the total amount of delinquency was found in homes that were poor or very poor. Overcrowding was important. Parental alcoholism, ill-treatment, neglect and vicious conduct were common. The highest coefficient of association ($\cdot 55$) was found for defective discipline; this was recorded in 61 per cent of the delinquents, as against 12 per cent of the controls. In 5 per cent of the girls physical development was excessive or inadequate. It is interesting that Burt comments on the physical over-development of many girls, who had records of being overgrown romps and tomboys at school, and burly hoydens and viragos in later years. Similar observations were made by Healy and Bronner (1926); and the Gluecks found better muscular development in their delinquent boys than in controls. However signs of bodily weakness or ill health were found in nearly 70 per cent of the combined sample, and more frequently in the girls than the boys; this took most commonly the form of malnutrition and respiratory disorders. On the intellectual side, there was a shift of intelligence to the left, with mean IQ (boys and girls) at 89 per cent; 8 per cent were mentally defective, with IQ less than 70. Educational backwardness was even more in evidence, with nine out of ten of the sample falling below the middle line of average educational attainment; three out of five were so far below it as to be classifiable as 'educationally backward' or worse, 20 per cent so 'utterly unable to read, spell, or calculate as to be classifiable as "educationally defective" '. The analysis of temperamental conditions is not conducted along psychometric lines; but the dominance of primitive and universal impulses over behaviour was found to be more prominent in the delinquents than the controls.

In resumé, Burt shows in his tabulated summary of conditions that the delinquent series are handicapped over a wide range of fields of observation: physically, intellectually, temperamentally; in their environmental conditions within the home and without; in the physical and the psychological state of their make-up. Only in a negligible proportion of cases (1·4 per cent of the girls) was no major factor assignable.

The work of *William Healy and Augusta Bronner* (1926) is of exceptional interest and importance, but much more so for the problems of delinquency in boys than in girls. The interest derives from the fact that parallel and comparable studies were made in Chicago and Boston, with very different results. The difference in follow-up results between the two cities could be related to differences in the ways in which the boys were handled administratively.

The primary samples were made up of 4,000 juvenile repeated offenders, studied personally by the authors, 2,000 in Chicago between 1909 and 1915, and 2,000 in Boston from 1917 to 1923. These constituted in each place an unselected series. However, the follow-up data are based on smaller numbers. A follow-up was made of 920 individuals from the Chicago series in 1923, and was successful in all but 18 per cent of cases. After omitting the dead (2 per cent), and those in institutions for the mentally abnormal (3 per cent), there remained 675 persons, 420 boys and 255 girls. The 420 Chicago boys were then compared with a series of 400 boys, as far as possible matching them in seriousness of delinquency, who appeared in the Boston Juvenile Court over the same years, 1909–14, successfully followed up to 1923. There was also a second sample of Boston boys, studied by the authors 1917–23, whose subsequent careers were known from routine procedure.

After-careers were classified as 'successes' or 'failures', with a very small number of 'indifferent' outcomes. 'Success' meant living in the community without known detriment to the community, and without engaging in criminality; 'failure' denoted actual delinquency, i.e. those with a court record as an adult, being adjudged guilty, and those committed to adult correctional institutions. The outstanding finding is the much more seriously criminal record of the Chicago boys than the Boston boys of the same epoch. There were adult court records for 50 per cent of the former, for 21 per cent of the latter. The crimes committed by the Chicago boys were much more serious, including for instance 14 homicides, totally lacking from the Boston series. Sent to adult correctional institutions were 37 per cent of the Chicago boys, 6 per cent of the Boston boys.

We need not follow the authors into the analysis on which they seek to explain this massive difference. Some of the administrative differences between the two cities may be briefly noted. What one might call ascertainment of delinquent boys was much better in Boston than Chicago, so that, proportionately to the population, there were four times as many. In Chicago minor delinquencies were being dealt with by the police to a much greater extent than in Boston, where even for these slighter offences appearance in court was usual. In Chicago there were often delays between the charge and the appearance in court; in Boston the two stages occurred on the same or subsequent days. Committal to a juvenile correctional institution followed in 40 per cent of the Chicago cases, i.e. more than four times as frequently as in Boston (9·5 per cent). Taking only the serious offenders, those repeatedly delinquent, in Chicago 74 per cent were committed, in Boston 30 per cent. In Chicago little use was made of parole, and there seems to have been very little supervision of past offenders; in Boston parole was extended to 21 years of age, and was supervised by groups of capable officers, for boys and for girls. Individual characteristics of the offenders had some relationship with the success or failure of after-history, but much less strikingly so than this huge community difference.

In essence, Healy and Bronner's work constitutes itself as a reasoned and annihilating indictment of current penological methods:

> The long array of data gathered in this book offers convincing evidence that the treatment of juvenile delinquency by some

prevailing methods is followed by an amount and an extremity of failure that is appalling. . . . This is represented by the astonishing figures of 61 per cent Failure for males (15 per cent being professional criminals and 5 per cent having committed homicide), and 46 per cent Failure for girls (19 per cent being prostitutes). (p. 201)

From all this it is a fair deduction that as a whole the treatment of delinquents is unwarrantably inefficient, particularly in the light of the fact that there is an abundance of evidence that careers of juvenile delinquency are in the main swervable. In both cities from which our data are gathered, the extent of Failure is such as could not be tolerated in business, industry or science. It seems perfectly clear that there was a time in the lives of the criminals we have studied when, if intelligent, forceful treatment had been undertaken, there would have been a fair, or even better than a fair chance that the delinquent career would have been checked. (pp. 210–11)

Now it may easily be known that through and under the law, a very poor business indeed is done in the handling of delinquents and criminals, for social offences seem certainly not to be diminishing and offenders who have once been in the hands of the law all too frequently do not cease their offending. One may readily argue that the difficulty is with the law itself, its machinery and procedure, in that it fails primarily to aim at maintaining itself as an effective social agent, or that the main trouble lies in the limits of legal education, study of the criminal law affording nothing of a scientific or business-like attitude toward the problems which the law attempts to solve according to its traditions and theories. (p. 4)

And, finally, one may say that perhaps of primary importance is the fact that, as yet, because of lack of application of scientific method in the field, there has been built up no large body of solid knowledge to be used as a guide to treatment. This accounts for the prevalence of the idea that justice is achieved, above everything, by the treatment of each and all alike, certainly a very pernicious principle, since it takes no account of the multitude of differences in human beings and situations, and brings about indiscriminate herding of individuals in institutions, with consequent tremendous moral contaminations and formation of anti-social grudges of which those who are students of offenders could give many examples. And, second, the judge very humanly influenced by his moods, notions, prejudices, has to make without aid from science many decisions which involve errors, if outcomes are the criteria. At any rate, science, which has such commanding victories to its credit elsewhere, has never, either as research or as practical guide, had its inning in this field. (p. 5)

This formidable charge rings just as appropriately to our ears today as it might have done forty years ago.

As noted above, Healy and Bronner found that delinquent girls did a very great deal better than delinquent boys. The delinquencies which brought them under observation were very much the same as in samples reported by other workers, i.e. 'immorality' in some form in the first place, stealing second, with running away from home, excessive lying, and general incorrigibility being charged in progressively lower proportions. The careers of girls were followed up only in Chicago. Their success rate (54 per cent) was markedly better than that of the boys (39 per cent); but they showed the same relationship between commitment and subsequent failure. The following table can be constructed:

	Not committed	Committed	Total
Success	61	77	138
Failure	25	92	117
TOTAL	86	169	255

The association of commitment with failure is highly significant ($\chi^2 = 14\cdot8$, $p < \cdot001$). Of the girls committed 54 per cent turned out Failures, as against only 29 per cent of the girls not committed. The authors point out some of the reservations with which one must regard the obvious interpretation of these figures (that commitment in itself has a bad effect); it is for instance fair to say that it will be the more serious offenders who will have been committed. This is more likely to have been a matter of moment in the boys than the girls. The comment can also be made that, even if the more serious offenders get sent to correctional institutions, the exceedingly high rate of failure would seem to suggest that this method of treatment is a mistaken policy.

Turning to the individual characteristics of the offenders, the peak age for appearance in court was 15–16 for girls, 14–15 for boys. No significant differences in the success rate were to be found between the various age groups among girls. Heredity is discussed in somewhat unsatisfactory terms, i.e. in terms of a positive family history for mental abnormality, alcoholism, delinquency, with the categories overlapping. However, the data provided show a phenomenon, which is not drawn attention to by the authors, i.e. a significantly lower proportion of cases among the girls (40 per cent) than among the boys (51 per cent) in which there was no family history of any abnormality. Delinquency in the family history is stated to have been present in 24 per cent of all cases, boys and girls, alcoholism in 32 per cent, and mental abnormality in 17 per cent. Presence or absence of a positive family history made very little difference to outcome, with the exception of mental abnormality, which increased the failure rate.

Some interesting statistics are provided about the distribution of sibships with one, two and more delinquents. Of families where there was more than one child, only one was delinquent in 62 per cent of cases, and more than one in 38 per cent. The economic level of the girl's family, whether destitute, poor, normal, comfortable, or able to afford some luxuries, bore no relation to outcome. The same was true of the family structure. Girls from homes broken by death, desertion or divorce (53 per cent of all cases) had very nearly as good a success rate as girls from unbroken homes (54 per cent: 56 per cent). In the same way, the presence of bad influences in the home, quarrelling, alcoholism, immorality, criminalism, worsened the prognosis by very little. This was so surprising to the authors, that they made a special study of 35 cases in which the girl came from a home in which there was criminalism or immorality. It was found that girls committed to an institution were equally divided between successes and failures; while of the 15 girls who had been placed out and not allowed to return home 13 had been Successes (out of the total of 18), and only 2 had fallen among the 17 Failures. This emphasizes the critical influence of after-care for success or failure. A similar effect is produced by marriage; the 121 girls (47 per cent of the total) who married had a success rate of 69 per cent, as against one of 41 per cent among the unmarried.

On the physical side, the interesting finding is made that both boys and girls were above weight standards for their ages; this was more marked in the girls than the boys, and 70 per cent were above the general age-weight norm. The authors attribute ætiological significance to this finding, and suggest that the physical over-development 'tends to draw a girl's attention early to sex life and that it leads her early to be attractive to the opposite sex'. Early onset of 'puberty' (by which one supposes menarche is intended) was not common. Physical illnesses and disabilities played no very important part; only 14 per cent of the girls had either gonorrhoea or syphilis.

Both for boys and girls, the mean intelligence quotient (base 16 years) was in the neighbourhood of 90 per cent, which the authors consider near the mean for the general population. The 255 Chicago girls who were followed up are classified into those who were mentally normal, 152; feeble-minded, 38; psychopathic personalities, 37; psychotic, 19; psychoneurotic, 8; constitutional inferior, 1. The success rate in the mentally normal girls was 62 per cent, in the others 43 per cent. There were 9 epileptic girls, of whom one was also psychotic. It is a great pity that the authors provide no account of the psychotic girls. Mental abnormality was slightly more frequent in the girls (40 per cent) than in the boys (35 per cent). Those who were actually ill psychiatrically, i.e. those diagnosed as psychotic or psychoneurotic, constituted 5·4 per cent of the boys, but 10·6 per cent of the girls. We shall have reason later in this work to emphasize the greater significance of psychiatric morbidity for delinquency in the female than in the male.

Girls from correctional schools

In the study by Katharine Lumpkin (1931–2), the really striking finding was one of very low average intelligence. She reported on 252 correctional school girls, 11 years and older and under 18, being consecutive commitments over a two-and-a-half year period. Tests of intelligence were given at the school, and showed that the mode of the group was in the IQ 66–75 class. They were mainly sexual delinquents, and 40 per cent were venereally infected; but there was a history of truancy and stealing in many cases. There was a high proportion of broken homes, in 40 per cent broken by death, with a break from all causes in 63·5 per cent. Social defective tendencies were prominent in the families, with alcoholism, epilepsy, mental defect and mental disease frequent, and showing a tendency to cluster; in 11 per cent of the families one fourth of the members were delinquent.

A very curious relationship was found when the girls were divided into those with major and with minor offences.

Unfavourable home factors were more prominent in the minor offenders, as shown in the table below:

No. of Unfavourable Home Factors								Major Offenders	Minor Offenders
None .	.	.	.	.	.	.	.	24	1
One .	.	.	.	.	.	.	.	34	14
Two .	.	.	.	.	.	.	.	61	26
Three	.	.	.	.	.	.	.	63	29
TOTAL								182	70

The author makes no attempt to explain this interesting finding. The most plausible explanation would appear to be that the major offenders were committed preponderantly because of the major or repeated nature of the offence; minor offenders were committed only if home circumstances were thought to be bad. This is an example of the difficulty, in research in this field, in distinguishing the causes of delinquency from the factors which are taken into account by courts in deciding on custodial care.

Delinquent women

We now come to the work of *Sheldon* and *Eleanor Glueck* (1934b). This is a very massive study of the life histories of 500 women paroled from a women's reformatory in Massachusetts, whose parole expired in the years 1921–25. The study is a very comprehensive one, including the family history and history before commitment, the personal record in the reformatory, history during parole, and follow-up history for five years thereafter. The reformatory in question was run by a pioneer in the work of reformation, and the records show a considerable improvement in the social histories of these women compared to their record in the year preceding commitment. The great mass of data supplied to the reader is statistical in nature; but detailed personal histories of 11 selected women illustrate the case material and bring it to life.

The offences for which these women were committed were preponderantly sexual in nature, including offences unknown to British law such as adultery and fornication. One fourth of the women had been sentenced for offences against public health and order, and one tenth for property crimes. Three quarters of them were native-born Americans, and 94 per cent were whites. They were mostly very young, but they were no longer adolescents; 41 per cent were aged 20 and under, and a further 23 per cent were 21 to 25. Despite their youth, nearly all of these women had previous records of arrest, probation, placing in correctional institutions, fines and other penal measures.

The women themselves suffered under a heavy incidence of practically every imaginable defect and handicap. They are described as a 'swarm of defective, diseased, anti-social misfits'. Their intelligence was shifted markedly to the left, with 11 imbeciles, 150 feeble-minded (IQ 50–70), and 76 borderline; 235 were in the normal and dull range. The bimodal distribution is of some interest, and will be discussed in Chapter 4.* The physical condition was mostly 'good' or 'fair', but four fifths of the women had venereal infections. A great variety of psychiatric abnormalities are diagnosed, including psychosis (10) and epilepsy (21); but in 73 per cent of cases there is nothing worse noted than 'emotional instability' or 'neurotic traits'. In 59 per cent there was a history of mental abnormality in the family.

The women had mostly come from impoverished families. Their fathers were inefficient or irregular workers, hardly able to support their abnormally large families; in many cases the mothers had had to go out to work to supplement the family income. The parents were of low mentality and in large measure illiterate; in less than half the cases were conjugal relationships between parents regarded as 'good'. Moral standards in the home were mainly poor; parental discipline tended towards laxity, and in only 8 per cent of cases was regarded as 'good'. In 81 per cent of cases there was delinquency or criminality in another family member.

The women fell well below average standards in educational achievement, both in length of schooling and competence. Many of them left their homes at an early age, and came early on to the labour market. The great majority of them misbehaved in childhood, truanting, running away, engaging in early irresponsible sexual activity, stealing; 95 per cent had 'vicious habits' by the time they reached adolescence. Over half the women had illegitimate pregnancies, and over half had been prostitutes before admission to the reformatory. Those who had married had done

* See also p. 30.

so in a casual and irresponsible way, and their husbands were often vicious or criminal wasters. Conjugal relationships were poor in four-fifths of the marriages, and three-fourths were broken by desertion, separation or divorce. In four-fifths of the cases the attitude of the women to their children was one of indifference or even hostility.

It is clear that the sample of delinquent women studied by the Gluecks is a socially extremely deviant group. There is so much abnormality of every kind, that one is compelled to wonder how much of it is relevant to the commission of an offence, and how much is more strictly related to the decision by legal authorities to confine the woman to a reformatory. Clearly, a delinquent girl coming from a stable family, which is prepared to take her back and look after her, would have a much better chance of escaping the fate that overtook the subjects of the Gluecks' study, than those poor exiles from an abnormal and broken home. What one may be seeing, in fact, may be not so much the relationship between these apparently ætiological factors and delinquency, but between them and the application of a particular set of social sanctions.

Comparison of delinquents and non-delinquents

An interesting study was carried out by *Healy and Bronner* (1936), comparing delinquents with their non-delinquent sibs; 133 families were studied with 145 non-delinquents and 153 delinquents, and eventually 105 matched pairs became available. The boys greatly outnumbered the girls (130 : 23). The report brings out the importance of familial factors. In 36 per cent of cases both parents had little or no education; in 20 per cent a parent had a court record; in 26 per cent the father was heavily alcoholic. In only 15 per cent of cases could one say that there was a reasonably good home, a reasonably good family attitude, and the neighbourhood was not inimical; in these cases there was a very high incidence of psychiatric abnormality or emotional upset in the delinquent child. There was disharmony between the parents in 54 per cent, and in 41 per cent disagreement about discipline of the children. There was a shift to the left in intelligence, with 36 per cent of cases having an IQ less than 90. Social relations within the family were unsatisfactory, with the delinquent children showing lack of love both for the mother as well as for the father.

The comparison of the delinquents with their matched non-delinquent sibs brought out some facts of medical interest. Many interferences were found in the early development of the delinquent children, head injury, a cross fussy babyhood, difficult toilet training, many or severe illnesses, enuresis, personality deviations, all much more commonly than in their controls. Distinctly good health was enjoyed by only 44 delinquents as compared with 75 of their sibs. There was little difference in intelligence between the two series. Temperamental differences were shown in a much greater prominence (in about one third of cases) of great restlessness or overactivity in the delinquents, who tended to be uninhibited and greedy for excitement. Ascendant traits, and not submissive ones, and feelings of inferiority distinguished the delinquent series. Feelings of rejection and insecurity, inadequacies and inferiorities, feelings of frustration, discomfort about family relations, jealousy, internal conflict and guilt, affected the delinquents much more than the controls; and 91 per cent of the former, as against 13 per cent of the latter, were or had been very unhappy. A psychiatric classification was carried out for treatment purposes, and approximately 20 per cent of the delinquents were regarded as having abnormal personalities, with very poor prospects for the future. About one third of the delinquents were thought to be in a hopelessly bad situation; and in fact practically all those who remained at home in such situations had a poor follow-up record. The rest were thought to have good prospects, and in fact 72 per cent of them had no repeat offence during the subsequent two years.

Criminological statistics

The monograph by *Ahnsjö* on 'Delinquency in Girls and its Prognosis' (1941) is of rather restricted relevance to our work. Ahnsjö devotes his first two chapters to a discussion of criminological statistics from the literature of many countries; and then reports his own work on 2,448 female inmates of the State Reformatory and of various detention homes in Sweden during the years of 1903–37. As his study is based entirely on official records, little use could be made of the scanty data on the psychiatric state of the parents and of the girls themselves. The mean age of the girls was 15·0 years, median 15·4. Sexual offenders were on average 1·3 years older than others. There was a high illegitimacy rate, 27 per cent to be compared with the expected figures for the general Swedish population of 21 per cent urban, 12 per cent rural. Perhaps the most interesting findings relate to the frequency of the 'broken home'. 75 per cent of the subjects (for whom information was available) were cared for by both parents immediately after birth, 16 per cent by the mother only, and by other relatives up to a total of 94 per cent; 5 per cent were cared for by foster-parents. At the time of admission to an institution years later, only 50 per cent of the girls were living with relatives, 23 per cent with their parents; 18 per cent were living with foster-parents; and a substantial proportion of girls had left home to go to work and live on their own. Of the 1,663 pairs of parents who had looked after these girls immediately after birth, only 55 per cent were still living with one another at the time their daughter was admitted to an institution; 11 per cent had been divorced, as against the 1 to 3 per cent which might have been expected from Swedish official statistics. Ahnsjö attributes considerable importance to 'bad homes' and broken homes as contributory causes of detention.

The report by *Bagot* (1941) is a comprehensive one describing work on a major scale which had been carried out in Liverpool. It has, however, much less significance for the problems of delinquency in girls than delinquency in boys. Bagot examined two samples, one of 1,263 boys and 95 girls in 1934, and one of 1,723 boys and 140 girls in 1936. The sample consisted of all cases in which over the two years chosen a juvenile had been found guilty of an indictable offence. The sample of girls, therefore, contains relatively few with sexual delinquencies, and nine tenths of the girls had been convicted of larceny. The material examined consisted of the reports on the family circumstances of the offenders made available to courts. Bagot notes that the juvenile delinquency rate was three times as heavy in Liverpool as elsewhere in England and Wales.

The sample described is obviously an economically depressed one. All but 2 of the 1934 sample of boys, and all but 6 of the 1936 sample, were elementary schoolboys. Medical reports, compared with those for a general school population, showed a considerably greater amount of malnutrition. Mental ability, assessed on headmasters' reports, showed a heavy incidence of backwardness though not of defectiveness. More than 50 per cent of the families were below the poverty line. Certain localities (wards) showed an incidence of delinquency up to ten times that of those with the least incidence.

A number of findings from this report will be used for comparative purposes in later chapters, and will not be discussed in detail here. The children came from large families, nearly twice the size on average of working-class families in Merseyside. Detailed data are provided about the proportion of families broken in specific ways, by the death of father, of mother, by desertion, etc; by and large these various types of disruption occurred more frequently in the families of the girls than the boys, and the total estimate of incidence of broken homes is given as 41 to 44 per cent for the boys, and 49 to 56·5 per cent for the girls. About one third of the families of first offenders contained other delinquents, with a higher proportion for the recidivists.

Bagot emphasizes the significance of defective discipline. He notes: 'where there are many children discipline tends to be weak owing to the many calls on the parents, and, especially when there are a number of younger children, the older ones are often left to fend for themselves.' 'It is definitely established that the delinquents are the older rather than the younger members of the family . . . this applies even more strongly among girls than among boys.'

A prognostic study

A prognostic study of great importance was carried out in Sweden by *Edith Otterström* (1946). She had the advice and help of Gunnar Dahlberg, at that time one of the world authorities on psychiatric genetics and epidemiology, and a statistical expert of the highest order. The poor lady was, accordingly, set to do her statistical work along the soundest lines, with the result that, though she complains of the laboriousness of the arithmetic, her estimates of expectancy of criminality in her sample are in the right form for comparison with corresponding expectancies calculated by Dahlberg for the general population.

Her sample consisted of 2,346 cases, i.e. 1,727 boys and 619 girls. The greater part of these children, 1,035 boys and 566 girls, had been removed from their homes by the Child Welfare Board in the years 1903–40; a smaller number, 692 young men and 53 girls, had been sentenced in a juvenile court at ages between 15 and 18, and after 1934 up to the age of 21 inclusive. This last group constituted Group IV of her material. Group I consisted of children, from extreme infancy to adolescence, who had been taken care of by the Board because of the badness of their homes and because there was a risk that they might develop into delinquents (246 boys, 244 girls). Group II were the children, from age 4 up to 17, who had been taken care of on a 'mixed' indication, i.e. with minor symptoms of delinquency made the more ominous by the discovery of bad home conditions (166 boys, 75 girls). Group III were all children, from the age of 6 upwards, regardless of the character of the home, so delinquent that special educational measures were deemed necessary for their correction, and also juveniles aged 18 to 21 who were found to lead a disorderly, idle or licentious life, and in need of special measures (623 boys, 247 girls). Otterström also divides her material into the cases ascertained in the two epochs 1903–25 and 1926–40. During the earlier time there was an upper age limit under the Delinquency Law of 15 years. All these children, while in private homes and other placements, were kept under supervision. Further information was obtained from parochial offices throughout the country, from the Census Office of Malmö, from Social Registers and Temperance Boards in the towns in which the children lived, or if in the country from vicars, district council chairmen, Temperance Boards and Poor Relief Boards; and records were also checked against the Central Penal Register, and against vagrancy warnings in the Police Gazette. In this way all children were followed up till death, leaving the country, or the 1 January 1944.

Otterström was able to make an estimate of the incidence of children falling into her four groups, as a percentage of the total number of children of corresponding age at risk. These percentages are for boys and girls respectively: I. 0·7, 0·7; II. 0·5, 0·2; III. 1·8, 0·7; IV. 2·0, 0·14. The striking feature about these data is the climb in the sex ratio boys/girls from 1·0 successively to 2·2, 2·6 and finally 14·3, with increasing degree of delinquency. There were other striking differences between the sexes. The age when taken care of (Group III) showed its peak in the boys at 15, in the girls at 17 years. There were of course sharp differences between boys and girls in the types of delinquency. In the girls, Otterström classifies them under four main heads: crimes against property and malicious damage, vagrancy, sexual offences and general delinquency, with vagrancy as the commonest both in Groups II and III.

Studies of home conditions during childhood showed the usual high level of disturbance and disruption; 35 per cent of the girls in Groups III and IV came from homes where the parents were not living together because of death or separation, i.e. slightly more frequently than the boys. Over the period of observation official Swedish illegitimacy rates would have led to an expectation of illegitimacy in the boys of 18·4 per cent and in the girls 18·7 per cent. In the boys Groups I and II, and in the girls Groups I, II and III showed much higher rates; and taking girls of all Groups 32·5 per cent were illegitimate. The children came mostly from the poorer homes economically and there was an excess of those receiving poor relief. Homes were classified into good, medium and bad, the last being found when there was parental neglect of the home, intemperance, immoral conduct, failure to care for the child; 45 per cent of the boys and 60 per cent of the girls from Groups III and IV came from such homes.

As regards criminality in the family, Dahlberg estimated the risk for men in the population of Malmö of finding entry in the Central Penal Register (for more serious crimes) as 9·3 per cent, for women 1·5 per cent. Approximately double the male incidence was found for the fathers and five times the female incidence for the mothers, the highest rates being for children in Groups I and III. There were rather more criminal mothers for the girls than for the boys. Incidence of delinquency and criminality in the sibs of the probands was not checked against official records, but about one in four of the boys and one in seven of the girls were known to have a delinquent sib. The alcoholism rates were high in fathers and mothers, more so in the earlier epoch, and more so in Groups I and II where bad home conditions predominate than in Groups III and IV where child delinquency dominates the picture. The data about psychiatric abnormality in the parents are very thin, probably owing to very inadequate ascertainment. The mothers who were known to be prostitutes constituted 40 per cent of the mothers of the girls in Group I, and respectively 16 per cent and 6 per cent in Groups II and III; rather smaller proportions were found in all groups in the mothers of the boys. In girls of Group III, who come closest to our Magdalen girls, the incidence of insanity was 2 per cent in the fathers and 0·8 per cent in the mothers.

Otterström has some thoughtful observations to make on the differences between boys and girls in their family backgrounds. At every point she finds the girls under greater disadvantages than the boys: broken homes, frequent change of home, poor economic circumstances, and homes bad in their total character were all more frequent among the girls than the boys. In Group III also, but not in Groups I or II, a higher proportion of the girls (37 per cent) than the boys (25 per cent) were 'weak' in intellect or actually subnormal. She offers the following explanation:

> It is conceivable that the girls are less hereditarily prone to delinquency than the boys, and therefore require greater influence from their environment to fall into bad ways. In other words certain genes, whose presence in an individual results on contact with certain environmental stimuli in qualities leading to crime and delinquency, might be sex-linked. Other characters such as prudence, timidity, lack of enterprise etc., which have always been considered particularly feminine—no matter whether they are conditioned by heredity or the result of early influence of environment—might be thought to be a guard both against delinquency and criminality, and girls only fall into bad ways when both these qualities and the intellectual equipment fail, and the external surroundings are particularly unsatisfactory. It thus seems as though boys are more sensitive to the influence of environment, and fall into bad ways even when this is only relatively bad, whereas far greater and harder pressure is needed in the case of girls.

We shall see later that, in its most general form, this is an idea which receives very considerable support.

The principal interest of Otterström's work lies in its prognostic aspects. The follow-up survey was confined to 2,206 cases, 1,637 boys and 569 girls (94 per cent of the total material). The risk of falling into delinquency or crime was calculated separately for each year of follow-up, and these risks could then be integrated to provide a total crime risk. For women in the Swedish general population this could be stated as 0·20 per cent by the age of 18, 0·41 per cent by 21, 0·67 per cent by 25, 0·82 per cent by 30, and then by diminishing increments to 1·11 at the age of 50. But the expectations of criminality within ten years after release from care was for women of Group III 5 per cent, and for women of Group IV 24 per cent. There are other calculations, each balanced against a properly calculated population risk, as regards temperance, vagrancy, self-support and social position. They may be tabulated as follows:

Per cent expectation up to age of 35, of:	Women from Group				General population
	I	II	III	IV	
Criminality . . .	5	12	21	37	0·80
Vagrancy	2	14	17	10	0·14
Poor relief	11	18	33	22	—

These figures are much more favourable than the corresponding ones for men. For comparison, the per cent expectations of criminality by the age of 40 were for men in the Groups I–IV respectively 24, 37, 47 and 51. The differences between men and women were much smaller in respect of expectations of vagrancy and of poor relief. Although the boys later on did so much worse, in respect of criminality, than the girls, yet compared with general population risks (7·7 per cent for men by 35, 0·8 per cent for women) the situation is not quite as black for them as first appearances suggest. One may calculate that the success rate, as a percentage of the non-criminal expectations of the general population, was for men of Group III 59 per cent, for women of Group III 78 per cent.

Otterström examines her data to find whether any of the personal or group data are related to failure or success on follow-up. A higher lapse rate during follow-up was found to be associated with the presence of criminal parents, with inebriety in the father and generally bad conditions in the home. Legitimacy or illegitimacy were without effect, and so were the degree of intelligence, the age of contact with social authorities, the age of being taken in charge and the period of detention. These results must be regarded as not very instructive; it may be that the main factors which decide social success or social failure for adults who have come from bad homes may be those which impinge on them in the course of adult life, rather than the hang-over effects of earlier years.

Delinquents and controls

The work of *Maud Merrill* (1947) suffers from the defect of not considering the girls she studied in isolation from the boys. Her sample consisted of 300 unselected cases of delinquent children referred to a juvenile court in a rural county in California between April 1933 and June 1935; and it was compared with a control group of non-delinquent schoolchildren from the same communities, attending the same schools, matched for sex, age and locality. In each series there were 252 boys and 58 girls, and the mean ages both of boys and girls was 15 years 4 months. Merrill also carried out a follow-up study of 100 each from the delinquent and from the control series, the delinquents then averaging 20 and the controls 19 years of age. The study is both statistical and clinical. There is an abundance of interview material and psychological test data; and the discussion is enriched with numerous sketches of individual children.

The principal findings fall in line with other published work. Disruption of home life was much more frequent in the delinquent series than the others, and both parents living together were found in the former in 49 per cent, in the controls in 73 per cent. Death of one parent, divorce, separation and desertion were all more frequent in the delinquent series. In home adjustment (measured by the Bell Inventory), there was some difference between delinquents and controls, but not a very large one; it was rated as unsatisfactory or very unsatisfactory in 35 per cent of the former as against 22 per cent of the latter. There were much bigger differences between the two series in respect of both affection and discipline at home. A parental relationship rated as definitely hostile is shown (in a histogram) in approximately 20 per cent of delinquents as against 2 per cent of controls. The difference in respect of discipline, rated as very lax, or extremely rigid, or very erratic, was even greater, being shown in the histogram at about a 77 per cent level in delinquents as compared with about 5 per cent in controls. An attitude of indifference or worse towards the home was found in 47 per cent of delinquents, and 19 per cent of controls. The child was fond of both parents in 30 per cent of the delinquents, 41 per cent of the controls; and to some degree hostile towards them in 26 per cent as against 12 per cent. No precise data on sibship size are given, but the delinquent boys came from larger families, and 40 per cent of them had delinquent siblings.

While data about home relationships are the most significant, some other findings are of interest. Although the delinquent and the control children were neighbours, their economic status differed, being regarded as 'comfortable' in only 12 per cent of the former, as against 32 per cent of the latter. The occupations of the parents were more frequently unskilled in the delinquent series. Both the conduct of the child at school, and his attitude towards school, were much less favourable in the delinquent series. The mean intelligence of the delinquent series was slightly the lesser, but the difference on the Stanford Binet (IQ 86·7: 89·3) is said to be non-significant. A very suggestive finding was made when intelligence was correlated with place in school. In the control series 29 per cent were regarded as placed too high in school for their intelligence level, and 28 per cent too low; in the delinquent series the corresponding figures are 40 per cent and 21 per cent. We know of no corresponding data from the reports of other workers; but it would seem to be desirable to enquire whether delinquency, which is certainly associated with poor performance at school, is related with an educational regime which tries the child's abilities too high.

Merrill's follow-up study is not very instructive. Needless to say the level of adjustment was much better in the control than the delinquent series. Of the 257 individuals in the delinquent series, for whom data were available, 123 (48 per cent) recidivated during the time span observed.

Retrospect

Looking over the work done between 1920 and 1950, we see that these decades were responsible for a number of important studies, some of them of sophisticated design. The outstanding examples are the contributions made by Cyril Burt, by William Healy and Augusta Bronner, and by Edith Otterström. In the case of all of them, as well as in other work mentioned, the focus is much more on the delinquent boy than the delinquent girl. In fact during this epoch there seems to have been little recognition that delinquency in the two sexes is such a different phenomenon, in its causes and its manifestations, that in planning and reporting on an investigation the two sexes should never be compounded. We shall find that this lesson is still far from having been thoroughly learned. Of all workers only Edith Otterström, probably under the inspiration of Gunnar Dahlberg, concerns herself with the male-female difference and offers a biological theory to account for it. Where boys can be compared with girls, it is the latter who have far the more serious handicaps, worse homes, lower intelligence ratings, more mental abnormality.

In the early studies much emphasis is placed on poverty and overcrowding and on the economic disadvantages of the homes from which delinquents came. The family history in its genetical aspects does not come in for much consideration, but workers are impressed by alcoholism and vicious behaviour in the parents. Some workers emphasize defective discipline and training, and unfavourable habit formation. Children are burdened by physical defects and more than an average amount of illness, but several workers note that both boys and girls are overgrown for their age. Educational standards are bad, and intelligence ratings are markedly lower than for control groups, and are indeed all the lower the further one goes back in the history of investigation.

By and large the reader is provided with the impression that delinquency is a psychologically highly abnormal phenomenon, affecting only a small subclass of the population, a subclass eking out its existence in circumstances of extreme deprivation.

II

Delinquency in Girls Since 1950

THE shift in emphasis that occurs as we enter the modern era shows itself only very gradually. Investigators are still confined to traditional methods of exploration; but they tend to become increasingly self-critical. Moreover, some interest is taken in the differences between the sexes.

Girls in borstals

We begin with the work of *Epps* (1951, 1954). In the first of these papers she studied 300 delinquent girls in borstal institutions, aged 16 to 23, with mean of 19 years; and then three years later she studied 100 of them who had been recalled for further training owing to unsatisfactory behaviour, or who had had prison sentences. Of the original 300, the largest number (182) had committed offences against property, such as larceny, 101 offences against the person; only 9 were regarded as sexual offenders. They represent, therefore, a more seriously delinquent group of girls than those studied in the present work. However, almost exactly half of the 300 had previously been in an approved school.

Epps records a number of sociological data, such as the frequency of broken or unsatisfactory homes, the high incidence of delinquency in other members of the family, the past unsatisfactory work record. Thirty girls were illegitimate. In this series there was no shift towards early birth order, as 65 were eldest children as against 85 youngest children. Apart from a high incidence of venereal infection, the physical state of the girls was fair, and their physique as shown in height and weight robust. They were however on average of low intelligence. On progressive matrices 144 were within normal limits, 134 subnormal, 11 superior; the average score was 35, below the lower limit of average intelligence. Neurotic symptoms (in 63 girls) and emotional instability (in 83 girls) were prominent.

In her review of 1954, Epps considered the cases of 100 girls who could be regarded as the failures of borstal training, and compared their records with those of the original 300, which earlier had included them. Very little in the way of differences between the two groups in the incidence of social and psychiatric factors was found, and probably none of the differences statistically significant. However, there was a higher incidence of homes broken by separation or divorce in the 1954 group of 100 girls, and somewhat higher incidences of emotional instability and neurotic trends. These are quite likely to be factors which interfere with satisfactory training. Epps points out that the majority of girls after training are likely on their own wish to return to their homes, however unsatisfactory those homes may be.

Girl and boy sex offenders

In the work by *Atcheson and Williams* (1954), information was gathered from a comparison of sex offenders among boys and girls with others arraigned for offences of other kinds. The authors state that 90 per cent of all sex offenders are referred by the Toronto Juvenile and Family Court for clinical investigation, and that during the years 1939 to 1948, 2,516 boys and 596 girls, all over the age of 7 and under the age of 16, were so referred; these included 6 per cent of the boys and 35 per cent of the girls arraigned for offences of any kind. The authors took 283 sex offenders, 116 boys and 167 girls, and compared them with non-sex offenders, 126 boys and 168 girls. Among sex offenders they included all those in which promiscuous sex behaviour was part of the charge with which the court had to deal.

There were important differences between the sexes, in that the sexual delinquencies of the boys were mainly in the nature of sexual deviations, while in the girls they were mainly in the nature of (psychopathologically) normal promiscuity. In both groups, of sex and non-sex delinquents alike, the boys were younger than the girls. Girls twice as frequently as boys were committed to a training school. Comparing sex offenders with others, no differences were found in the incidence of three measures of socio-economic stress (less than marginal income at home, unsatisfactory home, broken home); and there were no differences in mean intelligence. In both sexes the sex delinquents were rather older than the non-sex delinquents. The incidence of serious personality maladjustment was related to the offence in a different way in the two sexes; whereas in the boys the sex delinquents were six times as frequently seriously maladjusted as their controls (20 per cent : 3 per cent), no significant difference was found in the females (11 per cent : 15 per cent). This study once again emphasizes the marked difference between boys and girls, when problems of delinquency are considered, and suggests that generalizations should not be stretched from one sex to the other.

Deprived children

Hilda Lewis's work (1954) on deprived children is concerned with a much younger group than ours (no boys over 12 or girls over 15), but nevertheless offers comparative observations of considerable interest. There were 500 children from 363 families, 277 boys and 223 girls; and they had been taken into the Mersham Reception Centre under care because of neglect (111), being uncontrollable (90), loss of parental care (78), pilfering (50), etc. Families were predominantly of social class V; sibship size was large with nearly 50 per cent of four and more; 23 per cent of the children were illegitimate. The relations between the parents were seldom good, and nearly as often 'bad' as 'fair'; cruelty, drunkenness, crime and sexual laxity were prominent; 264 fathers and 328 mothers suffered from severe physical and mental disabilities (36 mothers had been in mental hospitals for psychotic illness).

The children, who were under psychiatric supervision from Dr Lewis, were classified as 'normal' (119), 'mildly disturbed' (155), and 'definitely disturbed' (226). Five background factors showed a statistically significant association with patterns of disturbed behaviour. They were: mother neurotic or psychopathic; mother lacking in affection for child; father lacking in affection for child; prolonged stay in public care; illegitimacy. It is noteworthy that some abnormalities were, paradoxically, found more frequently in the background of the normal children than the disturbed ones. This surprising relationship is not commented on by Lewis; but from her data the following table can be constructed:

Per cent of cases in which	Child		
	normal	mildly disturbed	definitely disturbed
Neglected by mother . . .	68	56	37
Mother dull or defective . .	36	24	17
Neglected by father . . .	51	32	30
Home dirty.	55	32	16

The explanation would seem to be a fairly simple one, and rest on the fact that each of these factors, including psychiatric disturbance in the child, had some effect in furthering admission to the Reception Centre. If that were the case, then, to take one case, a higher degree of dirtiness in the home would be called for to secure admission in the case of a normal child than in the case of a disturbed child. The statistical argument is presented in a more precise form in Appendix B.

It was found that a mentally unhealthy mother tended to produce a neurotic reaction in the child. Unsocialized aggressive behaviour was more likely to have developed if either the mother or the father were not affectionate, or if the child had been in public care; this was also associated with illegitimacy. It is interesting that none of these background factors were associated with socialized delinquency, presumably because there the social factors would be more important than the home ones; neglect and bad company had often preceded socialized delinquency.

An interesting feature is Lewis's failure to find support for the theories associating psychiatric disturbances of all kinds, including delinquency, with separation from the mother during childhood. In her case material, unless separation from the mother had occurred before the age of two years, and had been lasting, it bore no statistically significant relation to the normality or otherwise of the child's mental state at the time of admission. No clear connection was evident between separation from the mother and a particular pattern of disturbed behaviour. Neither delinquency nor incapacity for affectionate relationships was significantly more frequent in the separated children.

Delinquents not yet charged

Wattenberg, with a number of different collaborators, has reported the findings of a delinquency study in Detroit in a series of papers, of which two are of interest here. The subjects of the enquiry were all those boys and girls under 17 years of age against whom complaints were made, and who were contacted by the Youth Bureau of the Detroit Police Department in 1952. The officer or policewoman routinely interviewed every such young person, and the parents, and in most cases visited the home, entering the data into a history sheet. Facts or ratings relating to 3,451 boys and 1,082 girls were coded, punched on cards, and analysed. Wattenberg claims that this group of young people are much more representative of juvenile offenders than the smaller number (only about one quarter of the sample taken) who eventually faced a charge in a juvenile court, or the still smaller number who would eventually be committed. This claim seems to be a fair one.

Differences between the boys and the girls are discussed in a paper by *Wattenberg and Saunders* (1954). These differences were wide ones and all-pervading; of the 68 tables prepared, only two (those relating to number of brothers and to number of sisters in the sibship) failed to show a difference significant at the ·01 level.

We need not follow the authors through all the differences they have elicited, but consider only those which are most relevant to the present work. The usual finding was made that the types of 'offence' committed by girls were very different from those of the boys: among the girls prevailing offences were incorrigibility, sex offences, truanting from home; among the boys, burglary, assaults, malicious destruction of property. Girls of 12 and under were much more like boys of the same age than the older girls were, and among these children larceny was relatively common. Recreation patterns were very different. The boys tended to be active and excitement-hungry, the girls less vigorous and rather aimless. Boys ran around in gangs and groups, often delinquent groups, much more than the girls. The girls in general tended to have poor interpersonal relations. Much more frequently than the boys they failed to get on with class-mates, and with teachers, and with adult neighbours. Though they did rather better in class, more of them hated school.

Relationships within the family were very much more disturbed among the girls than among the boys. From the figures supplied, the following tabulation can be drawn up:

	Per cent of	
	Boys	Girls
Came from intact families	56	41
Living with step-parent	16	22
No father in the home at any time	26	35
Marked quarreling in the home	20	32
Dislike of father expressed	5	16
Hostility to mother expressed	1	7
Punitive action and open rejection by parent	5	15
Eventual forgiveness shown by parents	28	7

In some respects the girls distinguished themselves from the boys, not in a shift to one side or the other of the average finding, but to both sides at once. Thus in socio-economic variables, the boys showed their peak distribution about the mean, while higher proportions of the girls came both from poor and from prosperous homes, both from slum areas and from areas above the average. A higher proportion of the boys were in the middle range of intelligence than of the girls, who exceeded the proportions of boys in the above-average and the below-average classes.

In a second paper (1955) the same authors discuss differences between girls with repeated offences and one-time offenders. Unfortunately the report is a short one, and the data made available are very scanty. Differences between recidivists and others reached a statistically significant level of ·01 in the case of 21 items, and of ·05 in the case of a further 7 items. These items are listed, with the appropriate level of significance of the difference; but this is the only information tabulated. The authors were able to detect two main clusters among these items, and, omitting the more miscellaneous ones, they were:

Cluster 1: girl repeaters were more in conflict with their homes than non-repeaters, i.e. significantly more frequently, (a) they expressed dislike or indifference towards their home,

(b) they expressed dislike of the mother or made no comment, (c) the parents gave them no money, (d) the parents were indifferent (not co-operative) towards police officers, (e) the mother spent no time at home, (f) the girl was not living with both her own parents.

Cluster 2: this related to life at school. Significantly more frequently than their controls, the repeaters, (a) were not attending school or were in special classes, (b) were estimated as 'below average', (c) had poor school marks, (d) disliked or were indifferent to school, (e) showed contempt for their teachers or made no comment, (f) were not friendly towards class-mates.

A similar comparison was made with recidivist and non-recidivist boys, and an attempt was made to see whether the pattern described was a specifically feminine one. No comparative data are supplied; but the authors state that girls more than boys were affected by present relationships within the home, particularly those involving their mothers. Relative neglect by the parents was more extreme among boy repeaters. Socio-economic variables were more closely related with repeating in boys, but conditions were worse for girls than boys.

Prostitution; the broken home

A short note on juvenile prostitution has been provided by *Gibbens* (1957) who, on going through the records of 400 girls aged 14 to 16, found 18 who had been living by prostitution at the time of their arrest. Eight of these 18 girls were very intelligent but very unstable emotionally; four girls were overtly homosexual, and more generally the attitude to men was one of hostility and contempt, with an incapacity to feel any real affection. Some girls were purely mercenary; some were very indolent and passive. Follow-up of these 18 girls with a further 13 from another series, showed only 6 who achieved success. It seems surprising then to read that 'all things considered, there is little to suggest that the outlook for juvenile prostitutes is any worse than for other wayward girls'. Gibbens emphasizes that for these girls prostitution is a very different thing from being promiscuous. He regards juvenile prostitution as a temporary phase, and thinks that few if any of these girls go on to become adult prostitutes.

A statistical study by *Monahan* (1957) is chiefly of relevance to the association between delinquency and a broken home. There is a critical review of the literature, tending to show not only a high incidence of homes broken in defined ways as a background to delinquency, but also a higher level in the case of girls than of boys. Monahan's own work is an analysis of 6 years of Philadelphia records, with 44,448 delinquents classified male or female, negro or white, first offenders or recidivists. Each of these dichotomies proved to be highly significant. Although Mohanan does not do so, we can get a clear idea of where his evidence leads by comparing the proportions of children living with their own parents (both of them), which is highest in the white boy first offenders at 72·4 per cent, and lowest in the girl negro recidivists at 19·8 per cent. Combining the percentages in the eight subgroups recorded into three independent pairings, we find that 20 per cent more of the white than the negro live with both parents, 12 per cent more of the first offenders than the recidivists, and 22 per cent more of the boys than the girls; the sex difference is in fact the biggest one. Monahan has no doubts himself of the validity of each of these differences, and says: 'One cannot ignore this evidence by assuming that there is a selective apprehension of youth on the basis of their home conditions rather than by a direct operation of the law.'

Answers by children to questionnaires

The study made by *Nye* (1958) is an attempt to learn about the causes of delinquent behaviour in the general school population. He points out that, in taking as one's subjects delinquents from an institutionalized population, as nearly all previous workers have done, one is making use of a seriously biased sample. Thus it has always been found that delinquents from training schools and other institutions show a preponderance of the lowest socio-economic classes. The actual occurrence of delinquent acts among teenagers may be much more evenly spread through all classes, and Nye quotes some evidence to support this opinion. Other observations, which are thought to have ætiological significance, such as the high frequency of a 'broken home' in the background of delinquents, may be less related with the causation of delinquency, than with the decision by magistrates to use institutional means of treatment.

Nye's theoretical framework is of considerable interest. He remarks in this connection that, 'It is now generally agreed that instincts play a minor if not non-existent role in human behaviour'; so that the instinctual causes of deviant behaviour, and psychiatric causes more generally, are allowed little place. His view, with which few will disagree, is that the causes of delinquent behaviour are many and various. Single causes have often been discarded, when they have failed to explain the whole of the phenomena, when they should be retained in explanation of some part. Typing crimes by a single cause, such as 'neurotic crime', 'socialized crime', etc., leads to categories which are no more homogeneous than delinquent behaviour as a whole. One should not think of delinquency as having been caused, but rather that there has been a failure in its prevention. The social controls which prevent delinquent behaviour are twofold; the internal controls which are built up within the personality of the developing individual by equipping him with a conscience and standards of behaviour, and the direct controls which impose some form of punishment for infractions of society's rules.

Nye carried out his investigation in three small Washington towns (pop. 10,000 to 30,000) by getting all the boys and girls in grades 9 to 12 inclusive to answer in classroom conditions but with guaranteed anonymity one of four different questionnaires; one of these questionnaires included questions designed to constitute a delinquency scale, so that the sample eventually used was a randomly chosen 25 per cent. Sociological data over a wide range were asked for, and in addition there were twenty-three questions relating to delinquency; seven of these constituted the delinquency scale. For this, the child was asked to place an X against 'no', 'once or twice', 'several times' or 'very often' in answer to the questions,

Have you:

1. Driven a car without a driver's licence or permit?
2. Skipped school without a legitimate excuse?
8. Defied your parents' authority (to their face)?
10. Taken little things (worth less than $2) that did not belong to you?
17. Bought or drank beer, wine or liquor? (Include drinking at home.)

19. Purposely damaged or destroyed public or private property that did not belong to you?
22. Had sex relations with a person of the opposite sex?

The validity of this scale is supported by showing that scores of 10 points and more are attained by 86 per cent of boys from training schools, scores of 9 points and less by 86 per cent of boys from high schools. In analysing the data the principal method used was to find whether the incidence of a sociological finding was significantly different in the two classes of 'most delinquent' and 'least delinquent' boys and girls. The 'most delinquent' and 'least delinquent' classes were distinguished by their scores, the 'most delinquent' constituting approximately 32 per cent of the boys and 28 per cent of the girls. The total sample consisted of about 2,300 children, boys and girls being about equal in number.

Socio-economic status was estimated on the basis of the father's occupation; no significant difference was found in delinquent behaviour of boys and girls in different strata. Lower delinquency ratings went with regular church attendance by the family, with small families and with rural and non-mobile families. There were small differences in delinquent behaviour between adolescents from legally broken and unbroken families; and it appeared to be a matter of indifference whether the break occurred before the age of 6, or between then and the age of 12, or later. Less delinquency was found in the broken homes than in the unhappy unbroken homes; the happiness of the marriage was much more closely related to delinquency than whether the marriage was an original or a second marriage, or whether the child was living with one parent only.

Data are provided about employment of the mother, and spatial mobility of the family. A series of interesting chapters discuss the data bearing on acceptance and rejection, not only of the child by the parent but also of the parent by the child. Both aspects of this reciprocal relationship showed themselves to be important, and mutual rejection was more closely related to delinquent behaviour than rejection by either side separately. Further chapters bear on discipline and punishment, freedom and responsibility, family recreation, parental disposition and character (moody, difficult to get on with, loses temper, truthful, honest), values, money, availability of parental information and advice.

Many of these findings are of much interest, but are not closely relevant to our work.

What is of relevance is the general nature of the sex differences. Girls commit only a fraction of the delinquent acts of the boys. They lead a more restricted life, in which control by the family plays a relatively larger part, and control by outside agencies a smaller part, than in the case of boys. Direct control techniques have greater significance for girls than for boys. The fact that the behaviour of fathers was more often significantly related to delinquency than the behaviour of mothers, is attributed to the greater homogeneity of maternal behaviour. Whereas mothers approximate to a generally accepted standard of conduct towards their children, fathers vary from those who see their role as close as that of the mothers to those who feel their duty is discharged by bread-winning.

The criticisms one is disposed to make of this study are of course very obvious. All the facts are seen through the child's eyes, and are taken as reported by him (in the framework of a rigid check-list), without any possibility of external confirmation. The delinquency scale is itself of dubious validity, and apart from items 10 and 19, is descriptive of uncontrolled rather than anti-social behaviour. A large part of even the 'most delinquent' children must have been well within normal limits by ordinary social standards. We are not told of the intercorrelations of these seven items; and it seems surprising that more use was not made of the entire range of 23 questions, with loadings based on a factor analysis. Nevertheless this remains one of the very few controlled studies of a non-institutional sample; so that where its findings agree with those of studies of institutionalized samples, they deserve a considerably enhanced level of confidence.

Wayward girls three years later

Gibbens (1959) followed up a group of 185 girls, whom he had himself examined at the court's request, while they were at a remand home between September 1951 and September 1953, and who had then been placed on probation or under supervision. Follow-up questionnaires were sent to probation officers in May 1954; and the officers were asked to say whether in general the girl's behaviour had improved, had shown little change, or had deteriorated. The results were rather disappointing, though the relatively small number of girls placed on probation did a good deal better than those placed under supervision. Of the latter 37 per cent were reported as having improved, 22 per cent no change, 37 per cent deteriorated. Supervision or probation were regarded as having failed if the girl was sent to a borstal or an approved school or training home after a breach; this happened with 41 per cent of the supervision cases and 16 per cent of the probation cases. Employment records were good in 84 per cent of the probation cases, 48 per cent of the supervision cases. In both groups about one in eight of the girls had an illegitimate pregnancy. Psychiatric treatment was necessary for about one girl in every six; most of the girls needing out-patient treatment were difficult neurotic girls from relatively good backgrounds, while the eleven girls who had to be taken into hospital as in-patients were extremely unstable, with a history of recurrent suicidal attempts and gross hysterical or pre-psychotic symptoms.

Gibbens observes of his material that it represents waywardness of late and sudden onset, and reveals nothing of the large numbers of girls who are diverted by the local authorities or moral welfare agencies at an earlier stage of disturbance. It is characteristic of girls that they nurse their grievances in silence until they burst into disturbed behaviour at adolescence. Wayward girls are also more likely than boys to stabilize suddenly and completely, given the right circumstances. A high proportion of those who did well had some period away from home; in many cases in which the girl stayed on at home, the problem went grumbling on, held within bounds by the exertions of the probation officers. Waywardness in almost all these cases represents fundamentally the first gesture for independence, and there is a large group who proceed rapidly to work out their own life away from home, and who need encouragement to do so. 'The psychiatrist is the last person to recommend removal from home unless it seems unavoidable'; but short-term removal appears to increase and improve the ties with home. Gibbens does not think that a larger proportion of girls should be committed to approved schools before the problem has become acute; but he appears to base this view less on the objective evidence, which tends in the opposite direction, than on the opinion of psychiatrists already quoted, which is derived from *a priori* theories. The belief, widely held as an article of faith, that it is prejudicial to the child to remove it from its natural home, even when that home is a bad one, and from its natural mother, even when she is neglectful, has come under severe criticism, e.g. from Wootton, criticism which has in fact never been met.

Deprived children again

The study by *Harriett Wilson* (1962) on delinquency and child neglect offers a parallel to the work of Lewis. The case material was chosen from families referred to the medical officer of health of 'Seaport', as showing evidence of child neglect over a certain period of time. Out of the 157 families notified eventually 52 were chosen for study on a point system, marks being given for defects in solvency, in health, in education, and in the event of a formal case being opened by the National Society for the Prevention of Cruelty to Children. Noteworthy features of these families were the large size of the family, averaging 7·4 children with a range from 3 to 12, and the low intelligence of the children, with average IQ of 82. Emphasis is laid on the 'extreme stress situations' of the parents, determined by low-wage incomes on the one side and the large numbers of children on the other, the situation often being made more acute by the bad health or frequent unemployment of the father. In the course of time, as the children get older, the extreme stress is gradually alleviated. Wilson considers the low IQ of the children as in part artificially depressed by the bad environment. The case material is such as to suggest to the reader that, while both parents tend to be of low intelligence, on average the mother tends to be lower than the father. The children were all educationally sub-average and bad school attenders (but bad school attendance was one of the criteria of selection).

Very interestingly, there was little evidence of maternal deprivation. The mothers were not affectionless, but mainly loving. The children in school were for the most part not disturbed, but rather shy, inhibited, listless, untrained. The families were cohesive, with strong loyalties even when living in conditions of appalling squalor.

There was a high rate of delinquency in these families. The expectation that a boy from one of them would be ascertained as delinquent by the age of 17 was 85 per cent, that of a girl 28 per cent. These expectations were eight times as high as in Seaport

generally, and double that of children living in the same neighbourhood. A fairly high rate of delinquency was also found in both
fathers and mothers. The question was asked whether the 27
families with criminal records produced more delinquent children
than the 20 with no records, this was found not to be so; indeed,
the opposite was the case to a statistically significant degree. A
policeman's interpretation of this finding was that the children of
criminal parents are more skilled at the job, when they become
delinquent, and more skilled at denying their guilt when caught.

Wilson develops the concept of 'neglect delinquency', contrast-
ing it with other forms of delinquency arising in more prosperous
families, which are thought to be ætiologically distinct. The causes
of delinquency are attributed to:– (1) poverty; (2) emotional
insecurity experienced by the children in the relationship with
their parents, primarily with their mothers. The mothers are not
always available when needed, or the mother may be mentally
retarded, or unable to cope with the demands of six or seven small
children simultaneously; (3) severance from the wider kin. There
is no grannie, no other relative to step in and help the mother at
times of illness, confinement, etc.; (4) important early training is
missed out. There is no systematic toilet training, no insistence on
manners, no conformity by parents to a code of manners. The
first disciplinary demand is made at school.

Balanced foursomes

An interesting experimental study was carried out by *Ruth Morris*
(1964), based on 56 quartets, i.e. individuals from each of four
groups, delinquent girls, non-delinquent girls, delinquent boys,
non-delinquent boys, matched for social class, intelligence, age,
and grade at school. The delinquent girls were taken from a
complete sample of all delinquent girls of 13 to 16 years, with two
or more police contacts, in Flint, Michigan (pop. 200,000).

The work was based on the sociological theories of Cloward,
who attributes the development of delinquency to difficulties in
attaining social goals along legitimate lines, when illegitimate
lines are open. Since the life of the female is so much involved
with personal relations, it was postulated that girls would be more
likely than boys to suffer under relational problems. Three
predictions were made: that delinquent girls would be, of all four

groups, most likely to come from broken homes; to come from homes with many family tensions; and to be at a disadvantage in personal attractiveness and grooming. In fact all three of these hypotheses were borne out by the findings. Differences between delinquents and non-delinquents among the boys, though tending in the same direction as in the girls, were generally statistically non-significant; in the girls, marked and significant differences were found between delinquents and non-delinquents. The data consist in questionnaire replies and interviewers' ratings; in the field of all three hypotheses the delinquent girls were at a marked disadvantage compared with other matching groups. It is a matter of some interest that there was a very large difference between the delinquent and non-delinquent girls in their attention to personal appearance and grooming, although (in both sexes) the actual frequency of dating was higher in the delinquents than in the others. Morris concludes that her results strongly support the view that girls are particularly susceptible to relational problems.

A population sample of 'experienced' girls

Another work of much interest to us, though not directly concerned with delinquents, is the report by *Michael Schofield* (1965) on 'The Sexual Behaviour of Young People'. His sample of adolescent boys and girls, taken by scrupulously fair methods of selection from the general population, included two age groups with modal ages of 16 and 18 respectively, and the 1,873 subjects were equally divided between these two ages and between the two sexes. The aspects of this work which concern us are those in which an attempt is made to characterize the background and personality of the experienced girls, since the girls of the Magdalen school, whom we have studied, have in large measure got into severe social difficulties, and have had to be sent to approved school training, just because of their active and ill-regulated sex lives.

Schofield found that there was a clear relationship between sex activity and the girl's relationship with her parents, both with her father and with her mother. Girls who got on well with either of them were far less likely to be sexually experienced. There was also a strong association between lack of sex experience and the girl's report on the happiness of her parents' marriage. Sex experience went also with the amount of freedom allowed to the girl by her parents, and was greatly increased in those who were allowed out late or to no set time. Girls who spent most of their time at home tended to be inexperienced, those who were out a lot had more sex experience. More experienced girls were found among those who had left school early, who did not like school, and had problems there; repeated change of job was also associated with sex experience. A record of delinquency was common in the boys of Schofield's sample, but much less common in the girls; 13 per cent of the experienced girls had a record of delinquency, as against 1 per cent of the non-experienced and 'inceptive' groups.

Summing up this part of the work, Schofield says that experienced girls were not found to have less favourable backgrounds than the others, and did not come more often from broken homes. But they more often reported poor relations with both the father and the mother and poor relations between the latter. In the analysis of the psychological tests of attitudes, three first-order factors were identified, with antipathy to family loyalty, dislike of home restrictions and preference for friends' advice. All these three were operative in the girls, but not in the boys. Experienced girls had gone much farther than experienced boys in rejecting family influences. At work (unlike the boys) they were more often discontented, more often unemployed, and more often in manual jobs than the other girls. There was evidence to suggest that physical development was more advanced than in the other girls of the sample. The girl, says Schofield, is more influenced by her family than is the boy. 'She must overcome these family pressures and derogate her family loyalty before she can be persuaded to agree to premarital intercourse.' One might add that one can also derive from Schofield's report the notion that a certain degree of social disorganization, outwith as well as within the family bounds, seems to exercise a strongly predisposing influence.

'Deviant Children Grown up'

The book of this name by *Lee Robins* (1966) provides us with by far the longest and best documented follow-up survey (apart perhaps from that of Otterström). The subjects chosen were those seen at the St. Louis Municipal Psychiatric Clinic early in its history, from its third to its eighth year, 1924–1930, omitting persons over the age of 18, and those with an IQ less than 80, and all negroes. What remained were 524 patients, 73 per cent males, coming predominantly from American-born Protestant parentage of low occupational status. At the time of referral only about a third of the children were living with both parents, and the girls had had an even more disrupted home life than the boys had. Despite the elimination of those with IQ less than 80, average intelligence was low; 30 per cent of the sample had IQs 80–89, the modal range, and 23 per cent IQs 90–99. The median age of these children was 13. More than a third of the children (37 per cent) had appeared before the Juvenile Court; an additional 40 per cent were referred for antisocial behaviour; and the remaining 23 per cent were referred for other than antisocial problems, mainly neurotic symptoms, learning difficulties, etc.

These children were matched with control cases, 70 boys and 30 girls, from St. Louis public elementary schools, of the same race, age, sex, IQ and socio-economic status, but without evidence of serious behaviour problems in childhood. A number of convergent lines were taken to locate both subjects and controls thirty years later; and it was in fact possible to locate or learn of the death of 88 per cent of the former patients, and 98 per cent of the controls. Once located, all available information was obtained, and 88 per cent of the target subjects were personally interviewed.

The amount of statistical information which is reported is so vast as to be digestible only with difficulty. The reader's task would have been easier if all differences not reaching an acceptable standard of statistical significance had been eliminated from the discussion. Many interesting findings are in fact not very well established since the number of controls is not great, and numbers are small in the subgroups of ex-patients, when broken down into males and females, and antisocial ones and others. What particularly diminishes the value of this great work, in which more than 40 people collaborated, is that it was not thought worth while distinguishing girls from boys throughout the study.

As perhaps might have been expected, the amount of antisocial behaviour, judged by whatever standard, was much greater in the antisocial group of ex-patients than in the neurotic group, and somewhat greater in the neurotic group than in the controls. Women from the antisocial group tended to marry young; and to choose husbands who drank, were arrested, were unfaithful, deserted. They had a higher rate of childlessness than other female groups, but those who had children had more of them. Women from this group were more subject to alcoholism, and more of them had some psychiatric hospitalization. Antisocial behaviour was commoner in the children of women in this group than in others; and it is interesting that, taking the two antisocial groups, men and women, who had children of school age, in 69 per cent of cases the fathers had children without antisocial or psychiatric problems, but only 42 per cent of the mothers.

General conclusions resulting from this study are that the clinic children grew up into more maladjusted and sicker adults than their controls; this was especially so in antisocial behaviour. Children referred for antisocial behaviour differed much more from controls in adult adjustment than did the children referred for non-antisocial problems (temper tantrums, learning difficulties, and problems in speech, eating, sleeping, etc.). The more severe the antisocial behaviour, the more disturbed was adult adjustment.

Attention is given to the delineation of the 'sociopathic personality'. Those so diagnosed in adult life showed themselves in earlier life to be:

boys referred for antisocial behaviour, especially theft also incorrigibility, running away from home, truancy, associating with bad companions, sexual activities, staying out late;

disciplinary problems at school
held back at least one grade
never graduated from elementary school;

described as aggressive, reckless, impulsive, slovenly, enuretic, lacking guilt, lying without cause;

most of them had a father sociopathic or alcoholic
homes broken by divorce or separation
mothers modally severely nervous, mentally ill or feebleminded;

as adult poor work history, financially dependent, marital problems
multiple arrests leading to prison terms
excessive drinking, impulsive, sexually promiscuous, vagrant, delinquent in paying debts
belligerent, socially isolated;

raised rate of injury and death by violence;

their children have a high rate of problem behaviour and failure to graduate from high school;

at time of follow-up 12 per cent had given up antisocial behaviour a further 27 per cent had reduced it markedly, the remaining 61 per cent were still seriously antisocial
commonest age for improvement between 30 and 40.

A finding of considerable interest, because of the way in which it conflicts with current psychodynamic theory, is that the fathers who were cold to their children had significantly fewer sociopathic ones; and this was also true of the fathers who were strict disciplinarians. 'Strict discipline may deter children from continuing their antisocial behaviour into adulthood,' 'coldness of the father appears to prevent sociopathy even in severely antisocial children.' A genetical relationship between the form of disturbance in parent and child is made improbable by the observation that antisocial traits in the mother are not associated with sociopathy in the child. Parental discipline and the degree of supervision are highly related to the later diagnosis of sociopathy. With both parents adequate or strict in their discipline there were 9 per cent of sociopaths; with one or both too lenient, 29 per cent; with one or both uninterested, 32 per cent. Harmony between parents was important; but the broken home that did not lead to discord was not found to lead to adult antisocial behaviour.

SUMMARY

Gathering together the conclusions which can be based on the work we have reviewed, we find that they can be ordered in a sequence which descends in certainty and importance:

1. Behaviour, stigmatized as delinquent, is much less common in girls than in boys. Delinquent girls make up a much smaller proportion of all girls than delinquent boys do of all boys.

2. The nature of delinquent offences among girls is completely different from the delinquent offences committed by boys. A large part of the delinquencies of girls consist in sexually ill-regulated behaviour, of a type not to demand social sanctions in the case of an adult. A large part of the indictable offences committed by girls

are of a relatively trivial kind, e.g. larceny. The spectrum of offences committed by boys is much more varied, and involves acts ranking much higher in their socially dangerous nature.

3. Delinquent boys and delinquent girls are most alike, in personal and social characteristics, in early prepubertal years, and begin to develop their own very different group characteristics with the onset of puberty.

4. The incidence of delinquency starts to climb, and reaches a peak, at later ages in girls than in boys.

5. Delinquent boys approximate to general population norms much more closely than delinquent girls, in all features which have proved open to testing.

6. In both sexes in the great majority of cases delinquent behaviour develops on a normal motivational and psychological basis; but psychiatric abnormality and morbidity are commoner in delinquent girls than delinquent boys.

7. Physical factors play a part in the development of delinquency in only a minority of cases, and then by some interference with central nervous function.

8. Delinquent girls (and boys) are usually found to be on average better grown than control series, and to be above population averages for height and weight.

9. Social factors have been found to be of very great importance in the causation of delinquency in boys; there is little evidence that they play anything like the same part in the case of girls. Subcultural delinquency seems not to have been explored at all in relation to girls. The effective motivational factors are connected, much more than with boys, with the intimate family, and with the girl's personal relations with her parents.

10. While earlier studies showed that delinquent girls came with more than the expected frequency from slums, from very poor homes, and from families suffering from economic disadvantages generally, more recent work allows factors of this kind an importance which has progressively diminished with time. It now seems probable that poverty, as an independent factor, plays only an insignificant part in predisposing to delinquency.

11. In the same way, while earlier studies associated delinquency with low intelligence, with the passage of time delinquent girls have been found to approximate more and more closely to population standards in the distribution of intelligence.

12. When one comes to consider education, the same secular change has not been observed. The delinquent girl, today as of old, is still more likely than her peers to have a poor school record, to have disliked school, and to have achieved a poor educational standard. The occupational record is also poor.

13. The 'broken home' is found more frequently with the delinquent than with the non-delinquent population, and more commonly with delinquent girls than with delinquent boys. The objective measures of a broken home show clearly significant differences; but it seems probable that tensions and disagreements between parents are more effective in causing delinquency than mere absence of one parent. There is no strong evidence that institutionally brought up children are at a special disadvantage. There is no evidence that 'maternal deprivation' plays an important part ætiologically.

14. Other features of the intimate family which have a predisposing effect are large size of sibship, and the presence of delinquents among parents and sibs.

15. Where they have been looked for, deficiencies in training, discipline and habit formation have been found to play an important role.

16. The delinquent girl is generally an unhappy girl, and her unhappiness is most commonly related to disturbed emotional relationships with the parents. However, children who are neglected by their mothers are likely to become delinquent, even when normally affectionate relationships hold.

17. The existence of opportunities for delinquent behaviour encourages its occurrence.

18. The attitude of the research worker towards delinquency has changed fundamentally over the last thirty years. Delinquent behaviour, which used to be regarded as abnormal in a pathological rather than statistical sense, is now looked on as psychopathologically normal. What are now sought are not so much the causes of delinquent behaviour as the conditions under which there has been a failure of prevention. Positive processes are called for to help the child develop its own system of internal controls, to which external social controls are added. Any process will increase the likelihood of delinquency which interferes with the first or relaxes the second.

III

Background to the New Inquiry

THE reader will have gathered from the previous chapter (if he did not already know) that there are large differences between the manifestations of delinquency in adolescent boys and girls. Boys and girls differ in their liability to delinquency, in the age at which they become delinquent, in the sort of delinquencies they commit, and also in the way in which the delinquent individual differs from others of the same age and sex who either do not commit delinquencies, or at least escape the notice of official records. Delinquency is an event of a different kind for the boy and for the girl. If we compare young schizophrenics, one sex with the other, the characteristics of the illness are much the same, even though they are seen against a different psycho-physical background. Delinquency is not like this. The problems that this sets us are difficult even to formulate; and so far very little has been done in a systematic way to find solutions. However one conclusion is obvious. The two sexes should not be considered together, but in isolation from one another. Every question that is asked, should be asked first for boys and then for girls; and all the data that are needed should be obtained twice over, independently for the one sex and for the other.

The authors of this book came to this field of enquiry with the training and the viewpoint of psychiatrists. A problem that particularly interested us was the question whether genetical factors might be incriminated. The sex difference suggested such a possibility. But at the time we began our inquiry we had no idea that the sex chromosomes could themselves be directly involved, as, at least in some cases, has now definitely been proved. We wished to explore at the genetical level the differences between psychosis, neurosis, and deviations of personality. We know that there is such a thing as a family predisposition to psychotic illness.

46

When present, does it carry with it a constitutional (genetical) liability to neurotic breakdown, or to behaviour disorders? One of us (V.C.) had carried out an investigation (1961) of the children of psychotic parents. She had found that these children are not constitutionally predisposed to neurotic illness; but the environment provided might have a predisposing effect, since children were more than normally liable to develop neurotic symptoms over the two years during which the onset of the psychotic illness in the parent had occurred. As a corollary, if we started out with a group of neurotic, psychopathic or disturbed children, would we find a heavy loading of psychotic illness in their parents? At this time one of us (J.C.) was the psychiatrist to the Magdalen Hospital Approved School; and the very representative series of delinquent girls that passed through that school seemed to us to offer an almost ideal field of study.

Unfortunately the deficiencies of the information available about the parents of these girls prevented us from reaching more than rather provisional (and mainly negative) conclusions about the significance of the genetical contribution to delinquency; but there was a wealth of data on a variety of aspects, with some bearing on the causation of delinquency.

It is our aim to offer what we have to the reader in as logical a way as possible. We shall begin by describing the Magdalen Hospital, as it was before it ceased to be a classifying school in 1966, what the girls were like and what their problems were, the services provided by the School and the sources of our information, and then how our inquiries were made. Subsequent chapters describe and analyse our findings.

The Magdalen Hospital

In his little book 'An Ideal in the Working' (1958), the late Rev. S. B. P. Pearce, Chaplain and Clerk of the Magdalen Hospital, gives an account of this old charitable foundation from 1758 to 1958. Its operation was considerably changed in 1934 by Home Office recognition as an Approved School, under the Children and Young Persons Act of 1933. The Committee of the Hospital made a total of 60 places available to the Courts, the agreement providing that there should be no change in the religious education of the inmates according to the beliefs of the Church of England.

The new status and new functions of the school brought changes, and, as Mr Pearce saw it, new problems:

> The pendulum has swung right to the other extreme. The girls today are given opportunities which would be given to few of them had their lives run a course which kept them in their own environment. There is now no thought of the emotion of penitence which was—perhaps often insincerely—an essential in the 18th Century. Instead the girl entering the Magdalen is resentful and rebellious. She sees not the great advantages given to her, but only the loss of her freedom and that often for the first time in her life, she has got to live by the rules. This is abhorrent to her and she is not slow to show this. The material is tough, and very frequently there have been several different attempts to cope with her all of which have broken down and which have culminated in the committal to an Approved School. There is little hope of her seeing this action as anything attractive, but as something which has taken her away from the life she had chosen and which has taken away from her the thing which she firmly believes she values above everything—her freedom.

The aims which the Classifying Approved School was intended to serve were many and important. Classification should diagnose the needs of each individual girl (and eliminate those unsuitable for Approved School training). It should select the training school best able to satisfy these needs, and it should provide the receiving school with notes on diagnosis so that training might proceed on the recommended lines immediately. In the short time the girl would be staying there the therapeutic aim would be limited, but an attempt should be made to create in the girl an attitude of purposeful collaboration in her training. Remoter aims would be the provision of factual and statistical information which would help to provide a basis for periodic review of problems and facilities, in the area served by the Classifying School and in the country as a whole.

In the course of time official policy gradually developed into combining classification procedures with those of assessment at the remand stage. Remand Homes which took on the functions of classification proved to be a more suitable and a more efficient means of providing a service for a local area. Bit by bit the Magdalen came to be an expensive anachronism, and was allowed to run down while new combined centres were being opened and developed in different parts of the country. However in the year 1958 it was still at its peak; and it is unlikely that in times to come any other centre will have such a comprehensive sample of the total adolescent delinquent female population of Southern England (see map, p. 55).

Some picture should be provided of the life led by the Magdalen girls from the time of their admission until discharge, usually by transfer to a training school. This life is a rather tightly organized one, but is a communal one with unlimited opportunity for exchanging ideas and experiences with one's fellows.

On admission a new girl and her escort are seen by the Principal or her Deputy for an introductory chat. She is then taken to the Infirmary Block and formally admitted by the Sister in Charge. Family and medical details are taken, she has a bath, is weighed, her eyes are tested and she is changed into school clothes. These are not uniform, and there is a reasonable element of choice. Girls do not wear their own clothes, but they are allowed to keep certain personal possessions—photographs, toilet accessories, knitting, books, etc. They have no money or make-up, and smoking is not permitted.

From the Infirmary the new girl is taken to one of the three Houses, each catering for a maximum of 10 girls. Here she is greeted by her House Supervisor and introduced to the other girls. The girls rise at 7.30 a.m. and help in the domestic work of their own House, or in the Kitchen, before breakfast at 8.30. There is a short service in the school Chapel each morning at 9.0, and on Sundays Morning and Evening Prayer is taken by the Chaplain or a visiting preacher. Bed-time is about 8.30 p.m., with lights out at 9.30 p.m.

For the first two weeks all girls attend the schoolroom in the morning, and for those who are still of school age there is full-time education as in an ordinary school. After the first two weeks, girls of 16 and over are divided into four work groups—Kitchen, Laundry, Sewing Room and Administration Block, and assist in the general running of that department. As the calls come, they are withdrawn for interviews with the Educational Psychologist, the Consultant Psychiatrist or for medical examination and hospital visits. Medical examination (by a woman doctor) includes blood tests, urine analysis and a complete gynaecological examination.

During the lunch break, where possible, the girls have a short time out of doors. Recreational classes take place three evenings a week from 5.0 to 7.0 p.m., and on Saturday afternoons. These take the form of Dancing, Movement to Music, Singing, Art, Netball, etc. Other evenings are occupied with T.V., indoor or outdoor games, hand-work, and Chaplain's discussion or film-strip talk. Normally girls do not go out during their stay at the Classifying School, unless this is of longer duration than usual; then they may accompany a member of the staff on a shopping expedition or the like. Visits are by appointment, but there is no special visiting day; visits are mostly confined to parents and other relatives.

Gynæcological problems

Every girl is examined gynæcologically on admission, and the full routine of the special clinic, with blood tests, is gone through. The proportion of girls found to be infected is very high; and it must be remembered that nearly every girl has been in a remand home or institution for several weeks before admission to the classifying school, and may have already had effective treatment. In the year under study the number of girls treated for non-venereal vaginal discharges was 139; one girl had gonorrhoea, and one had syphilis, (and one congenital syphilis). The number of girls transferred, who needed further treatment, was 46. In 1958, 62 babies were born to the total number of girls resident during the period of the Approved School order, and 14 of the mothers were married at the time of confinement. Babies born during the period of supervision, including the time after leaving the training school while the order still continued, totalled 79; and of this number 39 of the mothers were married at the time of confinement.

Almost without exception every girl examined at the classifying school has been exposed to the chance of pregnancy. If a girl is pregnant, she offers yet another psychiatric problem, in addition to the medical one; she is anxious to discuss her predicament and her hopes and fears for the future.

The care and management of pregnant girls is an ever present problem in Approved Schools; and the problem is a bigger one with the younger girls than with those who become pregnant after the age of 16. Society automatically condemns the father of a baby conceived by a girl of under 16, and any ideas she may have of continuing her relationship with the father of her baby have to be shelved to some indefinite far off future date. The schoolgirl mother is also handicapped by not being able to offer to work, in order to help to support her child, in the event of a relative agreeing to look after the baby until the mother becomes self-supporting and independent.

As a general rule, pregnancy is more psychologically and physically disturbing to younger mothers than it is to their mature contemporaries. Often the early onset of puberty has caught the girl emotionally unprepared. Depressed, deprived girls may seek comfort in sexual fantasies and masturbation; and accidental or contrived circumstances may lead them towards experiencing their fantasies in reality. Very often the initiating partner of the younger girls has been an older man.

Sometimes there is a strong desire for pregnancy; and if then the girl does not become pregnant either by accident or design, perhaps because she is in a relatively infertile phase of development, she may believe she is genuinely infertile. This notion is often expressed by adolescent girls; and some of them, in their attempts to disprove it expose themselves to repeated chances of becoming pregnant. This may be the beginning of promiscuous behaviour which leads to committal. A disturbed girl whose promiscuity is motivated in this way will not consider practising contraception, although she may have full knowledge of the techniques. Becoming pregnant, she will often keep her secret, and the pregnancy is only discovered indirectly at a later stage. The more mature girl who becomes pregnant, on the other hand, adopts a more realistic attitude, and straightforward medical care is usually sufficient for her needs.

Reactions to committal

Committal means loss of freedom; the girl loses her independence, and her parents lose all right or power to try to control her. On the girl's part the reaction to such a catastrophe is intense and often stormy. On a background of insecurity and anxiety provoked by the unknown future, there is likely to be seen a mixture, fluctuating in colour and intensity, of despair, resentment, deprivation and rejection, and depression. The outward reaction may show as defiant shouting, aggression, weeping and appeals for sympathy, help and advice, or perhaps an unreal elation. Individual reactions vary widely, and each calls out a counter-response from the adults who are involved with her at that time; all professional workers are put on their mettle to try and help her to adjust to the new situation.

The time factor, the expectable duration of the new life without liberty, is made obvious to the girl from the beginning. Magistrates and the authorities following them, exhort the girl to be 'good', and thus shorten her stay in the training school. These girls look on committal as a prison sentence, and talk of 'doing their time'.

Girls who are not psychopathic, nor overburdened with neurotic symptoms, usually adapt fairly quickly to the situation. Such a one is not unduly guilty about past misdemeanours, since for that she is being punished and requital is being made. She quickly gets the message that if she is 'good' her time in the training school may be shortened; and the idea of 'goodness' becomes equated with the idea of early freedom. Part of the Approved School system encourages passive conforming behaviour; and the system of rewards for 'good' behaviour, while making life easy for the conformer, may make it intolerable for the non-conformer and the rebellious, unless she is placed in a school that is suited to her particular needs. However, if rightly placed, the halo that shines over freedom and independence illuminates the new school environment.

However, after learning to enter with enthusiasm into school life, and after adjusting for a time so well, when the time of her release approaches the idea of freedom once again becomes the focal point of her thinking. Now it is the world outside that is idealized, and during the last weeks of training sometimes intolerable tensions build up. The school is then seen as a frustrating barrier between her and her freedom. Behaviour may deteriorate, and the girl may abscond just when release is within sight.

Girls with neurotic symptoms

Girls with neurotic symptoms have often come from situations of exceptional stress; in the Approved School they have a haven where they can settle down. Once their symptoms have subsided, they often make a better adjustment even than the 'normal' girls, some of whom have grown up and into a delinquent way of life to which they have become well adjusted.

However, some girls with severe and long-standing neurotic symptoms may compulsively 'act out' their neurosis, perhaps in bizarre ways (such as hiding soiled articles in odd places). One of the big problems with which the School has to deal is aggression. This may take unexpected forms, as when a girl smashed the picture of a Madonna and Jesus belonging to one of the Anglican nuns of whom she was especially fond. A girl who felt particularly rejected by her group surreptitiously cut the electric lead to the sewing machines on which the party were making dresses for a Christmas pantomime. An unpopular girl can be made the subject of group aggression; and some masochistic girls seem to provoke and enjoy group disapproval. Aggression can more commonly be shown by singing and shouting, or by disruptive behaviour in class. Aggression and rebellion are near allied, and some girls spend a lot of time planning revolt against authority and in plots and fantasies.

The girl who has been kicked around sees the world as a jungle which she must fight in order to survive. She is resentful of correction, or advice, or encouragement. After repeated failures at her job, at school or at home, she decides she is no good, they are all against her, what does it matter. She isolates herself from those who would help her, and allies herself with similar misfortunes. One such girl was not yet fourteen. Both parents were in prison and her brother was in a borstal. She was placed in many foster homes, hostels and remand home, but from each she absconded. She especially requested to be placed in a 'closed' school, where the challenge to escape would be a worthwhile one.

Nearly all the girls are very touchy, and at times it may take very little to spark off an outburst of aggression, with verbal and physical violence. A real or imagined injustice, or anything that looks like sarcasm or cynicism, is found especially wounding. To be called 'nothing more than a prostitute' is about the worst possible insult, and it is taken as meaning total and uncompromising rejection on the part of the adult.

Some of the girls have learned their aggressiveness from identification with the violent characters that have dominated their environment. These girls may be bullies, but they often show great tenderness to the defenceless, to babies and animals. They can be loyal to adults and to a chosen few among their fellows, and they may in their turn be regarded as rough diamonds with hearts of gold.

Aggression also arises from a background of psychiatric abnormality. When it occurs in outbursts that are short-lived and follow a consistent pattern, or in response to minimal provocation in a calm atmosphere, there may also be other tell-tale signs of physiological brain dysfunction, such as epilepsy, epileptic equivalents, or specific and non-specific disturbances of brain rhythms. Girls who have a lower threshold to stress than other members of their families, and are sometimes described as the black sheep of the family, are often found to have a history suggesting the possibility of damage about the time of birth or a minimal chronic brain syndrome. When violent behaviour arises in a way that seems quite out of character with the previous personality and temperament, and itself has an irrational and unpredictable quality, it should arouse the suspicion that one may be witnessing the early stages of a psychotic illness.

A common pattern that has been emerging since the war is shown by the girl who is constantly seeking excitement. This tendency may be combined with many types of personality; but many of these girls are imaginative and indulge in daydreaming, in which they play lurid mental charades. Pathological lying may result. These girls are often promiscuous, and they readily become addicted to drugs. If faced with their peccadillos all too directly they may turn aggressive; they promote conflict among others, and themselves get caught up in the entanglements they have woven. Some inadequate girls, occasionally only children or the only girl in the family, try to cast themselves in a male role. One girl, with an indefinite self-conception of this kind, used to use tooth-paste as shaving cream, and 'shave' it off by scraping with the beaten out lid of a cocoa tin.

The active lesbian is extremely rare in girls in Approved Schools. In these communities there is usually an active heterosexual interest smouldering all the time. The girls who abscond or go on home leave, and the new girls coming in, bring in with them the fuel to keep a healthy glow of heterosexual interest warmly alive.

The investigation

In the investigation to be described in the following pages, 318 delinquent girls were studied. They represented the intake for the year 1958 of the Magdalen Hospital Classifying Approved School, London. This School (before it was closed on 31.3.66) admitted girls, from 14 up to 17 years of age, and very occasionally a little younger, who had been committed to Approved Schools by Juvenile Courts in the Southern half of England, South Wales and the Channel Islands. The provenance of the girls who

FIGURE I. Geographical origins of Magdalen girls and location of the training Schools to which they passed on.

were admitted in 1958 is shown in the illustrative map (Fig. 1). One of the features of this map is the heavy concentration of cases from such urban centres as London, Birmingham and Bristol, and the deficiency from rural areas, and from the West country.

In 1958, girls committed from Courts in the North of England were admitted to two schools, the Magdalen Hospital Classifying

School in London, and the Shaw Classifying Approved School, in the North. This latter school was closed in February, 1960. During 1958, there were admitted to the Magdalen 322 girls, and to the Shaw 181 girls. For comparative purposes one may note that during this year there were also 189 girls admitted to Junior Schools, directly, without passing through any classifying school. Roman Catholic girls also went directly to their own schools, and during 1958 there were 115 senior and intermediate girls who missed going to Classifying Schools on this account. There were in addition 32 senior and intermediate "Protestant" girls, who by-passed the Magdalen and Shaw schools for a variety of administrative reasons. It would seem that the girls admitted to the Magdalen were a broadly representative group of delinquent adolescent girls committed for Approved School training, apart from the omission of the Roman Catholics.

The relative magnitude of the delinquency problem in the two sexes is illustrated by the fact that whereas 766 girls of all ages went to Approved Schools in England in 1958, the total number of boys doing so was 3,709, or nearly five times as many. Over the previous twelve years the number of girls admitted to the Magdalen increased in a fluctuating manner year by year. Beginning with 1947, the figures for that year and succeeding years to 1957 are: 159, 175, 199, 276, 258, 303, 331, 321, 288, 303, 332.

One of us (J.C.) was the Consultant Psychiatrist to the Magdalen Hospital School; and he examined, assessed and reported on every girl in the series. Data were available from the Records of Information from the Courts of Committal. These included a report from a Probation Officer about the home and family background, and a teacher's report from the girl's school. In some cases there was additional material from Children's Officers, general practitioners, psychiatrists and mental hospitals, Child Guidance Clinics and other sources. At the School every girl was examined by an Educational Psychologist, and individually tested for intelligence and educational standard. The physical health of the girls was supervised by the Medical Officer of the School. The final assessment and classification was completed by the Headmistress, who could make use of reports from the members of her staff as well as from those of technical specialists. On this basis she selected the training school which she considered to be most suited to the needs of the individual girl.

These schools vary a good deal from one to another. Some are larger, some smaller; some are for older girls, others for younger; some have a staff of one religious denomination (e.g. Salvation Army, Anglican Sisters); some take a special interest in girls of retarded intelligence, or in girls with psychiatric problems, or girls who are offenders (e.g. larcenists) rather than those with sex delinquencies. The locations of these Schools are shown by Capital letters on the map (Fig. 1).

The Training Schools reported back to the Classifying School twice during the course of training, and again a year after the girl had been licensed. In this way follow-up information covering most of the girl's period of committal was automatically available to the Classifying School. For the present investigation further and later information was also sought. During 1962 a request was made to the Headmistresses of the Training Schools for the completion of a form asking for information on the girl's progress during training and subsequently, under the following headings:

General behaviour during training
Details of any psychiatric breakdown
Any special vocational training
Response and counter-response to:
    Adults
    Contemporaries
    Parents
Placement on license
After-Care agent, name
                address
Changes in family situation during training (e.g. death, divorce, separation, physical illness of parent, siblings, etc.)
Has any member of the family had mental illness or psychiatric treatment during time of girl's training?
    Yes ....   No.....................   Not known ....
    If answer YES, please give details
Response during license
    Work (indicating if any special vocational training is utilized)
    Social behaviour (e.g. married, co-habiting, pregnancy, etc.)
    Any further Court appearances (details please)
    Court appearances of parents or siblings since girl's committal
    In your opinion what kind of response has this girl made to training (very good: good: fair: poor outlook: hopeless)
Remarks

The response to this request for follow-up information was excellent, in that a completed form and additional information were returned relating to all but four of the girls. In the cases of three of these four girls, closure of their Approved School precluded any return from there; but we still had the routine follow-up information sent previously to the Classifying School. In the case of the fourth girl, the Approved School Order had been revoked. Additional follow-up information was obtained in special cases from the medical records of mental hospitals, from after-care agents and probation officers.

The 322 girls admitted to the Magdalen Hospital School during 1958 included four girls who stayed only a day or two. We have no information about them. On all the remaining 318 girls there is a mass of information which is fairly consistent in degree of completeness from case to case. We had the data of the Record of Information, the Psychiatrist's (J.C.s) case notes and reports, the Psychologist's test results and reports, reports of other staff members, reports of psychiatric hospitals and psychiatrists elsewhere in cases where such contacts had been made, and the follow-up data. It is this material which is analysed in the following pages.

The most noteworthy deficiency of the material is the lack of a family history taken from a psychiatric point of view. The Magdalen Hospital School had no psychiatric social worker, who might have made a variety of useful enquiries in the London cases; and in general the psychiatric aspects of past history and later life are very deficient in those cases where the girl did not actually come under special psychiatric observation. One of the plans we originally had in mind was to make an estimate of the frequency of psychiatric ill health, especially psychosis, in the parents of delinquent girls. The poverty of the material on this side precluded this possibility.

The role of the psychiatrist in the classifying school

Part of the data which are described and analysed in the following pages were obtained by the Psychiatrist (J.C.) attached to the Classifying School in the ordinary course of his work. The nature of his relations with these girls is accordingly of some consequence and needs a brief description. The School was closed on 31.3.66

having been empty for some months previously, but the routine followed up to that time may be described as follows.

The psychiatrist is responsible for the mental welfare of every girl admitted, his first contact occurring when an admission date is sought and the girl's Record of Information is made available. Even then he may have to make provisional arrangements for a psychiatrically orientated programme, if this is indicated by the facts in the Record. The girl may be epileptic, or psychotic, or unusually aggressive or potentially suicidal, or for some other reason she may need to be involved in a ready-made plan of action immediately she is admitted.

The relationship of the psychiatrist to the girl is that of doctor to patient. The psychiatric examination conducted soon after admission is confidential, and the notes are retained in a private file. A lot of private information never gets beyond this file, and does not get entered into the Record of Information. The psychiatrist accordingly feels entirely free to ask for confidential information from other doctors to expand the medical history, and can pursue his own enquiries outside the official sources of information. The parents and relatives of a girl who visit her while she is in the classifying school are interviewed by a member of the senior staff of the school, and information is obtained which is often useful psychiatrically. These interviews would, however, be much more valuable if they were conducted by a psychiatric social worker, especially one with wide sociological experience.

Each girl is examined at least once during the time she is in the classifying school. The interview covers much the same ground in every case. It is in fact 'structured' to scan the psychical areas in which one is most likely to get a glimpse of the psychopathology and the motivations which led to the present situation. But these interviews are also potentially helpful therapeutically, and they are accordingly so conducted as to free the girl of her inhibitions and let her express herself with the least anxiety or embarrassment. It is advantageous to base the interview on the same lines of enquiry in every case, as it provides the psychiatrist with an instrument of comparison and relative assessment. Moreover, because every girl is interviewed in the same way there is no question in her mind that she is being singled out as being 'mental' or different from her peers in any way. The girls seek out information, and enquire into each other's offences, family backgrounds and relationships and their experience of love, companionship and sex. By such means they allay their anxiety and depression, or resentment and suspicion; and they may in this way 'talk out' a situation, rather than act it out in aggressive, anti-authority and rebellious behaviour.

The psychiatric interview comes to be regarded with all too much importance in the girls' view. The girls believe that their future placement depends largely on the impression they make during the interview. Rarely does a girl come for interview who has not been primed by others about what to expect, and rarely does she leave without being quizzed by her friends about what has occurred. They cross-examine each other about any enquiries made by adults into the psychosexual aspects of their lives. It has a reassuring effect when they find, on comparing notes afterwards, that they have all had broadly similar interviews, with an equal interest shown in each.

The interview technique may be described as follows. As it is important to obtain some idea of the girl's peer status and to learn something of her group behaviour, the psychiatrist usually collects the first girl from the group, and the group reaction is noted. Subsequently, the first girl collects another girl, and so on until the number is complete. The reaction of the guide towards the next girl to be interviewed is noted; and it is possible by seemingly neutral questions to get an idea of the girl's status within the group, and their reactions and attitudes towards each other.

The first half of the interview is conducted 'blind', and the clinical impression is recorded. Particular attention is paid to manneristic behaviour, distractibility, hyperkinesis, uncoordinated and clumsy movements, avoidance of direct gaze, tension habits, and other motor expressions of intrapsychic tensions and conflictual anxiety. The interview usually begins with a few neutral questions, such as asking the girl's age, her length of stay in the Magdalen, and about various house activities. No attempt is made to establish rapport until a factual account of the reasons leading up to admission to the classifying school has been gained. Her verbatim story is recorded, and this often gives valuable clues to causes and motivations, and is helpful in the general assessment of the girl at later stages.

When the 'blind' half of the interview has been completed, the Record of Information is read, and forms the basis for subsequent enquiries. The second stage of the interview focuses attention on the delinquent acts. Stealing, for instance, has to be evaluated in the same way as symptoms of any other kind. The change and development of the symptom over the whole course of its duration has to be studied. It is important to know the extent of material, or neurotic gain that is being derived from the symptom, and its psychological and physiological accompaniments. Affective and obsessive-compulsive factors seem to be of especial importance.

Prior to classification, very little attention seems to be given to a study of these acts. A bald description of socially deviant behaviour is given in sufficient detail to help the Court in deciding what to do. The psychiatrist reporting to the Court is mainly interested in the girl's personality and her emotional development, and in finding where he can evidence of neuroticism, brain damage, psychosis, or other factors which might need and might respond to medical attention. The girls who are remanded for a medical report are often sent for psychiatric examination by the Court because of a history of emotional instability, or because of sexual behaviour which is hardly to be understood in the individual setting except in terms of psychiatric instability. The Courts also like to have psychiatric reports on girls with repeated offences. Because of this, the psychiatrist often starts from a biased position and has preconceived ideas. He is likely to credit his patient with less control, judgment and sense than she actually has. Psychiatrists have ideas of their own, often not universally agreed. Some, for instance, consider parental deprivation in the earlier years as all-important, and then in their endeavours to unearth factors of this kind may neglect the wider longitudinal and cross-sectional survey. The danger is all the greater when, as is often the case, he is seeing the girl for the first and last time. A psychiatric diagnosis is expected, and specific recommendations based upon it. The psychiatrist's duty at this stage is to help the Court to find the best practicable solution.

The task of the psychiatrist attached to the classifying school is a different one. His first duty is to care for the girl's mental health while she is in his hands. Secondly he has to provide, to the Head of the training school selected for her, information which will have long-term value. A more refined psychiatric assessment is needed than was possible in the precommittal stage, and the psychiatrist will have the more detailed knowledge to make it possible.

The commonest reason given by the girls to account for their committal is absconding from home, hostel, lodgings or institution. Running away is an act charged with emotion. Sometimes it is intended as a final rejection of the home (at that time), and is sometimes in turn met with counter-rejection by the parents, who may wash their hands of the girl and declare she is beyond their control. At the time of this study they could and often did take her to Court on this account. In the Criminal Justice Act 1963, power of direct referral to the Courts is removed from the parents.

The attitude of the girl towards authority is a key point in the examination. Her school work is discussed, her status among other girls of her age, and her relationship with her teachers. Persistent truanting is frequent, and the record in this respect is an important guide to assessment. Of the present group only 4·5 per cent had an 'excellent' school attendance record, while in 34 per cent the record was 'good', in 23 per cent 'fair', in 22 per cent 'poor' and in 16 per cent 'very irregular'. Comparable figures for the school population as a whole are unfortunately not available. The girls who truanted a lot explained it by a frank dislike of school, often for no clear reason, and by their inability to get on with other girls and with their teachers. A common complaint is that they are not accepted by the other girls because they cannot compete with them intellectually or in material possessions. In this group there were no cases of school phobia. Many of the girls were actually encouraged to stay at home by mothers who were themselves tired and overworked, in poor physical shape after having a large family, or neurotic. The kind of separation anxiety that forms the basis of most cases of school phobia was not present, or was lost in the antisocial and anti-authority attitudes, shared with the parents, fully expressed and present in direct conscious awareness.

As a considerable majority of the whole group are deemed to be in moral danger and in need of care and protection, some assessment of the depth of psychosocial maladjustment has to be made. This has to be approached with tact and sensitivity, by way of a discussion rather than cross-examination on specific details. All these girls have been heavily cross-examined already by parents, police, probation officers and others, and are ready to take a defensive attitude. It is easier if the approach is made obliquely by way of relatively unemotional medical matters.

A beginning is made with enquiries about menstruation and any difficulties concerned with it; this leads to enquiries about the time of onset and the extent to which the girl was prepared for it, under what circumstances and by whom. Nearly always this brings out basic attitudes towards her parents, especially her mother, and to other sibs and other girls. Fantasy and reality attitudes towards pregnancy and sex in general emerge. In our group the mean age of menarche was 13·15 years; but in many cases no regular pattern was established for several months. The age of sexual initiation (mean age 14·15 years) is another turning point, which may have special significance in the history. Although many girls admit to prepubertal sex play, it is not common for full sexual initiation to occur before the onset of puberty, the exceptions being almost exclusively in cases of incestuous relationships or in 'non-voluntary' relationships with older men. The age of the initiating partner is very important. The older he is, the more damaging it proves to normal psychosexual development and adjustment. The longer the interval following menarche before initiation, and the closer her age to that of her partner, the less the damage that occurs. Most girls are initiated by lads of nearly their own age, and the mean of the stated ages of the initiating partner was found to be between 18 and 19.

The nature of the emotional relationship to the initiating partner often reveals general attitudes of importance, and fantasies about the opposite sex, about courtship, marriage, children and family life. Apart from the small group of cases classifiable under incest and rape, three main patterns emerged. One of the most frequent is the relationship with the steady boy friend, i.e. the boy who is regarded by the girl and by her companions as her more or less regular partner, to whom all priorities are given (over a period of at least two months). Forty per cent of the girls said that they were initiated by their steady boy friend, and 50 per cent of them said that they had been unwilling and had been overpersuaded. Fifty per cent of the girls said they had been initiated by an acquaintance, usually a member of the 'gang', or a neighbour or a school friend, and in only 10 per cent of these cases was the girl an unwilling partner. The commonest single stated motivation was to satisfy curiosity, or to win favour from a male member of the gang. In about 10 per cent of cases initiation occurred, with a casual partner, while the girl was on the run from home, or at a party. In about 15 per cent of these cases the girl said she was actually unwilling, although she was in a position in which she had virtually no choice.

The main impression which one forms on seeing a group of these girls is that of lack of grace or beauty; in technical jargon, they tend to be of dysplastic physique. A large proportion of them are large-boned powerfully built girls, nearly all overweight, and some grossly obese. A smaller number are small, thin and poorly developed girls with pinched and sometimes shrewish faces. Their quick ferret-like movements are in strong contrast with the elephantine gracelessness of the bigger girls. There are, of course, well-proportioned girls, sometimes handsome in a Junoesque way; but even then one is likely to see physical deformities such as squints, or skin-blemishes or scars, the evidence of childhood neglect or of the wounds of battle in their jungle background. It seems quite likely that physical defects and lack of physical attractiveness have played a part in causing delinquency. With such a disadvantage, a girl will be all the more likely, one supposes, to become miserable, angry, rebellious or resentful when adolescence compels her to take notice of it.

During the individual interview, the quality and the degree of energy of the personality make an immediate impression. Nearly always the girl is under tension, and shows that this has been her state for some time. Very many of them are nail-biters, and nearly all have this or other tension habits. In the interview they are distractible, avoid direct gaze, and fidget in the chair. Some particular technique of handling a situation, which has been learned in the past, may then be displayed; and they may be negativistic, sullen and aggressive, or gay, frivolous, coquettish.

Some of the more inadequate, insecure and anxious girls have disfigured themselves with tattoo marks on their arms and other accessible parts of their bodies. Usually these are scratch marks only, but at times they have been made more permanent by pricking in ink or boot-polish. The names of boy friends predominate, with 'Mum' or 'Dad' as second favourite. Hearts pierced with arrows, entwined hands and female figures are the commonest designs; they may show a nautical interest and a seaport domicile. Sometimes the girl has asked her boy friend to inscribe his name on her skin, and thus mark her as his exclusive property and warn off competitors. Asked what this meant to her, one girl said: 'When I am scratching his name I feel he is near to me and it is like being married to him and he has become part of me and I am not lonely any more.'*

Most of these girls have no real awareness of themselves as individuals. They have no long-term aspirations, no dominating interests, and are content to drift along on a diet of pop music, pep pills and parties, using sex as their credit card. When they come into the Classifying School they are deprived of their usual background; the façade they have adopted can no longer be maintained, and they have nothing to fall back upon. For a time they will seek to recreate the façade in fantasy, and they will be able to use themes from their actual and their fantasied experience of life for communication with each other. The more normal girls quickly abandon such attempts at escape from reality, and begin to make positive relationships with adults around them, and to develop realistic aspirations for the future. The more aggressive girls tend to act out their fantasies by attacking adult authority and planning to abscond. When frustrated, they become stubborn, sullen, negativistic and provocative. Inadequate, anxious and passive girls, on the other hand, show regressive traits and may indulge in attention-seeking and testing-out techniques. Sometimes real depressive features show, with feelings of guilt, tears and self-reproach, and changes in appetite, sleep rhythm and mood. Suicidal gestures and attempts are common in this group.

The psychiatric findings and their use in classification, and the girls who have made suicidal attempts, are discussed in later chapters. The three thumbnail sketches following, consecutive cases taken practically at random, may serve to illustrate the variety of persons and problems with which the psychiatrist had to deal.

* Projection of feeling also occurs through the medium of graffiti on toilet walls, books and furniture. It is noteworthy that graffiti at the Classifying School are more copious, lurid and sentimental than the similar productions made by the same girls at their Training Schools a little later on. The change may be in part a result of growing up and settling down. In the Training School the girl goes into a settled group, with a group tradition, where she will have increased security. In the swiftly changing population of the Classifying School there is no time for such group traditions to develop.

3244. Aged 15y 11m; IQ 127. Father sales-manager; mother part-time factory worker. Alice has one younger sister. Home, well kept and comfortably furnished. At her grammer school Alice is reported to have lied constantly, to have shown a negative attitude to persuasion and punishment, to have failed in effort and to have truanted. Her ability was thought to be low average for a grammar school; she left prematurely at her parents' request. Subsequently she had a number of jobs in superior shops, but proved an unsatisfactory worker. Her first court appearance was at the age of 15y 7m: beyond control, stole from employer, mixing with bad associates; second court appearance: larceny, false pretences. Psychiatric opinion at Classifying School: extremely shallow, with fantasies of being a brilliant artist; personality defect.

3245. Aged 15y 2m; IQ 115. Father salesman, Plymouth Brother, lacking affection, very strict and narrow; mother died after a long illness when Beryl was 10 years old; step-mother. Beryl has one younger sister and an infant paternal half-sib. Home, a 5-roomed house on a new estate, in excellent condition. At school she was regarded as being attention-seeking in the extreme but a delightful little girl. She was greatly unsettled by her mother's long illness and death, and later was upset by the step-mother's pregnancy, during which she first showed concern, and then became less friendly, turning her attention towards young men. One court appearance only at 15y 2m: care or protection, promiscuity. Psychiatric opinion: her promiscuity was a final rebellion against her father's fanatical restrictiveness.

3246. Aged 15y 5m; IQ 98. Father, collier, with gypsy blood, will not work; much discord with mother; mother press operator in factory. Christine is the eldest of 3 sibs of which the youngest, aged 9, is mentally retarded. Home, clean comfortable council house. School, very irregular attendance, disobedient, latterly isolated. Employment, frequently dismissed, impudence, pilfering. Three court appearances, first at 15y 3m for larceny, last: beyond control, exposed to moral danger, had run away from home, was associating with coloured men. Psychiatric opinion: a restless, unprepossessing girl, hiding inner tension under a façade of being self-assured, strong attachment to father.

Circumstances leading to committal

From the annual report of the Magdalen Hospital for 1958 Table 1 has been derived, showing the reasons for committal of the 322 girls admitted during that year; 314 were direct committals, 5 second committals, and 3 were transfers from other schools. There were 321 disposals: 313 transfers to other Approved Schools (46

REASONS FOR COMMITTAL	
Care or Protection	88
After Supervision	86
Brought back by Local Authority (after Fit Person order) . .	28
Beyond Control	25
Refractory	8
Non-attendance at School	4
Absconding from care of Fit Person	1
Care or Protection and Beyond Control	1
TOTAL OF SEX DELINQUENCIES	241
Larceny	65
Breach of Probation	5
Forgery	1
Vagrancy	3
Wilful Damage	3
Indecent Assault	1
False Pretences	1
Larceny and Care or Protection	1
Larceny, Possession of Offensive Weapons and Assault . .	1
TOTAL OF INDICTABLE OFFENCES	81

TABLE 1. Reasons for committal of the 322 girls admitted to the Magdalen Hospital in 1958.

requiring special treatment for venereal disease, 21 transferred to Duncroft for psychiatric treatment, and 12 needing maternity care). In 2 cases the Secretary of State ordered discharge; in 2 cases the order was revoked on appeal; 4 girls were transferred to the Shaw for classification.

As will be seen from the table, in three quarters of the cases the delinquency was in the nature of misbehaviour, mainly sexual, of a kind not subject to legal sanctions after the age of 17; in the remainder there was an indictable offence. Authorities are agreed that not too much should be made of this difference. Gibbens (1959) has commented on the close relationship between waywardness and antisocial behaviour, noting that girls who

before puberty steal from home or from shops, later turn to dis-
obedience at home, staying out late and making undesirable
sexual relationships. In our material practically no statistically
significant differences between the wayward girls and the offenders
revealed themselves, though the latter were on average about
three months younger. Among the sexually delinquent group there
are girls who are known to have stolen; but larceny, if it has
occurred, has been regarded as of much less significance than
aspects of the case calling for care or protection. It has often been
instigated by male companions, and sometimes has been the
means of independence in bestowing or withholding sexual
favours.

In the cases where larceny is the main charge, sex aspects have
played a relatively minor role. Stealing may be a simple result of
dishonesty, without any noteworthy psychopathological basis.
Nevertheless psychiatric aspects were just as prominent among
larcenists as in the rest of the girls, and just as frequently as the
others they had a psychiatrically positive after-history. It is in this
group that one finds relatively often a history of separation from
the mother or mother substitute, and a history of unusual mobility.
Girls with a history of stealing appear to find greater difficulty
than others in fitting into a new school environment; and they are
reported to be more prone to truanting. Repeated moves are often
indicative of unsatisfactory families; and they impose additional
stresses on the girl at a time when she is particularly vulnerable.
Stealing seems to be all the more likely when feelings of deprivation are combined with feelings of inferiority and inadequacy. If
the act has been ill-planned, crudely carried out and easily detected, with the need for material gain not a pressing one, a
neurotic motivation is likely to be present. One has to enquire
about the kind of objects stolen, and their manner of disposal. On
the other hand if the girl shows familiarity with the slang of
criminal subcultural groups, one can judge how much she has
been the victim of contamination through association. These are
matters of prognostic importance both for training and subsequent
rehabilitation.

The bulk of the sex delinquencies arise as a result of disturbed
parent-child relationships. The evidence for this admittedly
common-place opinion will be presented later. However, evidence
can often be gained from the individual case history that the

beginnings of such a disturbance go back to pre-school years. The disorder is a progressive one, and is usually accompanied by deterioration in school relationships. The girl is then open to the pressures and persuasions of schoolfellows and contemporaries with similar problems. From them she learns that the simplest and easiest way to deal with her problems is to try to avoid them, and if they are not to be avoided, to run away from them altogether. In its simplest form, the reaction starts as a phase of sulky rebelliousness, followed by a phase of testing out her parents by staying out later and later. Finally she may abscond from home. From this point chance plays a decisive part: she may find herself pregnant, or forced into prostitution, or involved in drug taking. Often enough she is debarred from returning home by the attitude of rejection taken by her parents; this rejection is usually maintained only until the girl is safely committed. However, many parents have tried by every means possible to guide and help their children along acceptable pathways, only to be defeated by a response that baffles them to the end. There is a hard core of girls who seem unable to respond to the help offered them; and we have not yet been able to evolve adequate ways of meeting their needs.

The role of the psychologist

The principal duty of the Educational Psychologist is to give an assessment of ability, both present and potential, and of scholastic attainments. If it is considered necessary, further diagnostic tests pertaining to personality are administered.

The attitudes of the girls to the test situation vary considerably. Some are frankly suspicious, and complain that they do not need to see a psychologist as they are 'not mad'. Others are nervous, and are inhibited by the memory of many a failure in school tests. The majority are anxious to do well, and with most of the girls rapport is easily established. A small number ask the purpose of the tests, but most accept it as a part of the classifying procedure which everyone must undergo.

The results of the tests, when treated statistically, show a distribution roughly comparable to that of the normal population, but with a preponderance of cases falling within the range 80 to 100 IQ. This ability level is normally catered for by the B and C streams of secondary modern schools, where there is an A, B, C streaming system; and it is this group of girls who generally have least interest in continuing with academic work. Many of them have received a formal education which has little bearing on their aspirations or practical needs, and they are almost unanimously glad to have left their schools. In contrast, the small number of girls of grammar school level are anxious to continue their education up to GCE level, and provision is made for them to do this.

When the test results are considered in relation to the girl's actual performance in school or at work, a strange contradiction becomes apparent. The girls of high IQ seem to have been persistently underfunctioning, while those of low ability, even the technically sub-normal, have reached a level of practical performance which is higher than one would expect from formal test results. A possible explanation of this is that the girl of high ability, whose home background is stable, must be 'disturbed' to become involved in antisocial activity, as there is no coherent environmental cause. This disturbance will naturally impair her performance. Conversely the girl from a poor cultural background, with little verbal facility or academic aptitude, will find the test situation harassing and will tend to underscore. In the practical field, however, she will more nearly approach an average level of performance.

Apart from the actual testing, each girl is interviewed informally about school, work and the family situation. Many of the older girls have held a long succession of jobs for short periods, and have no special interest or ambition. The main factor in their inability to hold jobs seems to be difficulty in face-to-face relationships with their superiors, and occasionally, their peers at work. Bad time-keeping is another factor, as is absenteeism. Many of the girls complain that their jobs have been 'boring'; but few of them have any special aptitudes sufficiently developed to apply to the work situation. The most common ambition given, usually by pre-school-leavers, is to 'work with children'. Work with animals comes second to this. These are typical choices of the insecure adolescent, since she imagines that the problems of communication will be cut to a minimum, and many jobs of this type are residential, thus providing a 'home' as well. Few of them have any idea of the qualifications or training necessary for different kinds of work, and the majority have been given very little vocational guidance at all. It is not, of course, the job of the classifying school to find the girls work; but it is useful to have an idea of their aspirations, to aid allocation to the schools which will cater for their needs.

SUMMARY

The group of girls investigated was a complete year's intake (1958) of the Magdalen Hospital classifying school. Girls committed to the school look on it as a prison sentence; after an initial emotional disturbance, the girl who is not psychopathic or severely neurotic settles down well. Further emotional disturbance is likely when the time for release from her training school approaches.

The number of girls investigated was 318, nearly all in the three year groups 14, 15 and 16 years. One of the authors (J.C.) was the Consultant Psychiatrist to the Magdalen Hospital School; and the investigation is based on his findings, the Records of Information, the reports of the School's Educational Psychologist, and also on a follow-up study conducted at the training schools.

The girls had come from all over southern England, as far north as Birmingham, Leicester and Peterborough, and as far west as Falmouth and Swansea. Of the 322 girls admitted to the School in 1958, 241 were committed for sex delinquencies (care or protection, etc.) and 81 for indictable offences, mainly larceny.

IV

Age, Intelligence and Attainment

Age

THE Magdalen Hospital School is for the intermediate and senior girls, with age range from the fourteenth to the seventeenth birthday. No girls were admitted during 1958 who were over the age of 17 years 0 months; but owing to exceptional administrative necessities there were 3 girls under the age of 14 (aged 13 years and 2, 5 and 11 months). The age distribution of the girls, together with other data, is shown in Table 3. Their mean age was 15 years 8·6 months with standard deviation 10·7 months.

We singled out the 53 youngest girls, i.e. the lowest sixth in age of the total of 318, for special examination. However they differed in only a few respects from the others. They were of significantly lower intelligence (IQ 92·4) than the rest; the nature of the charges made against them was relatively seldom classifiable as sexual (Table A1); and a relatively high proportion of them came from poor or institutional homes (Table A2). The relative deficiency of sexual misbehaviour is probably no more than a reflection of their greater immaturity. The other two observations may be understood when we reflect that young children are better protected than older ones, not only by their families and friends from getting into trouble, but also by other social agencies from being taken away from their homes. The relatively low intelligence may have predisposed these younger girls to getting out of hand; and their history of a poor home background may have been a consideration to the Courts in deciding to remove them to an Approved School.

Taking all 318 girls together, the relationship between age and intelligence shows up in Figure 2. The relevant figures, which are statistically significant, are available in Table A3. This suggests that it is principally for the youngest children that deficiency of intelligence increases the risk of delinquency. As the age of 15 is

I.Q.	No.	Mean size of sibship including patient
51— 52 58— 59 60— 64 66— 69	2 4 4 8	4·56
70— 74 75— 79	16 21	4·81
80— 84 85— 89	30 27	5·16
90— 94 95— 99	40 44	4·23
100—103 105—109	23 28	3·76
110—114 115—119	19 17	3·51
120—124 125—129	13 9	3·52
130—132 135—138 141—143 146—149	5 3 2 3	2·83
TOTAL MEAN S.D.	318 96·23 18·15	

TABLE 2. Distribution of intelligence quotients (Stanford-Binet Terman-Merrill). The mean size of the sibship into which the proposita was born is given for a rougher grouping.

approached, disturbed behaviour of the delinquent type becomes more and more within the span of normal reaction, taking the emotional instability of puberty into account. At this age there is a sharp rise in the incidence of delinquency in girls; and in this series we find that the children who are coming under observation are of almost exactly average intelligence. A year later, the mean intelligence of girls coming under observation has approximated to the mean of the group as a whole, and the indications of interaction between

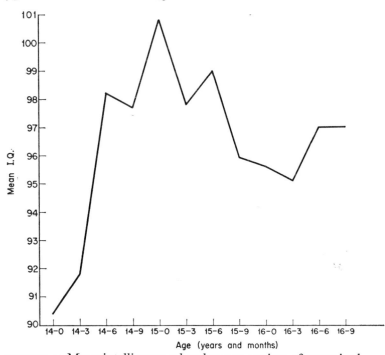

FIGURE 2. Mean intelligence related to age at time of committal.

age and intelligence have disappeared. Dividing our material into only three age classes, we see this change very clearly:

Age grouping	N	Mean IQ
13·2 —14·7	49	91·9
14·8 —15·10	116	99·1
15·11—17·0	153	96·8

The following may be taken as an example of the way in which low intelligence, in a setting of severe deprivation, can bring about a need for institutional care, even when the girl is too young to have developed the more adult forms of misbehaviour.

3189. Aged 14y 1m; IQ 59. Father died when Doreen was aged 6; the mother married again, a farm labourer, when she was ten. Mother and step-father are both of low intelligence, and there are many quarrels. There is one younger brother of nine, and the mother has a baby of eighteen months. Home conditions are sub-standard;

the family live in a tied cottage in a bad state of repair, dirty and ill-kept, in an isolated village. Doreen was brought up by her maternal grandmother until she was thirteen, and ran wild; she spent a happy childhood with her, and only since her death has she been in trouble. She was very backward, in an ESN class, school attendance poor, difficult relations with other children. She has been sexually precocious since the age of eleven. At the classifying school she impressed the psychiatrist as making the best of herself as far as her intellectual ability allowed; it did not seem that emotional factors had interfered greatly with her educational development. She claimed that her difficulties had arisen because she was unable to accept or tolerate her step-father, and she blamed him for causing her mother to reject her. Court appearance: care or protection; had run away twice.

Intelligence

Tests of intelligence, and of reading and arithmetic ages, were carried out by a qualified Educational Psychologist. The Terman-Merrill Stanford-Binet, WISC and other intelligence tests, and the reading tests, were given individually; the arithmetic tests were given to groups. Seventy-one girls of the sample were given the Raven's Matrices Test in addition to other tests. These girls were selected for this test because their powers of formal reasoning were not thought to be sensitively assessed by the other tests given. Of these 71, about 50 per cent produced scores equivalent to those they made on the Binet, some 35 per cent produced scores significantly lower, and 15 per cent significantly higher. The final IQ used for statistical purposes was that taken to be the best estimate. Very frequently other psychological tests, e.g. those of a projection type such as the TAT, were done as well; but we have made no statistical use of this. The mean distribution of IQs is shown in Table 2, with other data. The mean IQ of 96·23 (SD 18·15) is significantly lower than the expected mean of 100. As the distribution is very nearly symmetrical, one may assume that this shift to the left is a general feature of the material as a whole.

Intelligence and size of family

In the population as a whole, sociologists have repeatedly observed that there is a relationship between intelligence and size of family.

It has been found, for instance, that rating schoolchildren by intelligence, the lower the child's intelligence the larger, on average, was the number of his brothers and sisters. This phenomenon holds true for the population as a whole, and is related to differences between socio-economic classes in the distribution of intelligence test scores, and different patterns of marriage and

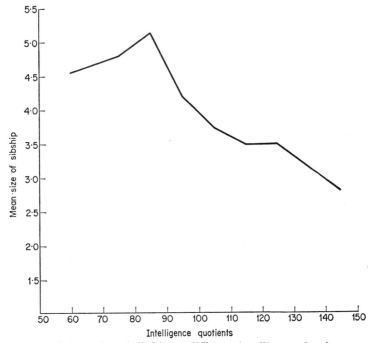

FIGURE 3. Mean size of sibship at different intelligence levels.

family building in social classes, as well as differences between the less intelligent and the more intelligent in family planning. The families of our Madgalen girls show the negative relationship between sibship size and intelligence very clearly (Figure 3, Table 2). The size of the sibship (including the girl herself) averages over 5 for girls of dull normal intelligence with IQs between 80 and 89. To the left, where IQs are still lower, sibship size falls off to some extent; but to the right, as IQs get higher, the fall in sibship size is very much sharper, reaching eventually a value of only 2·8 for girls with IQs between 130 and 149. The same phenomenon can be looked at in another way: if we take out of the whole series those 156 girls who were brought up in a home sibship of one to three (including the girl herself), their mean IQ was 98·7, significantly higher than for the group as a whole.

The most intelligent girls

A striking finding in our material was the large number of girls of very good intelligence. To see whether further light could be thrown on the relationship between intelligence and delinquency, we took out the records of the top sixth in intelligence, i.e. 53 girls with measured IQs between 114 and 149. Not surprisingly, they were better educated than the others, and they also tended to come from smaller sibships (average 3·1 instead of 4·2 for the material as a whole). Other differences between the most intelligent girls and the rest did not reach statistical significance.

However, among these girls there were indications of subjection to more than the average amount of environmental stress. They contained within their number more than the expected number of illegitimate children, of adopted children, and of cases of maternal deprivation. They also tended to come with particular frequency from the eldest members of the sibship. The interesting relationships between delinquency and birth order are discussed on p. 122. One can expect the average member of the population to be about halfway along the sibship, from eldest to youngest, with a position that averages at 0·5. Among these intelligent girls, the mean birth order (born sibship) was 0·37, and in the home sibship 0·28. Although this shift to the left is a large one, numbers were too small for statistical significance.

If it is true that the most intelligent girls had been subjected to more than the average degree of environmental stress, one could explain it by supposing that a good intelligence tended to protect a girl against delinquency, this degree of protection only being overborne if other factors are increased in severity.

The relationship between delinquency and dullness of intelligence

Most authors who have reported on delinquents do not give any estimate of the mean IQ, but draw attention to features of its distribution, such as the proportion of children with IQs lower than 70, 80, 85 or 90. These figures vary very much; and they are often not given in a form permitting of easy comparisons. The proportion of delinquents with IQs lower than 90 is given by different authors as anything between 16 per cent (Litauer, 1957) and 58 per cent (Dunsdon, quoted by Woodward, 1955). This proportion in our girls was 33 per cent.

The most important reference in this field is the review by Woodward (1955) of significant work to that date, which however led her to somewhat inconclusive results. She considered that early studies showing marked lowering of the mean IQ were unreliable because of technical inadequacies; and that even the best and most recent work was unable to eliminate cultural effects which suggest a relationship which may not in fact exist. She thought the best estimate of the mean intelligence of delinquents in the USA was 92, and in this country not less than 90. It is accordingly interesting that our material based on individual tests, shows a mean much nearer still to that of the general population.

Woodward stressed two factors which might tend to depress the test results of delinquents in an artificial manner. First, delinquents tend to come (as ours did) from larger sibships than most children do. Secondly, delinquents are commonly emotionally unstable, and emotional upsets may reduce the level of performance under stress. We do not consider that emotional upset played any noteworthy part in lowering the IQ score in our series. As is reported later (p. 141), the girls diagnosed as showing neurotic symptoms had a mean IQ which was almost exactly the same as that of all the girls together.

One of the possibilities which Woodward did not take into account was that there might have been a secular change in the intelligence of delinquents. Such a change is shown by the Magdalen material, the estimates of the mean IQ of the yearly intake, as shown in the annual reports being for six successive years:

1953	89·5
1954	91·5
1955	93·0
1956	92·0
1957	94·1
1958	96·7

These figures suggest that in more recent times the risk of delinquency may have increased for adolescents of average and
superior intelligence, more than for those of less than average
intelligence, so that the preponderance of the latter has diminished. This is a speculation that deserves to be tested, since it
might have consequences for public policy.

In some series, mental subnormality may have acted in its own
right in the selection that goes to constitute a research group. The
500 women studied by the Gluecks (1934b) were of remarkably
low intelligence as a group. None were of higher IQ than 110,
and only 22 per cent were over 100. Below this, 28 per cent were
dull (IQ 81–90), 16 per cent borderline (71–80), 32 per cent
feebleminded (50–70), and there were 11 imbeciles. The distribution has a bimodal appearance; the numbers of feebleminded
are very large, but there are fewer in the borderline group than one
might expect from the total shift to the left. An effect like this
could have arisen if mental deficiency had been a selective factor,
independently of its association with delinquency.

It may well be that mental subnormality plays a larger part in
adult female delinquency than in the delinquencies of girls, since
the adult aberration is the rarer and the psychologically more
deviant. The Gluecks' finding calls to mind the observations of
Penrose (1963) on the relation between crime and subnormality.

In all studies, he says, it has been found that a higher proportion
of women criminals than of men fall into the borderline defective
range. There is a striking connection between the number of
persons admitted to hospital as defective, or epileptic, or mentally
abnormal in any way, and the numbers sent to prison. This is
highlighted when there are administrative differences in handling
white and coloured populations in a single community. For
instance in the Union of South Africa in the year 1935, 3·72 per
thousand of the European population and 3·38 per thousand of
the non-European population were institutionalized. In the case
of the Europeans this was 3·27 in the mental hospitals and 0·45 in
the jails, in the case of the non-Europeans 2·56 in the jails and
0·82 in the mental hospitals. In European countries, also, there is
an inverse relationship between the number of beds provided for
the mentally ill or defective, and the number of people in prison.
'On the average, the provision of two mental hospital beds will
make one prison cell unnecessary'(!)

The fact that the mean IQ of our girls, at 96, was significantly lower than the expected population mean of 100, means that in this respect they fall into line with the results of others. There are few who would yet go so far as Woodward in thinking it unsafe to suppose that lowness of intelligence plays any role in the causation of delinquency. But most writers tend to the view that the part played in the causation of delinquency by a relatively low level of intelligence is not a very important one. As a rule, views on causation are not precisely formulated; it is usually implied as much as stated that a relatively low intelligence constitutes a handicap for the child of a kind to increase the risk of delinquency, and is on a par with other handicaps. If this is the way it works, it cannot be the same for all cases. As will be shown when we discuss the psychiatric classification of the girls, those who were diagnosed by the psychiatrist as showing abnormality of personality actually had a higher than average mean intelligence (100·7).

Educational standard

If the intelligence of these girls did not deviate very sharply from general population norms, we cannot be so confident about their educational level. Indeed the universality and the massive degree of educational retardation which was found was such as to suggest educational neglect. Table 3 shows the distribution of reading ages and arithmetic ages; and it shows that while the mean chronological age was over 15, the mean reading age was 12 years and the mean arithmetic age less than 11.

Using Burt's definition of technical backwardness in educational attainment, over 50 per cent of the girls were technically backward (or worse) in reading, 20 per cent of them being retarded by more than 30 per cent of the chronological age (notional maximum 15 years). In arithmetic, the standard of attainment reached was even worse: 78 per cent of the girls were technically backward, and 40 per cent of them were retarded by more than 30 per cent of their chronological age (notional maximum 14½ years). Only 18 per cent of the girls were technically backward neither in reading nor in arithmetic; and 147 out of the 318, or 46 per cent, were technically backward (or worse) in both. Naturally, there is a high degree of correlation between one kind of retardation and the other; and this is shown in Table A4.

Age in years and months	Chronological age	Reading age	Arithmetic age
4·0— 4·11	—	1	—
5·0— 5·11	—	2	—
6·0— 6·11	—	2	—
7·0— 7·11	—	10	20
8·0— 8·11	—	18	32
9·0— 9·11	—	18	60
10·0—10·11	—	29	77
11·0—11·11	—	39	41
12·0—12·11	—	56	41
13·0—13·11	3	81	25
14·0—14·11	75	60	22
15·0—15·11	100	1	—
16·0—16·11	126	—	—
17·0	14	—	—
TOTAL	318	317	318
MEAN VALUES	15 yrs. 9 mo.	12 yrs. 1 mo.	10 yrs. 9 mo.

TABLE 3. Distribution in respect of chronological age, reading age (Schonell) and arithmetic age (Burt).

It is difficult to discount these findings, but they have to be taken with some reserve, for two reasons. Both the Schonell reading test and the Burt arithmetic test, which were used, would not now be regarded as very up to date; and, unlike some modern tests, it is not possible to find for them the required standards from representative national samples:

Comparison with normal standards

Comparative material from samples of the general population can be found for reading ability, but not for 'numeracy' or ability with tests of arithmetic. It seems that educational standards show a good deal of secular variation, so that at some epochs children, on a national basis, are better educated than at others:

Shortly after the war a committee set up by the authority of the Ministry of Education inquired into the question whether the reading ability of children had been affected by the war ('Reading Ability', 1950). A new test, the Watts-Vernon test of reading ability was given to 3,500 children aged close to 15.0 years, and to 2,800 children aged close to 11.0 years. It was found that the reading ability of the fifteen-year-old was 22 months behind that of their fellows of ten years earlier, and that of the eleven-year-old was 12 months behind. Similar tests were carried out in 1952 and in 1956, as reported in a Ministry of Education pamphlet ('Standards of Reading 1948–1956', 1957). This showed that by 1956 the fifteen-year-old had recovered 5 out of the 22 months of relative retardation, the eleven-year-old 4 out of the 12 months. This leaves the fifteen-year-old in 1956 still 17 months behind on the basis of pre-war standards.

On this basis, it might be that our Magdalen girls should not be regarded as very seriously retarded educationally in comparison with their peers. The detailed comparison is shown in Table A5. The 1957 report does not give fractions of a per cent, but otherwise makes use of the same standards as the report of 1950. This classifies readers into superior, average plus, average minus, backward, semi-literate and illiterate. Backward readers were those whose reading ages were more than 20 per cent below their chronological ages; illiterate readers those whose reading age (regardless of chronological age) was less than 7.0 years; semi-literate readers those whose reading age was 7.0 years or greater, but less than 9.0 years. The Watts-Vernon test was calibrated against other tests, including the Schonell test. Schonell and Watts-Vernon reading ages were found to be on the average identical over the 8.0 to 12.0 years range; below 8.0 years the Watts-Vernon test was thought probably a little too difficult, while over 12.0 years the Schonell test probably became too difficult. From the conversion table provided, one sees that the Watts-Vernon limit of 17.0 years, dividing the superior from the average readers, corresponds with a Schonell age of 14.5 (in years and tenths of a year); and the Watts-Vernon age of 13.8 dividing the average plus from the average minus, corresponds with a Schonell reading age of 13.2. In these terms the 239 Magdalen girls aged 15.0 years and more in 1958 are seen to be significantly but not very markedly behind the Ministry of Education sample of girls aged 15 in 1956. The difference between the Magdalen girls and what might be expected from a fair sample of fifteen-year-old girls in the general population is affected in two different directions. On the one hand by 1958, when the Magdalen girls were tested, standards of reading should have made a further improvement from those obtaining in 1956; so that one might think we are underestimating the difference. On the other hand the Ministry's sample of 1956 will have presumably had a mean IQ of 100, whereas our girls had a mean IQ of 96. (Pearce)

We are probably justified in concluding that the Magdalen girls have suffered educationally in comparison with their peers; and that rather more than their peers they show a marked deficiency in reading ability by standards current before the 1939–1945 war. Their abilities in arithmetic are even lower; but we have no comparative material to show whether in this respect they have suffered more educationally than the population in general. It would seem proper to stress the fact that, on an absolute scale, they are seriously educationally deprived.

The effect of intelligence on educational attainment

We now have to consider what contribution was made to this educational retardation by lowness in intelligence. The mean IQ of the Magdalen girls was 96, and some degree of educational retardation was accordingly to be expected. In Table A5 reading age and arithmetic age are correlated with IQ; and by inspection one can see that a considerable part of the variance in degree of educational retardation can be explained in terms of the variance in measured intelligence. But it can also be seen that this is not the whole of the story. Of the 122 girls with IQs of 100 and over, only

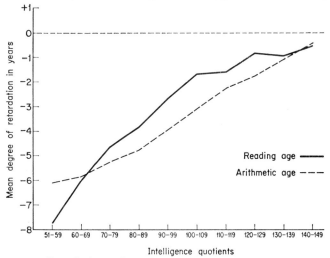

FIGURE 4. Correlation of intelligence with degree of educational retardation.

three were level with their chronological age, or ahead of it, in reading; and only 14 were ahead or level in arithmetic age. One expects a regression towards population means, when one selects a sample at one extreme of a quantitative variable, and measures performance in respect of a correlated variable; in other words, girls who did well on intelligence tests would be expected to do not

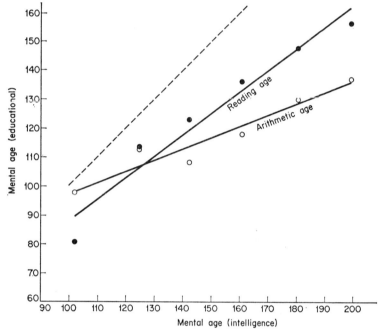

FIGURE 5. Educational mental age against mental age in intelligence.

quite so well on an educational test. But one would still expect them to do better than averagely well. In the present material, this is not so. Intelligent girls have done badly, and less intelligent girls have done worse.

The extent to which educational retardation has occurred, which cannot be accounted for by variation in intelligence, is demonstrated in Figure 4 and Figure 5. In the first of these we see that the number of years by which the girl's educational age lagged behind her chronological age (with notional maxima at 15 and $14\frac{1}{2}$), which is about seven years at the lowest IQ classification, gets less as intelligence improves, but persists through the entire intelligence range. Even at the top, with girls of IQ over 140, there is still an educational lag.

The same point is made in an even more convincing way when the effect of intelligence is eliminated by comparing attainment ages with mental age (Figure 5). The regression lines for reading age and arithmetic age against mental age lie far below the parity one would expect, and the slope in each case is less steep. As mental age increases, standards both in reading and arithmetic (but in the latter much more than the former) fall more and more behind.

There is a consensus of opinion among all workers in this field that juvenile delinquents of both sexes are more educationally re-tarded than their peers. Sir Cyril Burt was particularly impressed by this. He wrote (1948):

> 'Nothing is so startling about the juvenile delinquent as his extra-ordinary lack of knowledge; it is, with him and his kind, more frequent and more profound than any other intellectual failing. He is ignorant alike in the narrower respect of the simpler scholastic subjects—reading, writing and arithmetic—and in all the wider spheres of ordinary information and culture.'

Ferguson (1952) took a similar view. In his study of 1,349 Glasgow boys, of whom 165 had been convicted, he noted that a low level of scholastic ability was probably the most powerful single factor associated with high incidence of delinquency, and operated with equal force during and after school days. *Gittins* (1952) applied Burt's test of reading accuracy, Schonell's silent reading test, and Hill's Southend arithmetic test to 1,000 boys consecutively admitted to the Aycliffe Classifying School. The intelligence factor was held constant by relating the reading age with the mental age; reading age was less by one to two years in 37 per cent, and by more than two years in 21 per cent; arithmetic was still worse, equivalent percentages being 23 per cent one to two years retarded, 47 per cent three or four years retarded, and 26 per cent even more backward than that.

The question arises whether there is a causal connection be-tween delinquency and educational retardation, and if so, which is cause and which is effect. Merrill (1947) compared 300 delin-quent children with a control series matched for sex, age, locality and school at which the child was attending. There were large differences between the two series, both in conduct and attitude to school. It is interesting that 40 per cent of the delinquents were placed in school too high for their mental age, 21 per cent too low, the figures for the control series being 29 per cent and 28 per cent. This suggests that the child's difficulties at school might be having a bad effect on his behaviour. In their studies (1954, 1955) of 3,451 delinquent boys and 1,082 delinquent girls, Wattenberg and Saunders found that more girls than boys hated school; and that among the girls, those who were recidivists distinguished themselves from the others by more frequently being non-attenders at school, or in special classes, more frequently being estimated as below average, by their poor school marks, and by their antagonistic attitude both to teachers and class-mates.

Taking the unequivocal nature of the evidence into account, it is surprising to find that *Lady Wootton* (1959) takes such a sceptical attitude towards it. She notes the general agreement about the higher level of truancy shown by delinquents than others, but points out that the majority of truants, owing to their numbers, cannot also be delinquents. She notes also the agreement on both sides of the Atlantic that those who are guilty of offences tend to have poor school records; but she complains that much of the evidence is based on the assessments of schoolmasters, which cannot be regarded as objective. This is hardly a fair summing up. Only a few studies, notably those of Ferguson and Bagot, mainly rely on assessments by teachers, of ability or of attainment. Most authors rely on the educational record, including the grade, class or standard reached by the time of school-leaving; this has always been found to be much worse for delinquents than for their peers. Many workers have been able to assess mental ability independently of the educational standard, and where this has been done all are struck by the gross disparity: while in intelligence delinquents are at a slight disadvantage, in educational attainment they lag far behind.

Educational deprivation

It seems almost impossible to disentangle the cause-effect relationship of bad education and bad behaviour. While it seems most probable that our girls had got into habits of thinking, feeling and behaving which would prevent them from enjoying school work, prevent them from attending and trying and so prevent them from progressing, the possibility also remains that, because they were making so little progress at school, discouragement and disgust turned into truanting from school and uncontrolled behaviour outside it. Either way round, these girls were being deprived of an education up to the standards enjoyed by others of their ability and social background.

This waste of human potential is shown most strikingly, perhaps, in the girls of highest intelligence. As illustrations we may take the eight most intelligent girls, all with IQs in excess of 134. Extracts of school reports are given:

3240. Age 14y 10m; IQ 138, reading age 13.6, arithmetic age 13.9. Away from school one year, *aet.* 11–12 because of health. At 14.10 transferred from County Secondary to another secondary school as she was not working well. At the latter, attainment was not equal to ability. Often apathetic, her mind far away. Quiet, though vaguely restless at times; courteous, well-spoken, very helpful; little effort in physical training and games. Approachable and well-liked by all the staff who regret that a girl of such intelligence and potential character should be handicapped by tragic circumstances. (Mother in mental hospital; pt. first came to notice when father was before assizes for having sexual intercourse with her since she was twelve.)

3330. 15.0; IQ 141, RA 15, AA 14.6. Grammar school; normal attendance; attainment average or just below, recommended for special educational treatment. Finds maths difficult. Good literary ability. Moderate ability generally but does only what she has to do. Does not join in voluntary games. Takes punishment with a bad grace.

3347. 15.8; IQ 148, RA 14.3, AA 14.6. Scholarship to grammar school. V. good ability; attendance not good; persuaded father to write notes excusing absence. Her attitude 'school is too childish'. Obviously the pt. had been allowed her own way at home, and even before mother's death was out on her own too much. Could have obtained a v. good pass in 7 or 8 GCE subjects, if attendance had been better.

3399. 15.5; IQ 149, RA 14.8, AA 14.6. Grammar school; good English and maths. Transferred to a second grammar school. Casual, careless, work showed no promise; no effort; declined to do homework; anti-authoritarian; pert to teachers, upset fellow pupils; awkward, moody, insolent. Caused much concern by conduct with opposite sex when out of school.

3418. 16.1; IQ 146, RA 14.7, AA 13.9. Grammar school; transferred at one stage because of unsatisfactory progress. Attendance very poor; truanted. Versatile imagination; easy to talk to; intelligent. Moved to farmhouse school to prepare for agricultural career.

3475. 15.0; IQ 137, RA 14.7, AA 13.2. Grammar school, but failed, 'too low a standard and a bad influence'; was to be transferred to a secondary modern school when she attended Court for the first time. Eventually to High School and commercial college.

3504. 15.9; IQ 135, RA 14.0, AA 14.6. Grammar school at first, then transferred to secondary modern school, no reason given. Above average intelligence; special aptitude for maths. Friendly but could be aggressive; trustworthy, honest; temperamental.

3519. 14.9; IQ 143, RA 13.10, AA 13.2. Secondary modern school; 'average ability for her age'. Showed signs of unhappiness.

From the above reports, it is clear that only in a minority of cases were the teachers aware of the mental calibre of these girls or in a position to appreciate their educational potentialities. When we come down to girls of superior but less outstanding intelligence, we find that their quality is generally underestimated.

SUMMARY

1. The mean age of the girls (intermediate and senior age classes) was 15 years 9 months, with range from 13y 2m to 17y 0m.

2. They were given individual tests of intelligence (Terman-Merrill Stanford-Binet and WISC), individual tests of reading ability and group tests of arithmetical ability; 71 girls were also given the Raven's Matrices Test. Mean intelligence was 96·23 with range from 51 to 149; this mean is statistically significantly lower than the expected mean of 100.

3. The result is discussed in the light of recent work, which has shown higher mean IQs for delinquents than the older studies. It seems possible that some of this change may be due to delinquency affecting a more nearly average sample of the population in recent years. From 1953 to 1958 there was a rise of seven points in the mean IQ of girls admitted to the Magdalen.

4. It has been suggested that a part contributor to the association between delinquency and less than average IQ may be the association between both of these phenomena and relatively large

sibships. The Magdalen girls showed all of these associations. The highest mean size of sibship (including the girl who was our index case) was 5·16 found for girls with IQs between 80 and 89.

5. There is a suggestion that a lower than average IQ constitutes a factor predisposing to delinquency for part only of our material, and not the whole of it. It appeared to have endangered the youngest girls, whose mean IQ was only 92, but not to have been operative in another sub-group, the girls diagnosed as having an abnormal personality, who had a mean intelligence better than the average.

6. The youngest girls distinguished themselves from the rest, not only by a lower average IQ, but also in a relative deficiency of sex delinquencies, and in coming, even more frequently than the others, from poor or institutional homes. The suggestion emerges that these younger children had been subjected to stresses greater than those falling on the remainder, before lapsing into delinquency.

7. Nearly all the girls were educationally retarded to some degree, and over the group as a whole the effect was a massive one. By Burt's standards, over 50 per cent of the girls were 'backward' in reading, 20 per cent being retarded by more than 30 per cent of the chronological age. In arithmetic 78 per cent were 'backward', 40 per cent being retarded by more than 30 per cent of the chronological age.

8. The mean retardation in reading age was 2y 10m, in arithmetic 4y 2m.

9. Correlating reading age and arithmetic age with mental age showed that educational retardation affected girls of all mental ages, independently of intelligence.

10. Reading ability could also be compared with the findings relating to fifteen-year-old girls published by the Ministry of Education in 1950 and 1957. On these standards, 28 per cent of the Magdalen girls were 'backward', 7 per cent were 'semi-literate' and 2 per cent 'illiterate' compared with 25 per cent, 4 per cent and 0 per cent in the Ministry's sample of girls aged 15 in 1956.

11. Taking all the evidence together, it seems very probable not only that the Magdalen girls were educationally deprived, but that they were more at a disadvantage in this respect than girls of the same age group in the general population.

12. Illustrative extracts from school reports are provided for the girls of very superior intelligence (IQ in excess of 134). The suggestion arises from these reports, as also from school reports on other girls of superior intelligence, that teachers were unable to appreciate the mental abilities of the more intelligent girls in our sample. This might be because of behavioural disturbances, in some cases at least.

13. While it seems nearly certain that the frame of mind involved in delinquency interferes in school work and attainment, it may also be the case that educational deprivation and deficiencies in school training play a part in predisposing to delinquency.

V

Parents and Home

The 'Broken Home'

IN his discussion (1955) of the relationship between broken homes and juvenile delinquency, *Smith* pointed out that what really matters is the psychologically broken home, and that it is very difficult to get information about this. One can be sure that it is much more frequent than is generally supposed, and that what may seem to be a high incidence in the background of children coming from special groups does not necessarily mean that they are in this respect much more unfortunate than others of their age from the same social background. In 1952, in the USA, there was a nation-wide poll under the auspices of the National Midcentury Committee on Children and Youth, to discover what problems young people actually thought were of greatest concern to them. 'Unhappy relationships between parents' and 'the draft and the threat of war', out of twenty-three items, were ranked equal first in order of importance. Smith himself was inclined to be sceptical about the significance of the 'broken home', in its conventional meaning, for the causation of delinquency. He considered that there were indications that the higher rates of delinquency among children from broken homes could be explained largely in terms of differential treatment by law enforcement and social agencies: children coming from broken homes would be much more likely to be made subject to, say, care and protection, than children from homes that were still intact.

Probably most students of delinquency would agree with these views. There was no doubt in the mind of the clinician (J.C.) that the great majority of the Magdalen girls came from homes in which the emotional atmosphere was far from reaching even what one might suppose to be average standards of happiness and stability. From the statements made by the girls themselves it was clear that even where circumstances were superficially normal, and the parents were married and living together, disorders of behaviour, tensions of all kinds, witting and unwitting unkindness and even cruelty, quarrelling and all kinds of unhappiness were common. However, the girls could only present one side of the picture, in a light coloured by their own preconceptions; and objective information about the family situation was very incomplete.

In addition to its uncertainty, our information suffered also from the disadvantage of not being easily expressed in a precisely definable form. To get over this difficulty, it seemed best to concern ourselves, for statistical purposes, with that particular form of disturbance or deficiency of the home environment which is shown in some form of 'the broken home', i.e. the absence of one or both parents or separation or rupture between them. This has the advantage of providing an objectifiable datum, even though it is one which is probably only important when it is symptomatic of a more basic disturbance of the emotional background in which the girl has had to live. It was desirable to do this, in order to correlate the presence or absence of a 'broken home' with other social and psychiatric data.

The criteria by which we tried to distinguish the cases in which there had been an effective break of the home background from others in which there had been moderate continuity were necessarily somewhat subjective, though we hoped they did some justice to psychological realities. Thus in the numerous cases in which an illegitimate girl had been adopted in early infancy, and the adoptive parents had provided a stable home, the criteria for a 'broken home' were not regarded as fulfilled. But in other cases, e.g. where the father was away for long periods on military service, or in which the mother was repeatedly admitted to hospitals, or where there had been gross neglect, the conditions were regarded as fulfilled.

On this basis a 'broken home' was found in 146 cases, 46 per cent of the entire material. Even higher proportions have been found by some other workers (e.g. Seagrave, 1926; Monahan, 1957); and it may be that our definition has been somewhat stricter than theirs.

We know of no work on the problem whether delinquent girls coming from broken homes differ in their personal characteristics, or in the pattern of their delinquencies, from delinquent girls from normal homes. In the Magdalen girls we found only one such difference of statistical significance: the girls from broken homes had a mean IQ of 97·53 and the others one of 95·10. This seems to be an example of a simple selective effect; deviant girls who have been abnormally stressed are likely to conform to population standards more closely than other deviants who have not been so stressed. The distribution of sex delinquencies and indictable offences did not differ between the two parts of the sample, girls from broken homes and others. The former included a higher proportion of girls with psychiatric symptoms; they came more frequently from families with a second delinquent sib; and their follow-up record was not quite so good as that of the others. But none of these differences were of a magnitude to approach statistical significance.

The 'Broken Home' in concrete terms

We can get away from the somewhat subjective judgment of a psychologically broken home, and aim at something more objective. The incidence of the various social characteristics which, singly or in combination, go to make a broken home, are shown in Table 4. Here are the 'hard' data. The incidence of illegitimacy (23 per cent) is definitely high, even for a delinquent population; the expectation of illegitimacy for an average member of the population is only about 5 per cent. Other studies of delinquent girls (e.g. Bagot, 1941; Epps, 1951) found figures from 4 to 10 per cent; but the maladjusted girls reported by *Pringle* (1961) were illegitimate in 18 per cent of cases. The high illegitimacy rate is not very easily understood, since the abnormalities of home life to which it may lead, such as living with a step-parent or foster-parents, are less strongly associated with delinquency than is illegitimacy as such. It seems quite possible that the illegitimate girl, who never is legitimated, is living at a special disadvantage, whatever the home in which she finds herself.

According to the figures provided by *Munro* (1965), about 21 per cent of children can expect to lose a parent by death by the age of 16 to 17, 14 per cent of them a father and 9 per cent a mother. Comparable figures for a variety of samples of the general population in the USA and Britain from 1940 to 1958, i.e. in the neighbourhood of 18 per cent, are provided by *Gregory* (1958).

Among our Magdalen girls 18 per cent were orphaned or half-orphaned—no more than might have been expected on a random basis. This is a remarkable finding which we discuss a little later.

Separation, divorce and desertion are probably best taken together, since divorce is an officially recognized form of separation and divorce rates differ between Britain and the USA, and change also with the epoch. In 19 per cent of our cases, the girl's parents had separated, with or without divorce. This corresponds fairly well with the observations of others on delinquent girls; *Monahan* (1957), *Epps* (1951), *Beane* (1931) give an estimate of 25 per cent, and *Pringle* (1961) one of 20 per cent.

It is perhaps rather more to the point to look at the opposite face of the medal: only 44 per cent of our girls were living with both their own parents. This figure falls into the middle of the range of observations of others (*Ahnsjö, Beane, Bingham, Chinn, Epps, Healy and Bronner, Lumpkin, Merrill, Otterström*), from 23 per cent to 68 per cent. In the bulk of cases in which the girl had lost one or other of her parents, she still had two persons acting as parents: her mother and a step-father in 15 per cent, her father and a step-mother in 8 per cent, two step-parents in 9 per cent. Still more unfortunate were the 25 per cent of girls who had only one mother- or father-figure or none at all. In Table A7 we compare our findings with those of Kellmer Pringle (1961). She obtained her information from replies to questionnaires sent to 55 schools for maladjusted children, the replies being filled in by psychiatrists and psychologists; in the group of 2,593 children aged 6 to 16 there were 537 girls. It will be seen that Pringle's figures are very similar to ours.

Family structure (Carr-Saunders)

Perhaps one of the best modes of classifying family structure was proposed by *Carr-Saunders, Mannheim and Rhodes* (1942), in the following terms:

(A) Normal family consisting of husband and wife, who are the parents of the case, and children (including the case) living at home.
(B) Normal family, as in (A), with the addition of others, relatives, e.g. grandparent(s), or non-relatives (lodgers).
(C) Other families with two heads of the household (male and female) e.g. uncle and aunt of the case, or step-father and mother

of the case, or father and mother cohabiting but not married, etc., and children (including the case) living at home, and others, relatives or non-relatives.

(D) Families with one head of the household only, e.g. widowed mother of the case, and children (including the case), and others.

The material reported by Rhodes consisted of nearly 2,000 delinquent boys between the ages of 8 and 17, with a corresponding number of control cases of like age, equally divided between London (seven different courts) on the one hand, and six provincial cities (Manchester, Leeds, Sheffield, Hull, Nottingham, Cardiff) on the other. The delinquents were selected as the first 1,000 cases brought before the Juvenile Courts in London after the 1st October, 1938; and the collection of cases was subsequently extended to the provinces. The controls were matched by age and school, being selected by the head teacher, boy by boy, as a 'mate' to the case. It is to be noted here that, as the delinquents were selected solely by being brought to Court, any in-built bias in favour of a broken home will be much less important than where the cases selected are those who have been sent by the court to some institution and taken away from their parent or parents. The different types of family structure were distributed in percentages as shown:

Type of Family		A	B	C	D	Total
				per cent		
London						
delinquents	(982)	71	4	8	17	100
controls	(1000)	80	7	3	10	100
Provinces						
delinquents	(964)	64	5	12	20	101
controls	(970)	76	5	4	14	99

From this table it will be seen that, compared with controls, an excessive proportion of delinquent boys came from classes C and D, with a corresponding deficiency of boys coming from families of class A. This finding was very consistently made in the seven independent London series and the six provincial ones. The mean excess of boys coming from families of types C and D was

11·3±1·5 per cent. In London 87 per cent of the controls but only 75 per cent of the delinquents came from normal families of type A or B; in the provinces 81 per cent of controls, but only 68 per cent of delinquents.

It is interesting to compare our material with that collected by Rhodes. We may take classes A and B together, since B is a small class and as far as we know just as likely to provide a normal home background as families of type A. In any case in our material we did not have the information to distinguish between A and B families. As is shown in Table 4, only 42 per cent of the Magdalen

		N	Per cent
I	Illegitimate	74	23
	Adopted	28	9
	'Broken Home'	146	46
	Institutional upbringing at some time . .	38	12
II	Parents separated but not divorced . . .	34	11
	Parents divorced	33	10
	Parent dead (father)	29	9
	Parent dead (mother)	23	7
	Both parents dead	6	2
	Total orphaned or half-orphaned . . .	58	18
	Total affected by one or more of above factors .	123	39
III	Lives with step-parent (step-father) . . .	47	15
	Lives with step-parent (step-mother) . .	17	5
	Lives with other substitute for father . .	4	1
	Lives with other substitute for mother . .	21	7
IV	Effective parental figures:		
	two, own parents	140	44
	two, own father, substitute mother . .	24	8
	two, own mother, substitute father . .	49	15
	two, both substitutes	28	9
	one, own father	8	3
	one, own mother	38	12
	one, substitute mother	12	4
	none (institutional)	19	6
V	Family structure, Carr-Saunders type A or B .	134	42
	Family structure, Carr-Saunders type C . .	93	29
	Family structure, Carr-Saunders type D . .	91	29

TABLE 4. Data relating to family background. In Categories III, IV and V, items listed are mutually exclusive.

girls came from families of type A and B, but 29 per cent from type C and 29 per cent from type D.

It is to be noted that we included in the D class some homes in which there were two parental figures, if not two heads of household as required by the definition, e.g. one in which a girl was living with her father and the prostitute with whom he was cohabiting. The biggest difference between the Rhodes series and ours is in the C class. Under this head are included the anomalous types of family with two heads, e.g. one a step-parent, or both being the natural parents but not married. In the general population, if Rhodes's controls can be taken as a guide, families of this type are relatively rare, and not to be expected in more than about one case in 25. Our material shows such a structure in nearly 30 per cent of cases.

Other abnormal home backgrounds

The figures already provided give a striking picture of the extent to which these children had been deprived of any stable family background. In all, out of the total of 318 girls, 199 or 63 per cent came from homes affected by at least one of the disturbing factors noted. Other observations could not be included in such a formal list, and no doubt our information was incomplete. In 18 cases the girl had simply been abandoned by the mother; five girls had been subjected to sexual interference by their fathers, and one girl by a step-father. Out of the 119 cases in which none of the items of Table 4 were recorded, there were only 59 in which there was no report of some gross abnormality in the home. In the remaining 60 cases there were 17 in which the father was psychopathic, criminal or both; 25 cases where the mother was psychotic, psychopathic, neurotic, criminal, or abnormal in more than one of these ways; and 8 cases in which both parents were classifiable in one or other of these ways. There were 5 cases in which one or other of the parents was a chronic invalid, or blind, or a deaf-mute; 4 cases in which one or both parents were known to be of low intelligence; 3 cases in which severe family tensions were known to exist; and 3 cases with parental neglect or incest.

The record shows, therefore, that in only 59 out of the 318 cases, or in less than 20 per cent, was the family background even superficially of the normal pattern. Among these 20 per cent there may very well have been abnormalities of which we have not heard. And, of course, it may equally well be true that in some of the families of an anomalous kind the emotional background may in fact have been perfectly all right. In such cases we should have to look further afield to find a plausible explanation for the girl's delinquency.

As an example of the grossly abnormal home, which yet would pass as normal by the usual criteria, we can cite the following:

3284. Age 17y om. IQ 90. The father is aged 75, an old age pensioner, very deaf, partially crippled from an accident, alcoholic and litigious. The mother, 55, is a laundry worker, obese but probably promiscuous, untruthful, rejecting. Enid is the sixth of a family of seven, five sisters and two brothers. The elder boy, 25, is probably mentally subnormal; he is repeatedly in trouble and seldom works. The younger brother, aged 22, is on probation. Of the five girls only the eldest, aged 26, has nothing known against her. A sister aged 20 is an ex-approved-school girl, has been in a borstal, and is now a prostitute. The next sister, aged 18, cohabits with a lodger in her mother's house. Enid's younger sister, aged 12, has been before the court for non-attendance. The family home is a very dilapidated terrace house, scheduled for demolition—'a dirty slum'.
Enid's troubles have been lifelong. At seven months she was in hospital for kidney and heart trouble. At 5 she was deemed maladjusted, and was sent to a school for the maladjusted. Later she has been fostered in homes for the maladjusted; and she was an inpatient in a psychiatric children's department at 8 and in an adolescent unit at 13. A 'fit person' order was made when she was 14, and after that she was in hostels and foster homes. She has been severely maladjusted throughout, restless, wayward and obstinate, and in trouble for stealing, lying and absconding. Her schooling, in schools for the maladjusted, leads to the report 'difficult, obstinate'; in employment 'unable to settle at work'. In the opinion of the psychiatrist at the Classifying School, a member of a problem family, a loosely integrated personality, lacking insight, with a form of personality disorder now fairly irreversible. First Court appearance at 14, 'fit person' order; second: brought back by local authority, absconding, promiscuous.

The 'Broken Home' as a causative factor

There are a number of observations that strongly suggest that it is in the psychological disruption of family life where we should look for the proximate and most effective cause of delinquency, in girls if not in boys. *Cavan's* figures, quoted by Monahan (1957) show a steady increase in the proportion of broken homes from control group boys (21 per cent), to predelinquent boys (35 per cent), institutionalized boys (49 per cent), to institutionalized girls (71 per cent). *Shaw and McKay* (1931) threw some doubt on the significance of a broken home by showing that, though it was a frequent finding in a sample of 1,675 delinquent boys (43 per cent), it was still pretty common in a sample of 7,278 control schoolboys (29 per cent). *Toby* (1957) criticized their views, and thought their conclusion was not warranted that in general the broken home was not of much significance. Analysis of the New Jersey figures showed that it was above all significant for the occurrence of delinquency among (1) pre-adolescents, and (2) girls. It might not show up in the older boys because, as he thought, such weak control was exercised over adolescent males in the modal American family, that there was little difference between the supervision in a well-integrated family and in a disorganized one.

Wattenberg and Saunders (1954) found a higher proportion of broken homes among female than male juvenile offenders; 56 per cent of the boys but only 41 per cent of the girls came from intact families. Psychological factors were well to the fore. Twenty per cent of the boys and 32 per cent of the girls came from homes in which there was much quarrelling; dislike of the father was expressed by 5 per cent of the boys and by 16 per cent of the girls; hostility to the mother by 1 per cent of the boys, 7 per cent of the girls. Here, as elsewhere, the stress factor is shown up in much sharper contrast by the girls than by the boys. Perhaps it was because she only considered delinquency in boys that Lady Wootton was so little impressed.

In her discussion of the broken home Wootton found herself dissatisfied by the evidence. She notes that the few investigators who have attempted comparisons with the population at large are still not unanimous in finding that this proportion exceeds that to be expected. Nevertheless, in her summing up, there is no overlap. British studies place anything from 22 per cent to 57 per cent of their delinquents in the category of coming from broken homes, while available control figures range from 11 per cent to 18 per cent. In American studies, the figures for delinquents range from 34 per cent to 62 per cent, while comparative figures range only from 14 per cent to 34 per cent. One has the impression that Wootton is leaning over backwards to be cautious.

Other criticisms she makes are that the evidence is imprecise, being based on a great variety of definitions of the 'broken home', and on offenders of many (and often unstated) ages. Inasmuch as everyone's home is eventually broken, the lack of data as to age is a particularly unfortunate omission. These criticisms seem to us misconceived. Lack of information about the age of the delinquent at the time his home was broken does not impair the value of a comparison between the frequency of a broken home in delinquent and control groups of the same age distribution. Of course information about the age at which a child suffered the loss of a father or mother would be of the greatest value and interest. If we had equivalent information about delinquents and controls, we should be helped towards answering the important questions, what sort of breaking of the home is significantly associated with later delinquency, and at what stage in the development of the child is it likely to be most dangerous in this sense. These problems are, however, different ones from that which is now under discussion.

The complaint that the evidence is imprecise, because it is based on a variety of definitions of the 'broken home', and on a variety of offenders, is clearly mistaken. The fact that, even when using different definitions, we consistently find a difference between delinquent and control groups, adds to our confidence that what is common to these definitions of a 'broken home' contains a factor of operative significance. The greater the range of types of offender from whose study this factor emerges, the more we are inclined to regard it as valid for offenders as a whole, irrespectively of other adventitious group characteristics.

If the main criticisms made by Wootton seem to us far from cogent, so it seems that she misses the real source of doubt and difficulty that underlies so much of this work. This is the criticism made in considerable detail by Smith (1955), i.e. that the higher rates of delinquency among children from broken homes (he might equally have said the higher rate of broken homes among delinquent children) can be largely explained by differential treatment by law enforcement and social agencies. He asks:—Are children guilty of minor infractions of the law more likely to be referred to the juvenile courts if there is evidence of lack of parental control? Is there a greater tendency among authorities to release children from unbroken homes with a warning, e.g. if in petty property offences the father agrees to make restitution? To what extent are child offenders from broken homes so dealt with by juvenile courts to ensure they receive needed social services, and other benefits of which they may have been deprived? What proportion of children involved in delinquent behaviour who are not apprehended, or whose offences are undetected, come from unbroken homes?

To this last question, something in the way of an answer was obtained by *Nye* (1958) who induced a representative sample of school children to answer anonymously questions about their delinquencies. By his definition, in the sample as a whole the frequency of a broken home was 19·7 per cent. Higher proportions both of boys and of girls, coming from a family background in which they were not living with their original parents, qualified as belonging to the 'most delinquent' type, than boys and girls living with their original parents; in boys the difference was not statistically significant, in girls it was. Girls from broken homes, more frequently than girls from unbroken homes, (1) drove a car without a licence, (2) truanted from school, (3) ran away from home, (4) bought or drank alcohol, (5) had heterosexual relationships.

Also relevant is the provisional communication by *Douglas* (1966) on the progress of nervous and troublesome children followed up in the National Survey. Comparing the delinquent children with the others, the former showed a small excess of broken families, but no greater incidence of separation from parents in early life.

The argument put forward by Toby (1957) would seem to be a sound one. The association between a broken home and delinquency is much more marked in the case of girls than boys, and in the case of pre-adolescents than adolescents. Both of these two groups are more socially protected than their contrast groups. If it is in their case that a breakdown of these socially protective forces shows up so markedly, then one is inclined to suppose that they constitute, as it were, a test case, and what is revealed thereby is a factor of more general validity. Toby writes:

> The family not only transmits socially accepted values to the next generation; it also seeks to prevent the child from being influenced by deviant patterns. The better integrated the family, the more

successful it is as a bulwark against antisocial influences emanating from the neighbourhood or the peer group. However, the difference between the protection afforded by well integrated and disorganized families is greater for girls and pre-adolescents than for adolescent boys.

It would seem to us that what matters is, as Smith said, the psychological break in the home, operating perhaps through tensions and unhappiness, competing claims, inconsistencies of discipline and many other ways that plausibly suggest themselves. Actual rupture of the home may involve only some of these stresses. But it would appear probable that the disorders of behaviour themselves (and not their official ascertainment) are predisposed to by patterns of family structure less ideal than the most accepted one; that the association will show itself in a more marked form when one comes to legally ascertained delinquency, as in Rhodes's study; and that the association will be more sharply marked still when one of the criteria of selection of the sample is the removal of the child from the home. We have no doubt that, in the series we have studied, it was often because there was no reasonably stable or affectionate home for the girl that she was sent for admission to an Approved School.

The occurrence of wayward and delinquent behaviour in adolescent girls might then be looked on as an indicator, of problematic sensitivity, of the real and more serious and widespread social evil, namely the family environment which thwarts or perverts character development along socially adequate lines. This may be the submerged part of the iceberg, of which we only see the tip.

Maternal deprivation

In her review of the effects of maternal separation or deprivation in causing delinquency, Lady Wootton (1959) quotes the formulation by *Ainsworth and Bowlby* which states that 'actual physical separation from the mother in early childhood, to the extent that it involves privation or deprivation of a relationship of dependence with a mother-figure, will have an adverse effect on personality development, particularly with respect to the capacity for forming and maintaining satisfactory object relations'. Wootton finds the evidential support for this thesis to be very weak; and she thought that the contention that maternal deprivation not only damaged the personality but did so irreparably was particularly vulnerable.

It is necessary to distinguish sharply between maternal deprivation, or separation, and the broken home. Findings on the broken home, a broader concept within which maternal separation is included, relate to the state of affairs at the time of ascertainment or the time of entry into the investigation series. What is interesting about Bowlby's hypothesis is that it relates the events of adolescence and of adult life with the organization of the family at a much earlier time, i.e. in the subject's infancy. In our analysis we have dealt with the concept of maternal deprivation, as we did with the broken home, in two different ways, using a subjective standard, and an objective one.

Among the Magdalen girls 'maternal deprivation' was a common finding, and it is recorded in 120 cases (38 per cent) of the total material. In this assessment we have tried to do justice to the psychological aspects of deprivation, so that children have been counted as deprived who have been greatly neglected by their mothers, or whose mothers have been away for considerable periods from the home, perhaps on account of illness, as well as those whose mothers handed them over to relatives, or separated from them in other ways. Taking into account the Bowlby definition which requires lack of a warm, intimate and continuous relationship with mother or permanent mother-substitute, we have not counted those girls as maternally deprived who were adopted, provided that the adoptive mother played a normally maternal role.

It is not possible to base any secure argument on this high figure of 38 per cent. Many of our girls must have been committed to the approved school because of disorganized home relationships; and any series of individuals so selected can be expected to show a more than normal incidence of family disorganization, including maternal separation, in earlier years.

It is more interesting to see whether the maternally deprived girls differed from the others in any measurable characteristic. Some authors regard larceny as a form of behaviour disorder particularly likely to be associated with maternal deprivation; and indeed *Bowlby's* monograph on 'Forty-four Juvenile Thieves' (1946) provides the classic presentation of the maternal deprivation hypothesis. In *O'Kelly's* study of 83 approved school girls, she found that three quarters of the thieves and only one quarter of the sexually delinquent had experienced maternal separation or rejection (p < ·001). Interestingly enough, sexual delinquencies were found to be preferentially associated with paternal loss or rejection. We could not confirm these results in our material. The figures relating offence to maternal deprivation are shown in Table A8. While there is a slight excess of the maternally deprived among the girls brought before the court for larceny, it might well be a chance phenomenon.

Williams (1961) found a significant lowering of the verbal IQ, in comparison with the performance IQ, on the Wechsler Intelligence Test for Children, in children who had to be removed from foster homes; the suggestion arose that maternal deprivation might impair the development of language functions. The mean IQ of our 120 maternally deprived girls was 98·8, compared with 94·7 for the rest of the group; the difference favours the deprived girls and is just significant at the ·05 level (F = 3·92). However, the mean retardation in reading age for the maternally deprived girls was 2 years 8·73 months, the mean retardation for the total of 318 girls was 2 years 9·76 months, i.e. almost exactly the same. Our material, therefore, does not support Williams's suggestion. The fact that the 'deprived' girls were actually more intelligent than the rest may be yet another example of the reciprocal relationships we have observed at a number of points in this enquiry. Deprivation of maternal care and dullness of intelligence, we suppose, may each play a part in predisposing to delinquency, but do so independently. Sampling processes will then produce as a statistical artefact the appearance of a negative association between them. (See Appendix B.)

The objective concept

It is possible to reach a more objective standard of maternal deprivation by considering only separation from the mother. Our records provide data about this, together with the ages at which it occurred. In using this criterion, it seems best to include among the girls separated from their mothers those who were adopted or fostered. If this is done 138 girls (43 per cent of the total investigated) were separated from their mothers for a period of six months or longer at some time or times in their lives. In the cases of 57 girls (18 per cent), separation was from the earliest weeks of infancy, in the cases of 81 girls from later ages. Some of these children, after a period of separation, were reunited with their mothers; but as a rule once separation had occurred it was not made good, and in some cases where a girl and her mother had been reunited, it was only for a time, separation occurring once

Duration of Separation	Number
1	17
2	8
3	4
4	5
5	6
6	6
7	4
8	4
9	8
10	7
11	6
12	4
13	5
14	14
15	23
16	15
17	2
TOTAL	138

TABLE 5. Duration in years of separation from mother. Girls who had been adopted have been included as separated. Where in any case there was more than one period of separation, the periods have been summed. No period of separation of less than six months has been included; the numbers of years recorded are correct to the nearest half-year.

again. We have neglected periods of separation of less than six months; duration ran from this minimum to a maximum of 17 years, with mean value 9·6 years. The distribution of durations of separation is shown in Table 5; and the analysis of the ages at which the girls and their mothers were separated is given in Table A9 (of which a graphic representation is given in Figure 6). From this it will be seen that the frequency with which separation is observed increases steadily with age, in accordance with the

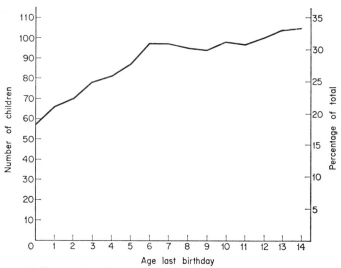

FIGURE 6. Separation from mother at given year of age.

principle that once it has occurred it is likely to be irreversible. There is no suggestion in these figures that separation at any particular age, e.g. during the first year of life, is more destructive of normal personality development than at any other.

Our findings, then, do nothing to confirm Bowlby's hypothesis, and though essentially negative provide no strong evidence in rebuttal. There is no blinking the painful fact that in a high proportion of cases the delinquent girl had been deprived of a normal level of maternal love and care. The deprivation syndrome is a much wider one than can be put into any precise definition. Even where she was living with her mother, the girl was often treated in a haphazard way, deprived of affection, or any consistent training, or otherwise not given her fair chance. At the time of their committal, many girls were living in a disturbed home environment—or without a family at all. From superficial appearances, one would have said that lack of maternal love and care was prominent as a current factor. This lack may have been lifelong, in which case there was also maternal deprivation in the Bowlby sense. But we found very few cases in which the girl had been deprived of maternal care in the first year or two of life, and later by adoption or fostering had come into a fully adequate and loving home. On Bowlby's hypothesis we should have found some cases like this. We cannot say that maternal deprivation, if effective in predisposing to delinquency, is more effective in the first few years of life than at a later time. But our material is not suited to providing a good test of this hypothesis. Indeed its probative value is open to attack, if used to support the importance of a generalized deprivation syndrome. Our girls may have come to our notice at least as much because they had no adequate home, on which ground admission to a training centre was called for, as because of the delinquent record.

One of the difficulties in testing the effects of maternal deprivation is lack of information about population norms. Gregory (1958) quotes the figures given by Oltman et al. for 230 state mental hospital employees, with 12 per cent deprived of one or both parents, by death, divorce, separation, desertion or psychosis, before the age of seven. *Oswald* (1958) found that of his young servicemen 3 per cent had lost their mother before the age of 5, and 6 per cent had had a separation experience of six months or more. The psychiatrically normal hospital population sampled by Munro (1965) had lost a mother by death before the age of 5 in 3·3 per cent of cases; but separation was much commoner. Excluding absences due to war-time service in the armed forces, loss of either parent for any cause before the 16th birthday was experienced by 33 per cent, loss of the father by 30 per cent, of the mother by 17 per cent, of both 9 per cent. Loss of a parent for any cause, which was also reported as having been emotionally disturbing, was reported by 12 per cent (father 9·5 per cent, mother 5·2 per cent). In this normal sample there was also a high incidence of disturbed relations with the parents, (with either 18 per cent, with the father 16 per cent, with the mother 7 per cent, with both 4 per cent). Munro's report emphasizes in fact how very common and widespread in the normal population are some of the psychic traumata which are often held specifically responsible for causing neurotic reactions and behaviour disorders.

The psychologically damaging nature of a separation experience is also far from settled. Hilda Lewis (1954) concluded that in her deprived children it was only when separation from the mother had occurred before the age of 2 and had been lasting that there was any significant relation with psychological abnormality in the child. No clear connection was evident between separation from the mother and a particular pattern of disturbed behaviour.

Neither delinquency nor incapacity for affectionate relationships was significantly more frequent in the separated children.

Heston (1966) in his prospective study of two series of children, one brought up in an institution and the other in foster-homes, found no differences between the two in intelligence, psychiatric disabilities, or overall adjustment; he thought there was some evidence of emotional trauma resulting from institutional care, but that this could be reversed by later experience of family living.

Incest and promiscuity

No estimate of the incidence of incestuous relationships, in this or any other material, can be anything but unreliable. The nature of the relationship leads as a rule to secrecy by all concerned, while at the same time false accusations are likely to be made where parental relationships are disturbed. Not only because the whole subject is taboo, but also because very serious legal consequences may result from investigating allegations of incest too closely, very little precise information is made available in the Record of Information, even in cases which were eventually authenticated. In the 318 Magdalen girls there were 8 cases in which the father was convicted of incest, and a further 6 cases which were investigated on this account but with insufficient evidence for prosecution. There were three cases in which the girl withdrew the charges and cleared her father; and in all three the girls said that they had been told by their companions that a charge of incest was a powerful weapon and a useful blackmailing tool to use against a restrictive father.

> 3259. Age 16y 5m. IQ 97. Florence's father is a general labourer, and is described as a weak character. The mother deserted when Florence was three weeks old, and was subsequently divorced by the father. Florence was an only child; she was brought up by the paternal grandmother. Her father was sentenced to six months' imprisonment for an offence against her when Florence was 14 years and 10 months. She was then committed to care, and was first in a children's home, then fostered, then in residential employment. At school she was slightly below normal educational attainments, gave fair attendance, but her conduct was regarded as very unsatisfactory: aggressive, truculently defiant, insolent, displays of temper, and alienated by the majority of the children. She failed to settle at work or in her foster-home; and after two resident domestic jobs,

which she kept for three months and one month, and a job as a storekeeper which she held for two months, she was brought back by the local authority. At the classifying school the psychiatrist thought she had a basically good personality, not vicious in any way, but had been disturbed in her attitude to the opposite sex by the abnormal behaviour of her father.

If a girl from the present series told the psychiatrist about incest at home, it was not thought advisable to try to establish the truth or falsity of the story. In the cases in which such an allegation had been made before admission, efforts to confirm or refute it would have already been made before committal. Every renewed effort to investigate the matter further would only add to the girl's anxiety. Furthermore no fresh information would be obtained from the visiting relatives, unless it was actually volunteered; and even then its main importance would be in relation to the family constellation to which the girl would return when due for licence from her training school.

So it was that the information obtained was largely limited to accounts given by the girl herself, and the data are not suitable for statistical evaluation. Psychiatric examination was particularly directed towards the practical end of finding out whether specialized psychiatric help would be needed after the girl was placed in her training school, as well as estimating the extent to which normal personality development had been diverted, and the degree to which family relationships had been disturbed.

Because of the large number of substitute fathers in the material, special attention was paid to allegations of sexual interest on the part of step-fathers, foster-fathers, male cohabitors of the mother, and other men living in the intimate family circle. Fantasied or actual incestuous relationships usually indicated an upset relationship with the mother; but they did not always produce lasting psychosexual disturbance in the girl. In none of these cases was overcrowding a factor. In none of the cases, suspected or confirmed, did it appear that the father was unfaithful to his wife with other women, and it may be that these men were not particularly tempted by extrafamilial opportunities. However, in two thirds of the cases the marriage was reported to be unhappy and the mother physically or psychologically sick. It must be remembered that the family structure and attitudes are seen through the eyes of the girl who is telling about them, and reflect her fantasies as much as the facts.

Nearly always incestuous relationships began prepubertally, with one exception in which the onset of puberty could be dated to the week after the girl's 11th birthday. The mean age at which incestuous relations began, as stated by these girls, was about eleven; the ages of the fathers varied between 38 and 56. The relationship also ceased when the father became aware that pubescence was at hand and feared that his daughter might become pregnant, or when she threatened to tell her mother or the police. Soon after puberty the girl is likely to seek heterosexual friendships outside her family, and often her boy friend is the first person she tells about her incestuous experiences. In one case in which the relationship began when the girl was eight, the episodes were fairly frequent, about once in every five to six weeks, but ceased when the girl was 10. She complained that her father had shown an equal regard for a female cousin of the same age. One might suspect that this father had paedophiliac tendencies.

In two of the cases of father-daughter incest a brother was involved as well. These seem to have been solitary episodes, and the brothers were not prosecuted. However, a number of other girls named a brother as their sexual initiator, and none of them ever complained to their parents or the authorities. In this subculture it did not seem that brother-sister incest was regarded as particularly abnormal, or as a matter for complaint. We can be sure that only a fraction of such cases were ascertained. Nor does it seem likely that, in this tacit social acceptance, such relationships were particularly traumatic psychologically.

Most workers have failed to notice the role played in the causation of his daughter's delinquencies by the father with unconscious, and unrealized, incestuous tendencies. Such unconscious longings are likely to show themselves in an over-determined concern for his daughter's welfare, which is seen by others as a sign that he is an ideal or even a martyred parent. Intuitively the girl herself penetrates the façade; and a defensive reaction on her side, met with the castigations of her mother, and reproof by other adults in authority, may end in mounting rebellion or escape by running away, and further sexual delinquencies. As a rule the parental relationship is unbalanced, most typically with a dominant domineering dogmatic self-opinionated father and an inadequate passive weak mother, often less well equipped socially and educationally. When this imbalance is further enhanced by the mother's ill health or neurosis, and the daughter approaches adolescence, the stage is set for the repressed incestuous drives to show in actual signs and symptoms.

The girl is likely to say that her father is over-restrictive, and that he insists on her keeping regular hours, often inconsiderately rigid. He may insist, for instance, that his daughter has to be home fifteen minutes before the local cinema show ends, or before the most suitable transport will bring her home from the evening's planned entertainment. This limits her chances of associating with her boy friends, and gives the father an excuse for grousing if his rules are infringed. The unconscious aim of these manoeuvres, as far as the father is concerned, is to block the girl's chances of forming a relationship with another male. The same end is deviously pursued in other ways. The father may go out of his way to find out all he can that is disparaging about her boy friend, and to criticize her friends generally, their dress and their habits.

It may be that by the time the girl has entered puberty, the marriage as a partnership has broken down. About this time the mother may be menopausal, and may become increasingly emotional. The father can often tolerate her emotional instability remarkably well; and many of these fathers act out an all-powerful tyrannical role towards their wives. In these circumstances incestuous approaches towards the daughters are not common. Organic illness, however, appears to be resented. Some husbands seem to look on such illness in their wives as, in some way, deliberately contrived; and if illness has led to her indifference to physical relationships, this is felt to be rejection. In some cases this 'rejection' is used as a justification for a search for a younger partner; and, on occasion, this may be their daughter. Rather rarely, the daughter is a willing participant, even a seducer; but when the denouement comes she will always claim that she was bullied, threatened and forced.

When such a relationship has begun, the wife may be aware of what is going on but may turn a blind eye to keep the family intact for the sake of the younger children. Sometimes she may be not only frigid but so totally indifferent that she takes no action, influenced also perhaps by the status she has achieved in the neighbourhood or with her relatives. She may be too anxious to be able to face disclosure and the consequences of official enquiries, trial and judgment. She may determine to break up the situation, regardless of her daughter's interests, and manoeuvre a situation by which the daughter finds herself committed to an Approved School.

A large majority of our girls answer the question 'why have you been sent to an approved school?' by saying 'because I ran away from home'. A disconcertingly large number of them say they ran away from home because of sexual advances made by near relatives. Next in traumatic effect, after the sexual advances made by fathers and father-substitutes, come those from other older men. It is only the very disturbed girl, or the girl of low intelligence, who willingly enters into such such relationships, although one should include here the tough and hardened young prostitute whose main concern is to see how much she can get from her partner. Some of our most disturbed girls have been victims of elderly paedophiliacs. On the whole, sexual relationships with boys of their own age, or with unmarried young men, or with men they pick up while on the run, do not cause obvious conflict or overt guilt reactions.

Relatively rare is the girl who acts out a role as a home-wrecker by associating with a married man, nearly always out of neurotic motivations. The man may be be quite happily married, with one or two children, until chance throws him into contact with the girl. In one such case, a girl of just under sixteen was having a relationship with a married man of twenty-five; and this came out when she was being questioned about other kinds of misbehaviour. The man was charged, and rather than face the Court proceedings committed suicide. The girl appeared quite unconcerned about the disaster she had brought upon this family. She was a selfish, shallow, egocentric and narcissistic girl, and played the role of the martyred and innocent victim of the unscrupulous male.

Running away occurs in a variety of other settings. After she leaves school the girl may find herself in a job unsuited to her, and she finds that she does not have the freedom to which she had looked forward so longingly in her schooldays. Curiosity and a desire for adventure may lead her on by small degrees, so that at night she stays out later and later. Then the parents react, too abruptly and too late, by imposing punitive restrictions; and one night she does not come home. Running away from home may also be an escape from unwanted reality into a fantasy world; one finds signs of a hysterical personality component in the early history of many persistent absconders. In other cases, particularly in the girls who start their wanderings at an early age rather than those who begin at puberty, obsessional compulsive features are to be detected.

One such girl showed this in her excessive cleanliness, and in her meticulous ways at work. She began to wander away from home at the age of 6. Her mother always knew where to find her, because she only went to certain familiar places. If she was not picked up in a short time, the girl would give her name and address to a policeman or other adult, and ask to be taken home. Eventually she was deemed maladjusted, and sent to a school for maladjusted children; and she had treatment for a number of years at a child guidance clinic. At the age of 15, she went to live in a hostel, and there again felt compelled to follow the patterns of her childhood. She said, 'I like to go to Hounslow, because I know my way there. I always do the same thing. I go to a café and have a feed of fish and chips and then I go to the public baths and have a jolly good scrub. Then I go to the pictures with a bag of sweets.' After that, she would wander about the district until it was late; and when public transport had stopped running, she would approach men with cars and ask to be taken back to her hostel. Throughout the night, she would wander about, changing cars and partners, allowing sex relations indifferently and without enjoyment.

Sometimes one suspects a basically endogenous change of mood as the source of the motivation in running away. Girls who run away from the approved school not infrequently say 'I was fed up, browned off', or 'I was bored'; and in some of them there was unmistakable disturbance of appetite and sleep, and a phase of apathy, anergia and contrariness as a prelude to absconding. Apart from the mood which precipitates events, there will be other contributory factors. In a study of fugue states in adults, Stengel found in many cases a childhood history of disturbed biological processes of domestication and of the 'relationship to the nest'. Trouble at home, a failure of parents to write, and anxiety about family matters often precede abscondings. The intention often is to get home and get reassurance that all is well. Once the girl is free, she may quickly forget this, and decide to enjoy her freedom first.

For the school managers absconding constitutes one of the most trying problems. There are few solitary absconders, and when two or more girls abscond together a feeling of tension in the entire school is aroused; often a spate of abscondings occurs before the school settles down again. If they are out for any length of time, the absconders always engage in sexual intercourse; and when they are returned many are found to have an infection requiring treatment at a V.D. clinic, and a few have become pregnant. Such medical problems have, of course, been met at an earlier stage (see p. 50).

SUMMARY

The Broken Home

1. Records showed that in 146 cases (46 per cent) the girl had come from a 'broken home', this term being applied as a matter of clinical judgment.

2. This corresponds fairly well with results obtained by others, which show a higher incidence of the broken home in delinquent girls than delinquent boys.

3. In this series, girls coming from broken homes did not distinguish themselves significantly from the others, except that their mean intelligence was closer to the population norm. This is what one might expect on the supposition that they had undergone a higher level of stress than the others.

4. Various aspects of the broken home, now defined in concrete terms, are exhibited in a table. Illegitimacy was frequent at 23 per cent; orphanhood was apparently no more frequent than might have been obtained from a population sample. The parents had been separated or divorced in 19 per cent of cases. Only 44 per cent of the girls were living with both their parents at the time of committal. Normal family structure (Carr-Saunders types A and B) was found in only 42 per cent of the cases, against a population norm of about 80 per cent.

5. Forms of disturbance of the home background, other than those which can be categorized as a 'broken home', were common. It is estimated that less than 20 per cent of the girls came from families which could even superficially be regarded as normal.

6. Investigations whose results appear to show a causative relationship between the broken home and delinquency have been criticized on a number of counts. It is considered that the only objection which throws serious doubt on the supposed

relationship, is that the mode of ascertainment of the delinquent involves a heavy selective bias: children admitted to institutions are, for instance, likely to be treated in this way, not so much because they have been delinquent, as because they have no normal home.

7. The importance of this objection is recognized, and it is noted that with many of the Magdalen girls the lack of a good home must have weighed in the mind of the court in deciding on committal. Nevertheless, it is considered that evidence from other studies supports a genuinely causative relationship between abnormalities of family structure and delinquency.

Maternal deprivation and maternal separation

8. It has been suggested that, if the child is deprived of the loving care of a mother (or mother substitute) in early infancy, the subsequent development of the personality may be permanently impaired; further, that this impairment may lead to an increased tendency to delinquent behaviour. This means that it is important to distinguish between the concept of maternal deprivation so formulated, and the broader but inclusive concept of the broken home, which is usually related to the state of affairs at the time the individual actually became delinquent. In this sense maternal deprivation in some degree is probably experienced over a limited period by a high proportion of normal individuals; and there is little evidence of a convincing kind in the literature that short-lived deprivation is a potent cause of delinquency.

9. Defining maternal deprivation in clinical terms to include not only separation from the mother in early years but also neglect or rejection by her, it was found that 120 (38 per cent) of the Magdalen girls had experienced this in some degree. In many more cases there were defective relationships with the parents; and a deprivation syndrome, in a generalized sense, was involved in a large majority, perhaps 80 per cent.

10. It is difficult to use these findings as convincing proof of the aetiological significance of maternal deprivation, since our selection of cases is a biased one: many of the Magdalen girls were sent to an approved school partly because their homes were broken and they lacked adequate mothering.

11. It has been held that maternally deprived girls are

preferentially liable to larceny rather than sex delinquency. In our material the deprived girls did not differ from the others in type of delinquency.

12. No support was found for a specific effect of maternal deprivation on the development of language functions, in so far as this could be shown in tests of reading ability.

13. Maternally deprived girls were significantly more intelligent than the others. This could arise as a statistical artefact if both dullness of intelligence and maternal deprivation had played some part as selective factors.

14. Maternal deprivation may be defined objectively (rather than clinically) in terms of physical separation from the natural mother. In this sense 138 girls (43 per cent) had been separated from their mothers for six months or longer at some time in their lives, 57 girls from earliest infancy, 81 girls from later ages. The mean period of separation was 9·6 years.

15. The numbers of children separated from their mothers at each year of age are tabulated; the proportion so separated increases steadily from year to year, apparently in accordance with the principle that once separation has occurred it is likely to prove irreversible.

16. The distribution of the figures does not suggest that separation at any particular age, e.g. during the first year of life, is more destructive of normal personality development than at any other.

Incest and promiscuity

17. No reliable estimate of the incidence of incest can be made in this sample, or indeed in any similar clinical sample. In the cases of 8 out of the 318 girls the father had been convicted of incest with her. This was as a rule a very traumatic experience. Incest with a brother must have happened in a higher proportion of cases, but rarely caused any severe emotional reaction in the girl. In general, seduction by an older man was traumatic in a way that was not true of sexual initiation by a boy of her own age. Sexual interference, not so much by fathers as by father-substitutes and other relatives, was a not infrequent prelude to running away from home. When the girl is on the run promiscuous sexual relations are almost inevitable, and this affects the girls that abscond from school, with consequences in venereal disease and pregnancy.

VI

Brothers and Sisters

Family size

ONE of the striking things about the families from which our girls came was the very great variation in size. This is brought out in Table 6. While 15 per cent were only children, the modal family size was one of 5 children, and 16 per cent came from sibships of

Sibship size	N	Sibship size	N
1	47	9	8
2	44	10	4
3	49	11	4
4	45	12	1
5	51	15	2
6	24	16	1
7	15	18	1
8	13	23	1

Total sibships 310. Total of sibs and patients 1,325.
Mean size of sibship, including patient 4·27, S.D. 2·94.

TABLE 6. Distribution of sibships, including index case, by size of sibship.

seven and more. The reader may get some impression of the problems which the all too prolific family creates for itself and others from a short sketch of the five biggest families.

3233. Age 14y 1m. IQ 91. This girl was one of 15 children, whose mother had died when she was between three and four. Her father was of gypsy origin, but in regular employment; verbally cooperative with the probation officer, he would actually take no positive action to support or to discipline his daughter. His family had given

trouble to the educational authorities for many years; and Grace
was brought before the court for non-attendance at school. She was
a quiet well-behaved girl, of good character and normal ability,
according to her school. To the psychiatrist she was pleasant, cheer-
ful, cooperative. She said she never liked school, did not mix with
children of her own age, and felt the teachers did not like her. She
made it clear that she would welcome the security of steady discipline.

3295. Age 14y 7m. IQ 105. She came in the middle of 16 children.
Her parents are described as both of them weak, indulgent, unable
to control their brood; living in a sparsely furnished 10-roomed
house. Two elder sisters have illegitimate coloured babies; two
elder brothers of 16 and 15, and a younger brother of 8 are on
probation. Hazel was before the court for non-attendance. The
school report is very bad: 'one of a group of badly behaved girls;
very poor at games and all school activities; work far below standard'.
She struck the psychiatrist as physically and emotionally immature;
she described feelings of inferiority and inadequacy, and a keen
sense of her failure in competition with other girls at school.

3368. Age 16y 2m. IQ 81. Irene came 19th in a family of 23 children
of whom 17 survive. Her father is an unemployed seaman, her
mother works in a steamer's galley. Of the sibs of whom something
is known, an elder brother of 19 has been on probation, and another
brother of 17 was at an approved school. Three younger brothers
of 14, 14 and 13 are all at approved schools. The family, previously
squatters in a camp, now inhabit an old-type council house; they
were allowed to run wild. Irene, found to be in need of care or
protection, was before the court having left home and attempted
suicide. The psychiatrist found her dull, myopic, with strong feelings
of inferiority; she said she truanted from school because the other
girls laughed at her. She had never been able to settle in
employment.

3474. Age 16y 9m. IQ 88. Joan comes in the middle of a sibship of
15. Her father, invalided from the R.N., works on shore as a donkey-
man. The family live in a well-kept terrace house with 6 rooms and
kitchen. Joan, first before the court for promiscuity a year ago, was
brought back after supervision. She told the psychiatrist of recent
marital disharmony at home, and said she believed her father was
not her father. All her sibs were delinquent. She presented delinquency and sexual promiscuity as a desired aim. She had been
thrown out of her last job in a seamen's store for dating men and
corrupting the daughter of her employer.

3478. Age 15y 7m. IQ 86. Kate is the third youngest in a sibship
of 18. Her father is a corporation cleaner; her mother was put on
probation when Kate was four for neglecting the family by failing to

provide medical aid for the children. The family have been known to the probation officer for the last 12 years. Five brothers are on probation; and at least one sister has been in trouble similar to Kate's. The family live in a council house, dirty and comfortless. From six until she was over fourteen Kate lived, together with one of her brothers, with a benevolent couple who took an interest in the family. During this time she was well-behaved. At school she earned a very bad report: 'disgraceful conduct; poor character; fails to respond to any type of approach.' After school she held a number of jobs for very short periods, and came before the court for care or protection (staying out late). The psychiatrist found her a dull girl, frankly impudent in interview, without any concern for the consequences of her behaviour (sexually promiscuous).

This selection might be taken to be extreme cases; but from a study of the whole material one receives a strong impression that similar problems appear in large sibships in general, and that here we are seeing a causative factor of some importance and widespread incidence.

A number of investigators have from time to time drawn attention to the size of the sibship from which the delinquent has come, and have considered that it tended to be a more than normally large one. Some figures from the literature are shown in Table A10. It has most usually been thought that large families tended to produce more than their share of delinquency because of overcrowding.

Unfortunately most of the data shown in Table A10 cannot be compared with census data, because of the need to carry out a statistical correction when sibship size is ascertained through a member of the sibship. Other things being equal, one is twice as likely to find an index case in a sibship of two as in a sibship of one. *Greenwood and Yule* (1914) gave a very simple method of correcting for this; and if one makes such a correction, data can be compared with sibships taken from the general population (e.g. sibships ascertained through a parent), provided one recollects that sibships of zero magnitude are excluded.

However, it seems fairly safe to compare one uncorrected estimate of sibship size with another. The results obtained by Rhodes in a model investigation are worth showing in detail (Table A11). His samples consisted of the first 1,000 boy delinquents brought before Juvenile Courts in London after the 1st

October 1938, and similar samples from six provincial cities, Manchester, Leeds, Sheffield, Hull, Nottingham and Cardiff. The total delinquent sample consisted of 1,953 boys aged 8 to 16 years inclusive. Each of these boys was matched by the head teacher of his school with another boy 'who could reasonably be regarded as a "mate" to the Case'. Rhodes's work has already been mentioned in the discussion on the 'broken home'; and here again he used the classification of families into types A, B, C and D, type A being the normal family with both father and mother at home. Rhodes gives the data about 'the average size of the family living at home', meaning thereby the size of the sibship; and it is these figures, for type A families, which are shown in the table. It is noteworthy that in twelve out of the thirteen samples, the average size of the delinquent families exceeds that of the control families. One can calculate a mean of all thirteen estimates of 4·4 for the delinquents and 3·7 for the controls.

We can make a direct comparison between our material and that of Rhodes by considering only the sibship size in intact families of types A and B, i.e. with both parents married and living at home. The mean sibship size (uncorrected) of the 134 Magdalen girls from families of these types was 5·08, i.e. exceeding the figure of 4·4 given by Rhodes for delinquent boys, and greatly exceeding his figure of 3·7 for controls.

There is no satisfactory information about sibship size in the general population. The 1946 Family Census and the GRO 1951 Census Fertility Report give no data on sibship size appropriate for comparison with selected samples. The age factor is an important one, as the spread of family limitation will have had an important effect on the younger groups in the population.

However figures of interest have been kindly provided by Dr J. W. B. Douglas from the National Survey of Health and Development. This is a follow-up study of children born in March 1946, and includes 2,190 girls. These children were rather younger at the time of the tabulation shown than were our Magdalen girls in 1958; but follow-up information available to the Survey does not suggest that there has been any very significant addition to the sibships of these girls since then. From Table A12 it will be seen that whereas 30 per cent of the girls in the National Survey came from sibships of four or more, 55 per cent of the Magdalen girls did.

One may also try to compare the Magdalen girls with other psychiatrically selected groups. Bagot thought that sibship size was above normal for families with a history of epilepsy, or mental deficiency, and for the blind. Taking Bethlem-Maudsley material we have found a mean sibship size (corrected):

all types of psychiatric patients aged 16-25	2·3
203 male exhibitionists	2·5
389 male homosexuals	2·5
318 Magdalen girls	2·6
320 epileptics of both sexes	3·0

This probably is not a fair comparison for the Magdalen girls, since most of the others must have come from intact families, and taking intact families only the corrected mean sibship size for the Magdalen girls was 3·5.

Large size of sibship as a cause of delinquency

Further support for the view that delinquents tend to come from relatively large families comes from the work of the *Gluecks* (1930), *Fortes* (1933), *Chinn* (1938) and *Ferguson* (1952). Some other points of interest arise from these researches.

Chinn groups his boys in ages 7–9, 10–11, 12–13 and 14–15. The mean sizes of sibship (uncorrected) in each of these groups is respectively 5·16, 5·20, 5·15 and 4·89. There is then a suggestion that the younger children are coming from larger sibships than the older ones. Taking the three youngest groups together against the oldest, there is a difference significant at the ·05 level. We make the same finding with the Magdalen girls. The mean sibship size (uncorrected) for the youngest sixth is 4·83, for the oldest sixth is 4·11. The explanation that offers itself is that while the younger children are by reason of their age less prone to delinquency than the older ones, this relative protection may be in part offset by large family size.

The findings of Ferguson are more striking. He studied 1,349 Glasgow boys who left school in January 1947 at the earliest permitted date after attaining their 14th birthday; 165 of these children were convicted at least once between the ages of 8 and

18. The proportion so convicted increased rapidly with increase in size of sibship:

Sibship size	Per cent convicted
1 to 2	7·8
3 to 4	8·1
5 to 7	13·9
8 and over	20·0

These figures are much the same as those given in Table 9, where it is shown that the proportion of all the sibs, brothers and sisters, of our Magdalen girls who had a record of delinquency goes up from about 7 per cent in the smallest families to 20 per cent in the largest.

In conclusion, it seems probable that the Magdalen girls came from sibships tending to be larger than sibships in the general population at a corresponding date and age. It also seems likely that size of sibship *per se* tends to increase the risk of delinquency, both among boys and girls. Further evidence would be required to show why this should be so. This appears to be a rather constant factor, which continues to have its effect as one generation succeeds another. It does not seem at all probable that overcrowding in the home has much to do with it. To us it seems probable that the greater the number of children, the more difficult it is for the parents to maintain adequate standards of upbringing. From the clinical illustrations given at the beginning of this chapter, it looks as if the larger families tend to run wild, and to be inadequately supervised and controlled, rather than actually to be treated badly. The improvidence which may go with an excessive number of children may also have some effect in producing a lax style of upbringing.

Birth order and maternal age

Birth order is closely associated with maternal age, so that in conditions in which there is a shift from average values in one of these characteristics there is, practically always, a shift in the other too. It is then up to the biologist, or the sociologist, to decide which is the important and primary effect, and which is merely a secondary consequence of the other. It has been found, for instance, that mongol children are likely to come towards the end of a sibship (and are indeed often the last child born), and that they tend to be born to elderly parents. The current theoretical position is to regard the birth order effect as secondary to the parental age effect. As will shortly be shown, delinquent children are more than averagely found among the earlier born in a sibship. One might accordingly expect that their parents, in particular their mothers, would tend to be younger at their birth than are the mothers of members of the general population.

Information about the age of the mother when the subject was born is only available in the cases of 91 of our Magdalen girls. For these the mean value is 26·5 years, with S.D. 6·5 years, which is about two years younger than the estimate of maternal age for the general population born in 1939, which is 28·5 years. Very few authors have recorded the age of the mother at the time of birth of delinquent subjects. The sample of delinquent women studied by Fernald et al. (1920) had a mean maternal age of 27·6, with S.D. 7·7. It seems to us that, when we are concerned with delinquent girls, the comparative youth of their mothers is not likely to have played an important aetiological role, while the possibility that the elder children of a sibship are more endangered than the younger ones seems very plausible.

The biological sibship and the social sibship

The sibship in which the girl was brought up was not always the same as the sibship into which she was born. Data relating to birth order and number of sibs (see Table A13) can accordingly be classified into (a) 238 sibships which were both born sibships and home sibships, (b) 72 sibships about which we have data, into which the proposita was born but in which she was not brought up, (c) home sibships, of which we have data about 77, consisting of unrelated individuals such as foster-sibs, etc., with whom the girl was brought up. With the first group, accordingly, she shared both heredity and early environment, with the second group heredity only, with the third group environment only.

It is hardly surprising that in the cases where the born sibship is not the same as the home sibship, the latter is on the whole smaller. It would naturally be in the largest sibships that the pressures would be strongest, which would lead to a child being taken into another family or into an institution. The low sibship size in class (c) is also affected by the inclusion of children from institutions, who have been classed as only children in their home sibship. The fact that mean birth order is rather high, in excess of 0·5, in class (b) may also have been partly caused by similar influences. One would expect the younger rather than the elder children of a large sibship to be the ones moved into other homes. However the mean birth order in class (b) does not differ significantly from the expected value of 0·5.

The concept of birth order which is used here may be explained as follows. If an individual arrives mth in a sibship of n, then his birth order is taken to be $(m - 1)/(n - 1)$. The value of this expression is indeterminate for sibships of 1, and in sibships of larger size has limits of 0 and 1, with expected mean value of 0·5. Mean values for series of observations, their theoretical and observed variances, are all easily calculated (*Slater*, 1962). It is accordingly easy to calculate whether the mean birth order of a series of individuals differs significantly from expectation, or whether the means of two series differ significantly from one another.

Taking the material as a whole, we see there is a tendency for the Magdalen girls to appear early in the birth order. Taking classes (a) and (b) together, i.e. all the born sibships, the mean birth order is 0·4404±0·0244; taking classes (a) and (c) together, i.e. all the home sibships, the mean birth order is 0·4130±0·0249. In the first case the mean differs from the expected value of 0·5 by a margin which is 2·4 times its standard error; in the second case the difference is 3·5 times its standard error. In either case the finding is highly significant. We are led to the conclusion that there is a systematic tendency for our girls to have come early in their sibships, i.e. to be among the elder members of them. The difference between the values for home sibships and for born sibships suggests that the influence of birth order is effective through the medium of the home background in which the child is brought up.

Comparable material, published in a form allowing calculation of the birth order statistic, is not abundant. The review of the literature by *Miller* (1944) shows this very clearly. The classic study was made by *Goring* (1913). He gives the order in sibship, for all sizes of sibship, for 1,377 male adult criminals, from which one may calculate the birth order as 0·425±0·009. Fortes (1933) has also given birth order data for 639 delinquents omitting only children, and families of 11+ lumped together; 607 sibships can be used for a calculation of a birth order value of 0·442±0·014. The values obtained both by Goring and by Fortes are very close to ours.

The interesting question then arises whether the increased tendency to delinquency shown by those born early in a sibship is of a general nature, or whether it is associated with a particular place, such as that of first-born. This can be tested by the method suggested by *Russell Davis* (1962). He divides the births into first or last, or second other than those already counted as last, or penultimate other than those already counted as second, or middle for all the remainder. Sibships of one only do not go into the analysis. This method has the advantage of classifying children in a psychological order, which has some constancy for sibships of many different sizes. Eldest is eldest, whether in a sibship of two or twenty; a child will feel himself to be a middle child whether he is the third of five or the tenth of twelve.

Using this method we can calculate whether the differences between observation and expectation are significant or not. We may also use these differences as a ratio $(O - E)/E$, which is a measure of the extent to which deviation occurs. Put in this form we have the figures of Table 7. Here we see a good deal of variation

	Deviation from Expectation: $(O-E)/E$		
	Goring	*Fortes*	*Present Material*
First born	+0·30	+0·16	+0·26
Second born	+0·40	—0·16	+0·06
Middle	—0·23	+0·38	+0·10
Penultimate	—0·31	—0·18	—0·04
Last born	+0·00	—0·30	—0·34

TABLE 7. Placing of delinquents in birth order; proportion of expected number in deficiency or excess.

between the several results of Goring, Fortes and ourselves; but it does not appear that there is an isolated tendency for one placing in birth order to stand out in a unique way. The consistent findings, that the first born is preferentially disposed to delinquency, and the penultimately born to be predisposed against it, seem to be merely part of a general tendency. We can get a rough idea of what this common trend is by taking the means of the three sets of figures. This shows, proceeding from first to last born, in turn $+0.24$, $+0.10$, $+0.18$, -0.18, -0.21, an unmistakable gradient sloping from one extreme to the other.

Why should the tendency to delinquency, as manifested in any single sibship, be greatest for the eldest member of the sibship and progressively diminish to reach its lowest level for the last? It seems to us that there is only one simple and plausible explanation, i.e. to relate the phenomenon with the stresses falling on the parents but especially the mother. It is when there are younger children engaging the attention of the mother that she is most likely to leave the older children to their own devices. When these younger children grow up in their turn, with none to follow them, the mother will then find them easier to supervise or control. The phenomenon seems to be as marked in small sibships as in large ones. If we combine the three series and take only the sibships of two, we find 87 first born and 67 second born; this gives a birth order of 0.435 which is much the same as the three estimates based on the whole material of each of the three samples.

There are, of course, other possible psychological explanations. *Lasko* (1954) gives some evidence to show that parents treat first born and second born children rather differently. As he saw it, while first born children started from a more favourable position, by the time they were three or four they were treated with less warmth, consideration and affection, than the second child received when he reached the same age.

Delinquency in the family

Of our Magdalen girls there were 62 who had one or more sibs with a record of delinquency. We think that this number would have been considerably greater if all the facts had been on record. In 6 cases there was no useful information about the sibs; and in the remaining 250 cases there was information, but none to suggest any delinquency. These sibships have been counted as non-delinquent, even though we may be sure that this is over-optimistic.

Information about the parents was very much poorer than about the sibs, even when the girl was living with her own parents and not with adoptive or foster-parents. Nevertheless we know of 19 fathers with records of delinquency, and of 8 delinquent mothers. Delinquency in the parental generation, and in the sibs, were associated with one another (Table 8).

		Delinquency among sibs		
		+	—	Total
Delinquency in father or mother }	+	12	15	27
	—	50	241	291
TOTAL		62	256	318

TABLE 8. Association between delinquency in parental and filial generations (χ^2 12.17, $p <$ ·0005).

Workers who have concerned themselves with the occurrence of delinquency in other members of the delinquent's family have always found evidence of some degree of familial concentration. In an early study, *Bingham* (1923) found that 19 per cent of 300 girl sex-delinquents had one or more delinquent sibs. But in these cases environmental conditions were very unfavourable, and she thought it was these debasing surroundings which were responsible rather than 'an inherited tendency to licentiousness as such'. Parallel findings have been made by *Beane* (1931), *Lumpkin* (1931), *Bagot* (1941), *Merrill* (1947), the *Gluecks* (1930, 1950), *Epps* (1951), *Ferguson* (1952).

The figures published by Ferguson are perhaps the most instructive. Of the 1,349 boys he investigated, 165 had been convicted; 69 or 42 per cent of them had families in which another member had been convicted, as against 16 per cent of the unconvicted boys. In most cases the delinquent relative was an elder brother, next most commonly a younger brother, then a father. Looking at the data another way round, Ferguson found that the chance that one of his boys had had a conviction went up sharply with the appearance of other delinquents in the family:

Other members of the family convicted	Per cent of boys convicted
No other member	8·6
Father but no other	9·8
Elder brother(s) but no other	26·7
Younger brother but no others	30·4
Relatives from two or more strata	62·5

The tendency of delinquency to cluster within families, and especially within sibships, can be taken as an epidemiological datum of the first importance. The way in which it occurs, and the reasons for which it occurs, will be further gone into. We can think of both heredity and environment as being responsible, and it will be necessary to try to disentangle their effects. If genetical causes were important, then one would expect to find some clinical difference between the girls who came from families with other delinquents from those who came from families clear of delinquency.

The girls from delinquent sibships

The girls from the sibships in which further delinquent sibs were known distinguished themselves from the remainder in only two respects to a statistically significant degree. They came from relatively large sibships, uncorrected mean size 7·0 as against 4·2 for the group as a whole; and they were of relatively low intelligence, mean IQ 91·37 as against 96·23 for the whole sample. There was just as much variation in intelligence, with range from 138 to 51, and standard deviation 19·58. The 62 girls from these sibships were of the same mean age as the rest, and did not differ from them in other respects in any noteworthy way. Of the statistically non-significant differences the most marked were a relative excess of the non-sexual types of delinquency, e.g. larceny, and an excess of girls coming from physically poor or institutional homes.

In these respects there is some resemblance between this group and the children studied by Wilson (1962) in the 52 'Seaport' families selected for child neglect. She too found very large sibships, low intelligence of the children, exceedingly poor and squalid homes, and the delinquencies she describes among the girls are exclusively non-sexual.

To get a reliable comparison between the size of the sibship in the families with and without a second delinquent, a statistical correction analogous to the Greenwood-Yule correction has to be made; the way in which this is done is shown in Appendix C. Applying this, we find mean sibship size for the sibships without a second delinquent 3·47, as against 3·88 for the sibships with a second delinquent. If we multiply sibships according to the number of delinquents they contain, mean sibship size rises to 4·32. The whole of this tendency seems no more than a manifestation of the connection between large sibship size and appearance of delinquency which was shown by the main sample. Sibship size, as an environmental stress factor, seems just as much in evidence in this sub-group as in the main material.

Searching further for data of value for hereditary/environmental discrimination, we looked at the 12 sibships in which we had information both about blood brothers and sisters with whom our index case had not been brought up, and also about unrelated foster-sibs with whom she had been brought up. There were 4 cases of delinquency in the 20 blood-sibs, and 8 cases of delinquency in the 49 foster-sibs. As the proportions are about the same, this information is not helpful.

Clustering of delinquency within sibships

However findings of considerable interest emerged when we examined the way in which delinquent sibs were distributed in individual sibships (Table A14). From this table it will be seen that there are a surprisingly large number of sibships with 2, 3 and more delinquent sibs. Part of this effect was found to be due to a tendency for the expectation of delinquency to rise as the sibships grew larger. This is brought out in Table 9. In the smaller sibships, in which the proposita had 1 to 3 sibs, the proportion of sibs with a record of delinquency was 7·5 per cent; as larger and larger sibships are considered, the risk for the individual sib increases steadily, to reach a figure of nearly 20 per cent in sibships in which the proposita had 9 or more sibs.

Sibship Size	Incidence of delinquency in sibs		
	Delinquent	Total	Proportion
2—4	21	280	0·075
5—6	32	327	0·098
7—8	23	187	0·123
9+	40	202	0·198
TOTALS	116	996	0·116

TABLE 9. Incidence of delinquency in sib by sibship size.

This effect, higher expectancies of delinquency in the larger sibships, is impossible to account for on a genetical basis. The fact that the rise is a steady one, as one passes from smaller to larger sibships, suggests a quantitative relationship. The larger the sibship, the more parental resources are likely to be strained; the more children there are, the less adequate will be the care and discipline that the mother will be able to provide for each of them. The phenomenon we have noted does, therefore, suggest that the concurrence of multiple cases of delinquency in single sibships is susceptible of explanation along environmental lines.

However, there is more to the clustering phenomenon than can be accounted for in this way. When we have made adequate allowance for the relationship between sibship size and expectation of delinquency, some clustering is still found (Table A15). It will be seen from this Table that there are too many sibships with no other delinquent (other than the index case), and too many sibships with two or more additional delinquents; while there is a corresponding deficiency of sibships with a single secondary case, as shown below. The deviation from expectation is highly significant (χ^2 for 2 d.f. 19·34, $p < ·0005$).

Numbers of sibships with other delinquent sibs:	Observed	Expected
No other	202	182·5
1 other	31	57·9
2 or more others	30	22·6

This finding seems to us significant not only in the statistical sense. The suggestion that arises is that delinquency in a sibship,

once it has appeared, is itself likely to be a part cause of its repeated occurrence. One might say that one delinquent sib predisposes his co-sibs to delinquency.

Delinquency and propinquity to a delinquent

If a delinquent individual has any tendency to predispose his sibs
towards delinquency, by psychic contagion or in almost any other
way that seems plausible, one might expect him to have the
strongest effect in this direction on sibs near to him in age and in
birth order. One would expect him also to have a bigger effect on
younger sibs than on older ones. The figures of Table A16 were
compiled from the sibships in which information was available
about the age and birth order of other sibs. It shows that the
chance of having achieved a record of delinquency is highest at
55 per cent for the 15–19 age group, i.e., the age group in which
the Magdalen girls were themselves placed. The most delinquent
group was, in fact, that age group nearest to the index case, and
the proportion of delinquent sibs does, in fact, tend to be higher
for younger than for older sibs. However, these figures have an
element of arbitrariness. Sibs in much younger age groups will
hardly have had much chance of developing delinquencies; and
information about older sibs may be less full than about the
younger ones. We can see what the situation is when we classify
the sibs by their position in birth order, one, two or more places
ahead of the proposita, or one, two or more places after her.
These figures are shown in Table A17. In this we see the comparable phenomenon, a risk of delinquency rising steadily as birth
position approximates to that of the proposita, and reaching a
peak at 69 per cent at the next place after her in birth order, after
which there is a fall. Again risks are higher for the younger than
for the older sibs.

It seems likely that both age and propinquity in birth order to
the Magdalen girl who was our index case are playing a part in
this aspect of clustering. However we can separate the one effect
from the other. In each birth order position, individuals are
assigned the expectation of delinquency appropriate to their ages,
so that for this ordinal position we have a total expected number
of delinquents and non-delinquents. Table A18 shows that the
observed number of delinquents is in deficiency in ordinal

positions remote from the index case, while there is an excess of delinquents in the three ordinal positions, one place and two places older and one place younger.

These findings must be taken with some reserve, as we may be better informed about delinquency occurring in next-elder or next-younger sibs than, say, in much older sibs. However, so far as they go, they tend to confirm the idea that a girl may acquire a delinquent mode of behaviour partly because of the example of an older delinquent sister or brother, and may herself pass it on to a younger sib.

SUMMARY

1. It is nearly always found that the sibships from which delinquents come tend to be of more than average size. This proved to be the case with the Magdalen girls, whose mean sibship size (including the index case) was 4·3 uncorrected, 2·6 corrected. Of the Magdalen girls 55 per cent came from sibships of four or more, as compared with 30 per cent of the 2,190 girls in the National Survey of Health and Development.

2. It is concluded that delinquency in girls probably becomes an increasing risk in sibships of increasing size. It is consistent with this that younger delinquents have been found to come from larger sibships on average than older delinquents. The suggestion is made that, if size of sibship *per se* tends to increase the risk of delinquency, this is because the greater the number of children the more parental standards of upbringing are put to strain.

3. The birth order statistic is defined, with limits of 1·0 and 0·0, and an expected mean for any randomly chosen group of 0·5; values in excess of this signify late arrival in the sibship, values below 0·5 early arrival. The mean birth order of the Magdalen girls was 0·41, signifying that they tended to be among the oldest in their sibship. There is evidence that it is the order in the sibship in which the girl is brought up, rather than the order in the sibship into which she was born, that matters. A plausible hypothesis to explain this finding would relate it to the degree of stress imposed on the mother. Older children are likely to get out of hand when the mother has younger ones to attend to; but when the younger grow into adolescence, with none to follow, she may be able to cope with them.

4. Previous workers have reported a greater likelihood of finding relatives with a delinquent record in the families of delinquents than in the families of non-delinquents. In the 312 cases in our material where there was information about the sibs, there were 62 cases in which one or more sibs had been convicted.

5. Girls with delinquent sibs distinguished themselves from the others by coming from relatively larger sibships and by being themselves of relatively lower intelligence (mean IQ 91·4).

6. The occurrence of delinquency in the sibs showed a marked tendency to cluster. There was a significant excess of sibships with two, three and more delinquent brothers or sisters, after making due allowance for the effect of sibship size.

7. A possible explanation of this clustering would be that delinquency, once it has appeared in a sibship, is itself likely to be a part cause of its repeated occurrence. The mechanism which suggests itself as the most probable explanation for this would be psychological contagion.

8. Psychological contagion from one sib to another would be expected to occur most readily between sibs next to each other in birth order. Observations tend to support the view that this actually occurs.

NOTE. Since this book was written, a paper by Price and Hare (1968) has drawn attention to a simple method for handling birth-order data in sibships which may be incomplete. If the youngest individual in the series is x years old, then the sibships should be regarded as having been completed within x years of the birth of the oldest member. If the index case itself is thereby excluded, the sibship has to be discarded. Treating the Magdalen material in this way, we are left with 226 'born' sibships, mean size uncorrected 4·13, mean birth order for the proband 0·4482 ± 0·02618. The tendency for these girls to be found among the elder members of their sibships is therefore confirmed ($p < ·05$). Price, J. S. and Hare, E. H. (1968). 'Birth order studies: some sources of bias.' *Brit. J. Psychiat.* awaiting publication.

VII

The Psychiatric Record

FOR statistical purposes the psychiatric reports were classified into those diagnosing a basic abnormality of personality development, those diagnosing only the presence of psychiatric symptoms, and those in which no important psychiatric abnormality was diagnosed. In the first group there were 101 girls (32 per cent), in the second 64 (20 per cent), and in the third 153 (48 per cent). The classification is admittedly somewhat arbitrary, and might be difficult to justify in individual borderline cases; but the three groups are found to differ from one another in a number of interesting ways. A few words are necessary to give some picture of the nature of the clinical differences between these groups.

Normal girls (153)

The psychiatrically normal girls, who had entered on delinquent behaviour without psychological abnormality of personality, and without the symptoms that go with conflicts and stresses, are mainly examples of what has been called 'social delinquency' or 'subcultural delinquency'; that is to say, they come from a section of society in which certain patterns of behaviour are normal and accepted, although regarded as deviant and delinquent by magistrates, probation officers, social workers and, perhaps, the world at large. The subculture, in which the deviant pattern is the accepted one, may be a very narrow one, within geographical, economic and age limits.

The children of this kind, who were seen in the present sample, mostly came from the larger towns and cities, and from areas in these towns in which there was a good deal of impoverishment and high delinquency rates obtained. Some girls came from problem families, classifiable as such. These girls had grown up on the streets, and were familiar with a background of bingo halls, dance halls and garish fairgrounds. Their natural companions would come to be café frequenters, prostitutes and their men, layabouts and wide boys. Many of these girls would have drifted into such company after rebelling against the domination of home; and this rebellion would make them all the more likely to pick up the values their new companions would instil. *Leshan* (1952) has pointed out that such young people live a life of quick sequences of tension and relief. Future goals are not envisaged, and indeed the future is 'an indefinite, vague, diffuse region, and its rewards and punishments are too uncertain to have much motivating value'.

Among these girls one will see abnormal adjustments, which must be distinguished from basic abnormalities of personality and from the signs of illness, and which are essentially of a temporary and reversible kind: attitudes of negativism, hostility and rebellion against authority; of evasiveness, suspicion and guarding; of pertness, attention-seeking or sycophantic submissiveness; of self-dramatization as the helpless victim of circumstances for whose predicament only others are to blame. Though no doubt in part determined by the personality, such attitudes are of little prognostic significance.

Of more prognostic significance are the more lasting forms of abnormal adjustment which have become fixed by habituation. In this category come the response to stress by a retreat into fantasy, habitual resort to a lie, habitual pilfering, short-circuit reactions uninhibited by any past discipline. Such patterns of behaviour as these readily grow up on a normal personality basis, given circumstances propitious to their doing so.

As a rule, though they have acquired an unsatisfactory way of life, these girls are not psychologically damaged, and many have managed successfully within a primarily antisocial culture. Then it is often a chance factor, such as the death or serious illness of a parent, which upsets the balance and draws the attention of authority to the girl's plight. Because they are not self-critical nor anxious about their behaviour, they do not respond to an individual orthodox psychiatric approach. They usually respond better to environmental and group therapies; and they make up a large part of those who do well under Approved School training.

Though the problem is not one of treating either character deviation or neurotic symptom, there is a hard task to be faced in changing the girl's attitudes. She is likely to have the feeling that she should be excused the obligations of life, while it would be unjust to deprive her of its privileges. If she is not doing what she is called on to do, this is because of special circumstances; to discriminate against her on this account would be but to add to the general unfairness of things. There is no sense of guilt; and she is not cast down by the troubles in which she has involved both herself and others. But she is likely to have a low threshold to frustration, to be impulsive, and to abscond.

> 3404. Age 15y 6m. IQ 101. This girl was the second of three children, having a brother of 17 and a sister of 13. Their father is a removal man, and their mother works as a hairdresser at a mental hospital. She is said to be rather hard and houseproud, while the father admits to spoiling the children. They live in a 5-roomed house on a council estate, in very good condition. Laura has attended a secondary modern school, and has average ability for her age and normal educational attainments. Her attendance has been regular. The school reports that she is sociable, but easily upset, occasionally sullen in inexplicable lapses though usually helpful. Since school she has worked as a coil-winder in a factory, a shop assistant at Woolworth's, and a mother's help. She has lost several jobs, because of silly giggling behaviour, or from being sleepy (through staying out late). Repeated staying out at night brought her before the Court as beyond control. The psychiatrist found her tall and powerfully built, frank, and quite ready to admit to promiscuity. It was thought that it would be some time before her emotional development caught up with her precocious physical development.

Girls with symptoms (64)

The group of girls who were classified as showing psychiatric symptoms exemplify a variety of neurotic reactions. Probably the commonest is one of anxiety, tension, insecurity and feelings of inadequacy. Some girls feel deeply inferior, and are more at home with coloured boys. Some of them are rejected children, emotionally starved, lonely and in need of love. Others are confused by the psychological changes of puberty, or bewildered by deep conflicts based on sibling rivalries or ambivalent and disturbed emotional   relationships with their parents. In interview these girls would show themselves tense, fidgety, hyperkinetic, jumpy, distractible, afraid.

A related syndrome is that of depression, with many different kinds of colouring: disgruntled defensiveness, whining self-pity, turbulent resentment or morbid suspiciousness and guarded hostility, or dull listless apathy to the point of psychomotor retardation. Paranoid traits of a mild kind are common.

3413. Age 17y om. IQ 89. The father is an agricultural labourer. The mother has attended a psychiatric outpatient clinic for the past three or four years suffering from fits of depression and delusions which make her behave oddly. Eventually the father could stand her behaviour no longer, and they have been separated since the time Mary was 16. Two older sisters and a brother have all in the past been before the Court as beyond control. Mary comes fourth, and a younger brother of 8 years is MD and attends an occupational centre. Mary herself was in a children's home for a time when she was 15. The family live with the mother in a 3-bedroomed old type council house, with primitive outdoor sanitation, spasmodically cleaned and tidied by the mother. At school Mary has been an irregular attender, not interested in school work. She has caused a lot of anxiety, though outwardly not a nuisance. She was once found carrying a knife at a time when slashing had been going on and all the evidence pointed to her. She was attracted to the opposite sex, and spent a night out at the end of her school career. Since school she has been a cinema usherette and has worked in a factory, but has proved an unsatisfactory employee. She was brought before the court for promiscuity and failure to work. The psychiatrist found her depressed, and weeping defensively. She admitted deliberately becoming pregnant to escape an intolerable home situation; but was extremely insecure and ambivalent to her pregnancy.

An incongruity between superficial appearances and deeper feelings is often noticed. Thus one may find that the pseudo-sophisticated and apparently self-assured girl is distracted by inner perplexities and miseries; and underneath the façade of rebelliousness against all authority may be evidence of a strong need to be accepted. Less frequent symptomatic syndromes are shown by the occasional girl who is living in a vague dreamy world which she has peopled with fantasies to the point where fact and fantasy are hardly distinguishable; the girl whose immaturity, dependence and poverty of initiative have been such that she has accepted every unfortunate vicissitude with total passivity; the occasional cases in which neurotic hypochondriasis, obsessional symptoms or paranoid manifestations have come to dominate the clinical picture.

The operation of mental mechanisms of a relatively simple kind is plain to see in a number of these cases: the girl who has used promiscuity as the means of buying group acceptance; the girl who is working out the strains involved in her attitude to her father by stealing from him; the girl whose delinquency represents a reaction to intense sibling rivalry and an aggressive jealousy of a brother or elder sister; the girl who has deliberately become pregnant in order to escape from home.

In many of these cases it would seem probable that there is a degree of instability of personality which cannot be entirely written off as the natural result of emotional immaturity on the one side and a stress situation on the other. Both these groups, classified as having 'symptoms' and classified as 'normal', shade off accordingly into the group classified by the psychiatrist as showing signs of abnormality of personality.

Abnormal personalities (101)

These signs are not as a rule in the nature of symptoms. The most important exception to this is the unusual case where symptoms suggest the imminence of a psychotic development or epilepsy. Thus a number of girls showed recurrent mood changes, usually depressive, with the clinical qualities that mark an endogenous depression, and suggest a basic cyclothymia. Some examples of this type will be found in Appendix D. Another girl was vivacious and volatile, with no modesty, and distractible and restless—the kind of state which is suggestive of hypomania. In two or three cases symptoms suggestive of a schizophrenic change have been noted, of which examples will also be found in Appendix D. The feared change has not always occurred. Thus one girl was noted to be stiff, affected, graceless, with postures which at times looked bizarre; she was estranged from feminine pursuits, but had a craze for lorries and long-distance driving, accepting sexual intercourse as a price to be paid for indulging her craze. At the time of classification she was regarded as pre-psychotic; but in the training school she settled down. Another girl was also manneristic, smiling incongruously and talking beside the point; despite the suspicion that this was a schizophrenic pre-psychotic stage, her after-history was negative psychiatrically.

Some insight into the type of observation which led the

psychiatrist into diagnosing abnormality of personality may be gained from the case history files placed with the Institute of Criminology (Appendix D). Among them, apart from graver conditions, are a number of girls who were diagnosed as of abnormal personality at the time of commitment, and whose subsequent career led them into psychiatric hospitals where a diagnosis of personality deviation or its equivalent was made. These girls can be very roughly grouped into two classes, those who are affectively disturbed, and those whose affective response is flat and shallow.

In the first class the basic abnormality is an instability of mood, which under stress leads to affective symptoms, irritability, aggression, deep depression, anxiety, etc.—symptoms, in fact, which have already been discussed in connection with the 'girls with symptoms'. However, in the group of girls with abnormal personalities, it has been considered that the basic instability is such that emotional responses, even to trivial stresses, are disproportionately violent, or persistent, or unpredictable and inappropriate. Much of this excessive lability will pass off in the course of leading an ordered way of life, and more of it as adult development takes over from adolescent immaturity. But some of these girls grow up into over-emotional, or aggressive, or depressive adults.

3378. Age 15y 7m. IQ 94. Her father is unknown and the child was illegitimate. Her mother married a postman, and has four younger children, the oldest eleven and the youngest an infant. She is described as an emotionally immature woman who reacts against Nora at her own level. The family live in a 6-roomed terrace house, clean and comfortable. As a baby Nora was cared for by relatives, and then from 18 months was in a day nursery. She was always a difficult child. When she was 6 her mother married and came to London to live. Nora then became restless, started nocturnal enuresis and bad tempers. At the age of 7 she was sent to a school for the maladjusted. Later on she stole both from her parents and from school, was untruthful and emotionally disturbed. A little before her thirteenth birthday she made accusations of indecent assault against a man, which were shown to be false. After school she was dismissed from a number of factory jobs for stealing or other unsatisfactory behaviour. She was brought before the court for vagrancy, stealing episodes and promiscuity. In her interview with the psychiatrist she was at once pert and sycophantic; she blamed her mother for everything. She was thought to show a severe degree of personality disorder, egocentric, narcissistic, unable to profit by experience, amoral, a liar. At the training school, when rejected by her best friend for another girl, she pushed her hand through a window and tried to cut an artery. This was thought to be a serious attempt on her life. There were two stays in mental hospitals. One ended after 17 days because she was not certifiable and was not willing to stay; at the other she stayed for 4 months (diagnosis: aggressive psychopathic personality). On follow-up she had a very poor work record, stole from work, engaged in prostitution, and was sent to a borstal.

In the second class of girls of shallow affects we find personality deviations mainly in the hysterical direction. There is usually a lack of self-criticism, a tendency towards rationalization and readiness to blame others. One sees a young person whose reactions are quick, superficial, without lasting qualities. Common sense, insight, foresight, judgment, loyalty to others, capacity for any deep emotional relationship, do not develop adequately, because of an affective rather than intellectual deficiency. Some of these girls are markedly lacking in initiative and spontaneity, and drift into lazy and slatternly ways. Others, more extraverted, become greedy for immediate sensation, exhibitionistic, erratic, totally selfish. A shift towards the schizoid brings us a sprinkling of girls who are cold, callous and calculating, who regard kindness as weakness, who have a record of cruel and sadistic behaviour. Colouring of other kinds may also be seen, e.g. obsessional traits, perverse sexuality and lesbianism. We have no data to show what the further developments are likely to be, when these girls pass out of adolescence into maturity. They do not seem to do much worse than the others while they are in their training schools, where their behaviour is subject to control. One doubts, however, whether they are fully trainable, and whether they are not more likely than most to relapse into antisocial paths on final discharge.

Differences between the three psychiatric groups

When we compare the three groups of girls ('normal', 'symptoms', 'abnormal') with one another, a number of statistically significant differences are disclosed.

Intelligence. As will be seen from Table A19, there were marked differences between the groups in respect of IQ. The girls of 'abnormal' personality had a mean IQ of 100·7, which is the average figure for the population, and they were the most intelligent group. The 'normal' girls had the low mean IQ 93·3; and girls with 'symptoms' took an intermediate position with a mean IQ of 96·1. One might say, the greater the psychiatric abnormality, the less the abnormality in intelligence. Such a finding would be just what one would expect if both temperamental abnormality and dullness of intelligence, each independently of the other, increased the risk of delinquency (see Appendix B).

Birth order. Table A20 shows that girls in the 'abnormal' class have a relatively high and nearly normal value (0·47) for birth order. On the other hand girls with 'symptoms' show a very low one, (0·29). This time it is the 'normal' girls who occupy an intermediate position with a mean birth order of 0·43. In our section on birth order, we have suggested that early position in birth order is to be understood as an expression of a stress factor operating on the mother. In this context, it is not surprising that the 'abnormal' girls show a negligible incidence of this stress. On the other hand that this stress should show itself so positively in the girls with 'symptoms' suggests that the stress of being an older girl reflects on the girl as well as on her mother, and may show itself in psychiatric symptoms as well as in delinquency.

Home background. Here also we find evidence that the girls classified into the group showing 'symptoms' tend to be those who are subjected to an unusual degree of stress. As may be seen from Table A21, there is a deficiency of girls in this group coming from 'good' and 'fair' homes, and a corresponding excess of those coming from 'poor' and institutional homes. Girls classified in the 'abnormal' group, on the other hand are found to come in excess from 'good' homes.

Among other stress factors, maternal deprivation also showed to statistically significant excess in the group of girls with 'symptoms'; in 34 cases this was marked as present (expectation 24.16).

Abnormality of the mother. One of the major aims of this investigation, when it was started, was to collect data about the incidence and the nature of psychiatric abnormality in the parents of these girls. Unfortunately the information available was extremely scrappy, in the case of the fathers even more so than in the mothers. So it is that in some cases we can reasonably assume that the mother is psychiatrically abnormal, e.g. because she has been in a mental hospital, or because she abandoned her children without making arrangements for their care, or because she lives the life of a prostitute or has been in prison or on probation. In other cases there is sufficient information about the mother for one to be able to hazard the conjecture that she is psychiatrically within normal limits. In yet other cases there is nothing known about her, or the information is so scanty or unreliable that no classification can be made. Along these lines, therefore, we have classified the mothers of these girls as psychiatrically abnormal in 83 cases; in 155 cases as probably within normal limits psychiatrically (but including as normal the mothers known to be mentally retarded); leaving 80 cases in which information is insufficient for any estimate. The distribution of these 80 cases between the three types of psychiatric diagnosis (26:15:39) is almost exactly what might be expected by chance ($p = \cdot 75$). This means that our sample of 238 mothers, about whom we have a reasonable amount of information, can be regarded as representative, and the 80 unknowns can be disregarded. We can now examine the relationship between 'abnormality' of the mother and the psychiatric status of the girl. This is shown in Table A22.

This table shows a statistically highly significant departure from expectation, which can be brought out more clearly in the figures below.

Magdalen girl	Per cent deviations from expectation	
	mother 'abnormal'	mother 'normal'
'abnormal'	+15	—8
'symptoms'	+46	—25
'normal'	—30	+16

The deviations of the observed from the expected figures are shown as a percentage of the expected figures ($[O—E]/E \times 100$). The most striking deviation is the large excess (46 per cent more than expected) of cases in which 'abnormality' in the mother is associated with 'symptoms' in the daughter. The girls classified as 'abnormal' also show an excess of 'abnormal' mothers, but relatively a much smaller one. The suggestion is a very strong one that psychiatric abnormality in the mother is operating principally as a stress factor, and not along genetical lines as a constitutionally predisposing one. If the latter had been the case, one would have expected to see the largest deviation from expectation in the class of 'abnormal' girls. Instead of that it is the girls of normal personality but with neurotic symptoms who are most likely to have an abnormal mother; in this series they do in fact have an abnormal mother more often than not.

SUMMARY

1. The psychiatric reports made at the time of classification (by J.C.) can be grouped into three classes. Abnormality of personality development of a basic kind or oncoming mental illness was diagnosed in 101 girls (32 per cent); psychiatric symptoms of some severity were found in 64 girls (20 per cent); and the remaining 153 girls (48 per cent) were regarded as psychiatrically normal.

2. The normal girls were mainly examples of 'social' or 'subcultural' delinquency. The world in which they had grown up had been such as to make delinquency a natural and normal response. Commonly found among these girls are adjustments and attitudes which are abnormal and antisocial in the context of a wider society, and ingrained habits of response and behaviour. These girls accept their own behaviour as natural and they are without a sense of guilt.

3. The girls with psychiatric symptoms were mainly troubled by tensions, anxiety, insecurity and a feeling of their own inadequacy. Other neurotic patterns occur, but are less frequent. In these cases delinquency is likely to be complexly determined, with the delinquent behaviour serving a neurotic purpose.

4. The girls with psychiatric abnormalities of a more fundamental kind included small numbers of the mentally ill (epileptic, schizophrenic, cyclothymic). Apart from them are the basic deviations of personality which approximate towards two types. The first of these are the temperamental instabilities which lead, on trifling stress, to extreme emotional reactions. The second is a quality of emotional shallowness, hindering the development of warm and lasting personal relationships, and leading to behaviour characterized by its selfishness, impulsiveness and lack of foresight.

5. The 'abnormal' girls had the highest mean intelligence

(IQ 101), the 'normal' girls had the lowest (IQ 93), and the girls with 'symptoms' took an intermediate position (IQ 96). This finding is compatible with the hypothesis that abnormality of personality and dullness of intelligence are largely independent of one another, and both increase the risk of delinquency.

6. The estimate of birth order was very low (0·29) for the girls with 'symptoms', nearly normal (0·47) for the 'abnormal' girls, while the 'normal' girls took an intermediate position (0·43). It has been suggested that a relatively early position in the birth order brings the child into adolescence at a time when the mother is under maximum stress. This evidence of stress on the mother is not noticeable in the cases of the 'abnormal' girls. The low value in the girls with 'symptoms' suggests that in their case stress on the mother and neurotic reaction in the daughter are correlated.

7. An examination of home background showed a 33 per cent excess of girls with 'symptoms' coming from poor and institutional homes, and a 26 per cent excess of 'abnormal' girls coming from good homes.

8. Maternal deprivation was also shown to excess (41 per cent) by the girls with 'symptoms'.

9. Psychiatric abnormality of the mother was associated predominantly with 'symptoms' in the daughter, and not with 'abnormality'. This suggests that the mother's abnormality is operating as an environmental stress rather than as a correlate of a genetically predisposing factor.

10. All these findings are compatible with the hypothesis that environmental stress predisposes to delinquency as a neurotic reaction, sometimes accompanied by psychiatric symptoms; delinquency in the unstressed individual is more likely to be associated with abnormalities of personality.

VIII

The Follow-up Record

THE information we had on the after-history of these girls was derived in the first place from the reports sent as a routine from the Training Schools to the Classifying School twice during the course of training and again a year after the girl had been licensed. In addition to this during 1962 a request was made to the Headmistresses of the Training Schools for the completion of a form giving information about each of the girls from our series who had come under their care. The Headmistress was also asked to rate the girl's response to training as 'very good', 'good', 'fair', 'poor' or 'hopeless'.

In the case of two girls, the Approved School Order was revoked, so that no attempt at follow-up was made. The follow-up findings to be described relate to the remaining 316 girls. In a few cases, the reports received are somewhat incomplete, so that in respect of one finding or another somewhat different totals appear.

No information about the work record of 15 girls was to be obtained. Of the remaining 301 girls, 172 (57 per cent) had a satisfactory record; 63 girls had a record which was not satisfactory, but showed some attempt to get and keep suitable jobs, even if not very successfully; 51 girls (17 per cent) had a frankly unsatisfactory record. Fifteen girls out of the total never went into employment, either because they had returned to their parents and stayed at home, or because they married.

Nothing is known of the social and marital history after discharge of 13 of the girls. Of the remainder 103 (34 per cent) were married at the time of the final follow-up; and 200 were single. Of the latter 28 were co-habiting unmarried; and 81 (27 per cent) had become pregnant while single, not subsequently marrying. The girls who married did better than the ones who stayed single. Their mean score on the Headmistresses' rating was 1·94 as against 2·87 for those who did not marry. And for those for whom data of

145

both kinds were available, only 23 out of 103 married had repeat delinquencies, as against 73 out of 202 in the unmarried, i.e. 22 per cent as against 36 per cent.

In the case of two of the 316 girls followed-up, it is not known whether there was any repeated delinquency during the follow-up period. Of the remaining 314 girls, 212 had no subsequent record, while 102 (32 per cent) did have such a record. Twenty-seven girls absconded, and a further five girls ran or wandered away from home. Thirty-five girls were in trouble for larceny, stealing, shop-lifting, etc., and most of them were put on a charge. Twenty girls were before a court for prostitution or soliciting. Other Court appearances were for breaking and entering (4), false pretences (2), insulting behaviour (2), drunkenness (2), and one each for arson, assault, attempted suicide, forging cheques, fraud, indecent behaviour, neglect of children, posing as District Nurse, taking away car, and in connection with taking part in an anti-nuclear bomb march. Some of these delinquencies were dealt with by re-committal. Seven girls came to live in probation hostels while put on probation, ten came to a borstal, and seven to prison.

The Headmistresses' ratings of the girls' response to training are shown in Table 10. Eleven girls were not placed, leaving 305 girls whose ratings could be analyzed. The Table shows that slightly less than half the girls reached the 'very good' and 'good' rating.

Response to Training	Schools		Total	Mean IQ	No. of repeat delinquencies
	Intermediate	Senior			
1. 'very good'	15	68	83	100	4
2. 'good'	16	43	59	98	12
3. 'fair'	25	44	69	93	18
4. 'poor outlook'	21	48	69	95	40
5. 'hopeless'	5	20	25	94	19
TOTAL	82	223	305	96	93

TABLE 10. Response to training as adjudged by training school, classified by age-class of school. Also shown are mean intelligence test result and number of girls with repeat delinquencies, showing decline in former and rise in latter as quality of response to training falls off.

These ratings are closely correlated with subsequent record, as is shown by the distribution of girls who had repeat delinquencies or had to go to institutions. The proportion of such failures increases from 5 per cent in the 'very good' class, successively to 20 per cent in the 'good', 26 per cent in the 'fair', 58 per cent in the 'poor', and 76 per cent in the 'hopeless'. As also appears from the Table, better response to training is correlated with better intelligence test results.

The records of the 82 girls who responded best ('very good') were taken out and analyzed. The most striking way in which they distinguished themselves from the rest was in having as a group a slightly higher level of intelligence (mean 99·6 as against 95·1). They were also, and probably for this reason, slightly better educated, with a mean reading age of 12 years 3 months (main series 12 years 1 month), and a mean arithmetic age of 11 years 2 months (main series 10 years 9 months). They had slightly more sex delinquencies; and personalities were noted as abnormal in 31 cases (Exp. 25·8). But only the class difference in intelligence can be taken as statistically significant.

The records of the 25 girls who were classed by their Headmistresses as being 'hopeless' were also examined. Their mean IQ was 94·5, mean reading age 11 years 10 months, mean arithmetic age 10 years 6 months. In these respects they showed a shift in just the opposite direction from the very good responders. In all other respects they conformed to the average.

The personal characteristics of the 102 girls with repeat delinquencies were also examined. By and large, they showed little sign of being anything but a random selection from the main series; they deviated from the average even less than the two groups just mentioned. Their mean IQ, for instance, was 96·3, exactly that of the series as a whole, and they had the same mean educational attainment. They were of the same mean age as the others. No evidence was found to support the hypothesis of constitutional criminality; 18 of these 102 girls came from families with delinquent sibs, as against an expectation of 19·9.

One might have expected that there would be some relationship between the psychiatrist's rating of personality and the follow-up record. No such relationship was found. Table A23 shows the distribution of Headmistresses' ratings against the personality classification, and against the incidence of repeat delinquency.

For both these distributions the probability value lies between ·50 and ·30.

Analysis of follow-up data in relation to the individual characteristics of the girls has, accordingly, proved very disappointing. Apart from the fact that a relatively good intelligence seems to be helpful, those who do well and those who do badly both seem to be a largely random selection.

Analysis by schools

The distribution of Headmistresses' ratings, shown in Table 10, is subdivided into those provided by Intermediate and by Senior Training Schools. Taking all ratings into account, there is no significant difference between the two groups of schools ($·20 > p > ·10$). However, it is noteworthy that the Senior Schools provide a higher proportion of girls with a 'very good' response, 30 per cent as against 18 per cent in the Intermediate Schools. This difference is significant ($·05 > p > ·02$).

When we pursue the analysis further, into the results obtained by individual schools, we get the data shown in Table A24. In this table, the Headmistresses' ratings have been used as if they were measurements. 'Very good', 'good', 'fair', 'poor' and 'hopeless' were marked respectively as 1, 2, 3, 4 and 5; and mean scores are entered in the Table against the schools, which are placed in order of relative success in this respect. From this the wide range in results obtained can be seen, as also the lack of correlation between these mean scores and other characteristics of individuals, though there is a tendency for the schools with the more intelligent girls to do better than the rest.

All these schools differ a good deal in the nature of their intake. Some of them are larger than others; and the results obtained by those with a turn-over too small to permit statistical comparison with the others, have been put together under the heading 'Miscellaneous'. These small schools did rather well. The main differences between the schools are drawn along the lines of age, intelligence and psychiatric state, all of which find expression in the Table.

Psychiatric oversight of some degree is available, but at a distance, or with difficulty, or seldom used at the Schools G, K, L, S, T, and W. The services of an outside Clinic are available at other Schools including E and I. Four Schools, including C, F and P are visited twice monthly by a psychiatrist (C and P by J.C.). At one School, D, an intensive effort is made along psychiatric lines. During the period covered by this study two psychiatrists were visiting this School for a total of four visits weekly. The intake was restricted to girls who were thought specially suitable for psychotherapy, who must have at least average but preferably good intelligence, who must have insight and must express their willingness for treatment. It is a remarkable fact that, with all these advantages, this School was only able to attain very middling results, whether one judges by the Headmistress's rating, by the percentage of repeat delinquencies, or the percentage of girls 'brought back' or made subject to a 'fit person' order.

Statistically significant differences from the general average in the psychiatric nature of the intake were shown by the Schools C, A and D. These differences are not related to their success ratings. The principles on which girls were selected for each of the Schools (in the order shown in Table A24), may be briefly noted as below:

Intermediate: P, 14-year-olds of immature or inadequate personality, likely to benefit by the small group in the Cottage system; I, girls of average and above average intelligence, who prefer town life, likely to benefit from outside classses; G, girls of mixed intelligence who prefer out-door work and a country life; L, girls of dull intelligence.

Senior: C, girls of roughly average intelligence, often emotionally unstable but not requiring D (or when D is full), all willing for or preferring community life; A, treatment girls of average intelligence who could benefit by secretarial training, dress-making, gardening, etc., and who have expressed their willingness to go to a Salvation Army school; E, girls who express definite preference for work other than domestic, sufficiently stable to be placed out in work during their period of training; D, girls of good intelligence in need of psychiatric treatment, must have insight and express their willingness to accept treatment; T, fairly stable girls interested in out-door work; B, girls of a tough amoral calibre, intelligent, presenting acute problems, needing treatment; F, intelligent toughs and girls who present acute problems; W, girls of low intelligence who have expressed willingness for a Salvation Army school; S, below average intelligence, likely to respond to the small group and the homely atmosphere; K, younger toughs of mixed intelligence.

On the whole the Intermediate Schools got slightly less favourable results than the Senior Schools. The Headmistress's rating of response to training has a higher mean value, indicating a relatively poor response; the proportion of girls put on a 'Fit Person' order, or 'brought back' after absconding is 22 per cent against 14 per cent; the proportion of girls with a repeat delinquency is 37 per cent against 34 per cent. None of these differences, singly, reaches statistical significance. However, as has already been mentioned, 30 per cent of the Senior girls achieved a 'very good' rating against only 18 per cent of the Intermediate girls (p < ·05).

Using the raw scores of the Headmistresses' ratings an analysis of variance was carried out. This did not show a significant difference between Intermediate and Senior Schools, but taking all Schools together there were significant differences between them individually (F = 3·14, p < ·001). It is not clear that all of this variation in rating scores is due to the results achieved; probably some of it is caused by the application of somewhat different standards. Some Schools, in fact, may be judging their girls by a rather severer standard than the others. Two other measures of success in training are available (1) the proportion of girls made subjects of a 'Fit Person' order, or 'brought back' from absconding, and (2) the proportion of girls with repeat delinquencies. These proportions are shown, as percentages, against the individual Schools in Table A24. It will be seen that, in respect of these measures also, there is a great deal of variation from school to school. There is only a rather loose degree of correlation between the different measures among themselves, and between them and the personal characteristics.

The fact remains, then, that we are unable to account satisfactorily for the wide range of results from success to failure, whether measured in terms of work record, repeat delinquency or in other ways. The differences in the results obtained from one girl to another bear rather little relationship to their personal characteristics. What does appear to determine the nature of the after-history are the circumstances in which life after discharge from the training school is lived; the stabilizing effect of marriage is noticeable. In the same way, different schools obtained very different degrees of success, which cannot be related to the nature of their intake. Probably some modes of approach and some methods of training are more successful than others. These would not be at all easy to define. The best results were obtained in a school run by Anglican Sisters. These ladies were found unshockable by even the most desperate and sexually misbehaved girls and yet they succeeded in instilling into them some idea of higher standards of behaviour. While in no way over-permissive, and while maintaining a disciplined structure of day to day life, they managed to create a friendly and intimate society, in which both the anxieties and the rebelliousness of the girls could be outgrown. The methods and techniques used in this school have been described and discussed elsewhere (*Cowie*, 1966).

Girls with a psychiatric after-history

We have discussed in the preceding section the discouraging fact that the personal characteristics of the Magdalen girls were so poorly correlated with their later delinquency record that, in the individual case, no useful prediction could have been made during their stay in the Classifying School. It is, perhaps, more encouraging to find that the psychiatric after-history was rather more predictable.

Of the total sample of 318 girls, 50 came under psychiatric care or supervision in the four-year period after Committal. As might have been expected, there was a significant excess among them of girls who had been regarded as psychiatrically 'abnormal' (A) by the psychiatrist (J.C.) at the interview at the Magdalen Hospital (see Table 11). What is much less expected is that there was also a significant deficiency among them of girls classified as having psychiatric 'symptoms' (S), but with basically normal personalities. This suggests that these latter girls had been going through only a temporarily difficult phase at the time of Committal, and settled down well afterwards. One might even advance the view that the production of psychiatric symptoms, at the time of such a critical event as compulsory admission to an Approved School, is a sign of grace, as it were.

The fifty girls with a psychiatric after-history are, however, worth some special attention. Background data provide some suggestive clues only here and there. The incidence of psychiatric abnormality in their mothers was no higher in this group than in the sample as a whole. Seven mothers had had untreated neurotic symptoms, one had been treated for neurosis, and two had had psychotic illnesses. Our scanty data about the psychiatric aspects of the family history are therefore insufficient to implicate a genetical predisposition.

Of those rated		Psychiatric After-history in:		
		Number	Per cent	Expected Number
'Normal'	(155)	18	11·6	24·37
'Symptoms'	(64)	4	6·3	10·07
'Abnormal'	(99)	28	28·3	15·57
TOTAL	(318)	50		50·01

TABLE 11. Girls with psychiatric after-history, classified by psychiatric rating on admission ($\chi^2 = 17·18$, 2 d.f.)

No significant differences were found between this group of 50 girls and the total sample with respect to age, intelligence and educational standards. Although this group contained some of the dullest as well as some of the brightest girls, the standard deviation in intelligence (16 points) was somewhat less than for the main series. However there is evidence of heterogeneity within the group, small as it is, and evidence also for a relationship between intelligence and degree of mental abnormality, most probably abnormality of personality. Excluding the three girls who were referred to psychiatrists as possibly certifiably mentally defective, the mean IQ of the remaining girls with positive psychiatric follow-up was 96·8, about the same as that of the main series (96·2). If we extract from these the 26 girls who needed hospital treatment, their mean IQ is found to be 98·7. If from these again we take those 14 girls who attempted suicide, their mean IQ is 102·7. If from the hospital cases we take the 19 girls who were rated 'abnormal' by the psychiatrist at time of classification, their mean IQ is 102·9; and the 11 among them who were also given a diagnosis of personality disorder at hospital had a mean IQ of 103·5.

The explanation of this finding is not far to seek. As is shown in

Appendix B, if a sample is selected on the basis of alternative criteria, A or B, then A and B may appear to be negatively correlated in the sample, when there is no such negative correlation in the universe from which the sample is drawn. Both abnormality of personality and a lowering of intelligence seem to have played a part in creating the problems for which our 318 girls were committed to the Magdalen. It follows then that, within this sample, indications of a negative correlation between the two may be seen, or, as stated above, evidence of a positive correlation between abnormality of personality and higher intelligence. Looking at the facts in yet another way, one might say that the indication is that for a girl of relatively good intelligence to become delinquent rather more than the ordinary level of personality deviation is required.

There was a difference between the 50 girls with psychiatric after-history and the rest in respect of the nature of the delinquency. This is best seen when one compares the girls who had a history of an offence (larceny, breach of probation, etc, as shown in Table 12) with the non-offenders (sexual delinquencies, etc.). We have included among the offenders not only those charged with an offence, but also those committed 'after supervision' with

	Psychiatric After-history in:		
	Number	Per cent	Expected Number
Offenders (95)	25	26·3	14·94
Non-offenders (223)	25	11·2	35·06
TOTAL	50		50·00

TABLE 12. Girls with psychiatric after-history classified by legal status of delinquency ($\chi^2 = 11\cdot47$, 1 d.f.)

a history of an offence earlier on. As will be seen from Table 12, there was a significant excess of offenders among the girls with a psychiatric after-history; and looking at the matter the other way round, one sees that the proportion of girls with a psychiatric after-history was twice as great among the offenders as among the non-offenders. This suggests that sexual delinquencies and such offences as larceny are not quite on a par psychiatrically, and that abnormality of personality or psychiatric disturbance may play a larger part in the latter. However, it is to be noted that no relationship was found in the main series between the psychiatric rating, N, S or A, and the nature of the delinquency.

Another interesting finding is that there was a relationship between psychiatric follow-up and home background. In this group of 50 there was a significant excess of girls who had come from homes rated as good and also of girls who had come from institutions, with a corresponding deficiency of girls from homes rated as fair or poor (see Table A25). This finding, like that relating to intelligence, has a paradoxical appearance; but a similar explanation in the two cases is likely to hold. In this case we might suppose that girls coming from good homes had less incentive towards delinquency than the others, so that if they did drift into misbehaviour psychological disturbance was the more likely to have played a part. If so, one would expect to find them relatively over-represented in a subgroup of the psychiatrically disturbed. Institutional homes, also, may have been relatively lacking in the motivations towards delinquency which would be prevalent in the less satisfactory homes. Put in another way, it may be that the defence afforded by a good home against falling into serious delinquency tends to fail in the presence of psychiatric disturbance.

Environmental effects which might have been expected to pre-dispose to psychiatric disorder, but which did not show up in this material, included maternal deprivation and broken homes. There was a tendency, just falling short of statistical significance, for these 50 girls to come from relatively large sibships.

Out of these 50 girls, 21 were classed as having a psychiatric after-history only because they had been kept under psychiatric supervision at their training schools or at nearby clinics. Most of these girls at the time of classification had been thought suitable for psychotherapy, and had therefore been selected for schools where the services of a psychiatrist were available. A further three girls were referred to a psychiatrist as mentally subnormal and two of them were certified.

Girls admitted to hospital on psychiatric grounds

Twenty-six girls were admitted to hospital on psychiatric grounds during the follow-up periods. A psychiatric epitome of each of these cases is available in the bound volume of appendices to this book (Appendix D) deposited with the Institute of Criminology. This case material deserves attention, as it gives an impression of the nature of the psychiatric symptoms and disorders of personality, in this group seen in extreme degree, which were widespread in the main series. A single example can be quoted here.

3151. Age 16y 1m. IQ 89. Her father is a railway worker, nervy, bad-tempered, and inconsistent in his handling of the children; her mother is described as normal. Olive is the second of four children, and the youngest, a boy of 9, is spastic. The family live in a council house, but we do not know how it is kept. At the age of 14 Olive had an illness whose nature is unknown, but which may have been meningitis. She went to a County Secondary School, but her educational record was below average; she truanted, had many short absences, and at school was reported as uninterested, disobedient and insolent. She later worked in a factory. She first came before the Court at 15y 4m for 'attempted suicide' and staying out late. Her second appearance was for breach of probation, violence, knife-throwing, setting a fire on the dormitory floor. At the Magdalen she impressed the psychiatrist as 'abnormal', a very disturbed girl; her behaviour was incongruous, she was preoccupied with the idea of suicide, and she had an intense jealousy of her elder sister. There was thought to be a suspicion of schizophrenia, in view of her paranoid attitude, her negativism, her inappropriate affect and poor empathy. She was the only girl in the series who was charged with attempted suicide. Her suicidal attempts had been made with aspirin, coal-gas, swallowing floor-polish, eating pins and needles, scratching her wrists with broken glass, and by drowning. Most of them were thought to be by way of gestures, in response to disapproval, frustration or rejection; but some of them were thought to have been serious.

While on licence from the Approved School, during the follow-up period, she made yet another attempt with aspirin. She was in hospital for ten months, with a diagnosis of 'schizophrenia'. She returned home, worked for nine months in a factory job, and then married an older man. Three years later the Probation Officer reports that she is a 'solid citizen', settled down with her four children.

Altogether fourteen girls in these fifty, equivalent to 4·4 per cent of the main series of 318, attempted suicide. Many of them attempted suicide on several occasions, and some of these attempts were very serious. One girl (3473) after a number of attempts finally successfully killed herself. Mental pathology on a major scale made a considerable contribution to this group. The girl who died was diagnosed by the hospital psychiatrist as suffering from personality disorder; but at the age of 15 she had had a baby and had suffered from a puerperal depression after it. Other girls diagnosed by the hospital psychiatrist as suffering from depressive illnesses were 3262, 3358 and 3514. Two girls, 3290 and 3312, were epileptic, and their suicidal attempts were characterized by the irritable impulsiveness that goes with epilepsy. Two girls, 3151 and 3555, were diagnosed as suffering from schizophrenia. The remainder received hospital diagnoses of personality disorder and, in one case, hysteria.

In all these cases the attempt at suicide, even when it was deliberate and dangerous, seems to have been impulsive and ill prepared.

Among these unhappy and frustrated girls, flaring up into a self-destructive outburst because of some temporary exacerbation of their miseries, one does not find a single case of the coolly desperate suicide who works out his plans to the last detail. In many cases we see mere gestures and demonstrations, which once done seem to have served their purpose, perhaps as a form of abreaction. Girls who behave like this are likely to do so again and again, until eventually they grow up and learn other ways of defending themselves against their emotions. In other cases the suicidal attempt bears the mark of what Stengel has called the cry for help (e.g. 3507); even a potentially dangerous attempt on one's life may be motivated in this way. These cases verge on those which look as if they had been carried out in despair and were fully intended to succeed (e.g. 3514).

Psychiatric diagnosis (Table A26)

The presenting symptom which most frequently called for transfer to hospital on psychiatric grounds during the follow-up period was violent, aggressive, suicidal or otherwise very disturbed behaviour. Six girls (3290, 3312, 3446, 3471, 3498 and 3521) were diagnosed as suffering from epilepsy. In two of these cases (3446, 3471) no typically epileptic fits were observed, but the EEG records were characteristic. In the remaining four cases both EEGs and clinical findings confirm one another. One of these four girls (3312) was recognized as epileptic at the time of classification; in another case (3521), although fits had occurred, there was no evidence of their epileptic nature, and they were thought to be hysterical; doubts about them persisted in the minds of clinicians over a series of hospital admissions, and it was only on the third hospital admission that the correct diagnosis was reached. In another case (3290) no fits nor any suggestive symptoms had been seen at the time of classification, although it is highly probable that disturbance of brain function of an epileptic kind had already begun to occur and had contributed to the delinquency. It was not very long after she went to her training school that this girl developed a severe epilepsy, causing status on one occasion. All of these six girls were extremely disturbed and very difficult to handle. One of them (3312) went into an epileptic psychosis with hallucinatory experiences.

It is interesting that among these six epileptic girls one (3498) had a temporal lobe epilepsy, of all types of epilepsy that most likely to cause psychiatric disturbance. Temporal lobe epilepsy is a focal epilepsy, and is caused by local damage or disease in the brain. One of the other girls (3446) almost certainly had a focal epilepsy also. She had had a severe head injury at the age of twenty months; her IQ was 75, suggesting intellectual defect from brain damage; and the EEG showed a unilateral preponderance of abnormal waves. A gross brain lesion is also a possibility in case 3354. However 'idiopathic' epilepsy (epilepsy of unknown origin) also contributes its quota. In cases 3290 and 3312, for example, intelligence was better than average, EEG results were compatible with centrencephalic epilepsy; and the mother of the first girl was psychotic, the mother of the second epileptic, suggesting the presence of a hereditary factor.

Schizophrenia was diagnosed, as the last effective diagnosis, by the hospital psychiatrists in three cases, 3151, 3405 and 3555. A diagnosis of schizophrenia at an interim stage, subsequently not confirmed, was made also in cases 3288 and 3462. In case 3405 we are unable to accept the hospital diagnosis, which does not seem to us to be based on objective criteria. The diagnoses in the other two cases have to be accepted. The first of these girls (3151) gave rise to a suspicion of schizophrenia at the time of classification. One might perhaps have expected a gloomy outcome; but after hospital treatment she settled down very well. The reverse process took place in case 3555. At the time of classification she looked like a selfish superficial girl, but with personality within normal limits; during training she became increasingly withdrawn, an attempt at suicide eventually necessitating admission to hospital. There she has not responded to treatment with ECT and tranquillizers, but has become increasingly paranoid. The hospital diagnosis is one of 'paranoid psychosis'; but as she has now been in hospital for four years without recovery, one must assume the illness is schizophrenic.

Depressive illnesses were diagnosed in cases 3262, 3358, 3505 and 3514. It is not easy to be sure of such a diagnosis when one is dealing with adolescents, with immature personalities and very unstable affective equilibrium. Having called the state one of depression, it is again not easy to say how far endogenous and reactive elements have entered into it. The endogenous factor cannot be entirely neglected, despite all the contribution from environmental stresses. In a considerable proportion of these girls cyclothymic traits of personality were to be observed.

The largest diagnostic group is that of the personality disorders. Eleven girls come under this head, or twelve if one includes 3358, who was also diagnosed as having a depressive state. In addition one might include 3405, who was diagnosed as a schizophrenic on very inadequate clinical grounds, 3387 diagnosed as suffering from 'hysteria', and 3439 who received no hospital diagnosis. However, there are also possible exclusions—3354 whose personality disorder may well be dependent on a gross brain lesion rather than being developmental, and 3462 who is quite possibly a schizophrenic.

Of these fifteen girls thirteen were classified (by J.C.) as having a personality disorder at the time of classification, i.e. as 'abnormal'; one girl (3323) was in the 'symptoms' class, and one girl (3405) was thought to be 'normal'. The conformity between independent diagnoses by the Magdalen psychiatrist and by later hospital psychiatrists indicates that a characterological diagnosis, even at such early ages, may not be without some predictive meaning.

Eight out of these fifteen girls made an attempt at suicide at some time after going to her training school; and nearly all of them were very disturbed emotionally, for the most part being persistently tense and anxious, with much emotional lability, and tendencies to impulsive and aggressive outbursts. One might expect that these girls would settle down in a stable environment; but the fact that their emotional disturbances continued throughout the greater part of their training period suggests that stronger emotional ties were necessary to secure them, than those available in school. The later follow-up of these girls is discouraging. One of them (3473) took her life; and eight of them have gradings of 4 or 5 on the Head-mistresses' rating scale. Those among them who married did better, as shown below:

Follow-up rating	1	2	3	4	5	?	Suicide	Total
Married	2	1	—	2	—	1	—	6
Did not marry	—	1	1	3	3	—	1	9
TOTAL	2	2	1	5	3	1	1	15

The number of girls in this group who were not markedly disturbed is a small one; 3244 shows a personality of the affectively shallow type, which leads her into a predatory existence; and 3405 is of somewhat the same type, though much more colourless, and proved ineducable and persistently delinquent.

SUMMARY

1. Of the 318 girls in the series, 316 were successfully followed up during the four following years to 1962. Follow-up information was not complete in every case, so that totals for statistical purposes range from 301 to 314.

2. Work record was satisfactory in 57 per cent, frankly unsatisfactory in 17 per cent.

3. A third (34 per cent) of the girls were married at the time of final follow-up. Of those still single 14 per cent were cohabiting unmarried, and 40 per cent (27 per cent of the whole sample) had become pregnant while single, not subsequently marrying.

4. Two thirds of the girls had no subsequent delinquency records, one third (32 per cent) did have such a record.

5. The response to training was rated by Headmistresses as 'very good', 'good', 'fair', 'poor' or 'hopeless'. Somewhat less than half the girls (47 per cent) achieved a 'very good' or 'good' rating; nearly one third (31 per cent) were regarded as having given a 'poor' or 'hopeless' response.

6. Those who did well and those who did badly on this rating seem to constitute a nearly random selection from the total series as far as individual characteristics are concerned, except that

there was a slight tendency for better results to be associated with better intelligence. Furthermore, the 102 girls with repeat delinquencies appear to be a random selection from the total series. These findings suggest that whether or not a girl responds well to training depends on factors which have relatively little to do with her personal characteristics or past record.

7. One of these factors might be the training school to which the girls were sent. There are highly significant differences between the schools both in respect of the type of girls admitted and in respect of the results obtained. But the nature of the results does not seem to be related to the nature of the intake. This suggests that the decisive factor lay in the different approach and methods of training in use at the different schools.

8. Apart from that, the most important influences in deciding whether or not a girl made a good response to training, and settled down afterwards, would seem to be associated with her life at that time, the hazards and stresses she then encountered, and the people with whom she became involved. One important feature of life after school is marriage. The 103 girls who married scored significantly higher on the Headmistresses' rating; and in them the incidence of repeat delinquency was significantly lower (22 per cent) than in those who remained single (36 per cent).

9. Fifty girls came under psychiatric after-care during the four years following Committal. Among them there was a significant excess of girls diagnosed as 'abnormal' by the Magdalen psychiatrist (J.C.), and a significant deficiency of girls diagnosed as having 'symptoms'. This suggests that in the latter temperamental difficulties had been only temporary and, once relieved, left better than average prospects of rehabilitation.

10. The greater the degree of psychiatric abnormality for which psychiatric after-care was needed, the higher the girl's intelligence tended to be. This can be explained as a statistical artefact; though it is possible that good intelligence has some effect in shielding a girl from the consequences of minor abnormalities of personality.

11. In the group of girls needing psychiatric after-care there was an excess of offenders (cases of larceny, etc.). Looked at the other way round, psychiatric after-care was twice as often needed for offenders as for girls committed as in need of care or protection, for sexual delinquencies, etc.

12. Among the girls needing psychiatric after-care there was also a significant excess of girls coming from homes rated as either 'good' or 'institutional'. This again could be a statistical artefact, or could be explained as a consequence of the protective effects of a good home, so that delinquent girls coming from good homes would be more than normally likely to be psychiatrically abnormal.

13. Out of the 50 girls in psychiatric after-care, 21 were only kept under psychiatric supervision at their training school; 3 girls were referred to a psychiatrist as mentally subnormal, two of them being certified as such; 26 girls were admitted to hospital on psychiatric grounds during the follow-up period. Out of these 26 girls fourteen (4·4 per cent of the main sample) attempted suicide, many of them on several occasions, sometimes seriously, and once fatally. Mental pathology was prominent in this group: four of these girls were subject to depressive illnesses, two were epileptic, two schizophrenic. Altogether among the 26 hospitalized cases there were 6 cases of epilepsy, 3 girls diagnosed as suffering from schizophrenia, and 4 cases in which depressive illnesses were diagnosed; the remainder were diagnosed at their hospitals as suffering from personality disorders.

14. The types of personality disorder noted were chiefly in the form of excessive emotional lability, emotional disturbances and spells of tension, anxiety, depression, aggressiveness. In these very disturbed girls the response to training was mainly not good, though those who eventually married had done rather better during training and seem to have settled down later.

IX

Conclusions

Clinical judgments

IN earlier chapters we have seen that our Magdalen girls differed from what could have been expected of a sample from the general population, both in their personal characteristics, and in the backgrounds from which they came. These girls tended to be of slightly less than average intelligence, but were much more retarded educationally than could be accounted for on the basis of intelligence. We concluded that they had in fact suffered educational deprivation, missing for one reason or another the training and development which the average girl at a modern or comprehensive school obtains. On the psychiatric side many of them, and many of those with the best prospects, showed neurotic symptoms which appeared to be the result of stresses coming from an unfavourable environment; and there was a greater than average amount of psychiatric abnormality of a grosser kind: more extreme deviations of personality and illnesses such as recurrent depression or epilepsy. Though these findings were sufficiently noteworthy, they were dwarfed in importance by the nearly universal evidence of grossly disturbed family life. Families tended to be unduly large; the home was more often than not 'broken', so that in only 44 per cent of cases the child was living with both her natural parents; delinquency was common in the sibship, and tended to occur in clusters, suggesting the significance of psychological contagion.

It is, perhaps, worth giving as an example of nearly all the more important hostile influences in a single case where many of them converge. The case is an extreme one, but every feature it shows can be found in a great number of others.

3352. Age 15y 8m. IQ 74. Phyllis has been before the court for seven offences of larceny, for the first time at the age of 12. Her father has a withered arm; he is a drinker, plausible, violent, and has made court appearances for assault, unlawful wounding and neglect to maintain. Her mother is obese, emotional, verbose, dirty, and has been treated for venereal disease. Phyllis is the sixth of seven sibs. The eldest brother, who has been convicted, has been for some years in hospital with schizophrenia; another brother has twice been on probation for larceny, and yet another brother has been in an Approved School. A 20-year-old sister has been fined for larceny, and another sister, who has been on probation for larceny, has three children, all in care. The parents, who were in conflict for years, are now separated. The family live in a 2-bedroomed house in a very dilapidated condition, with not a whole pane of glass in the house. Phyllis went to a secondary modern school, where she was regarded as a good-hearted girl, with good health and good attendance, but dirty and slovenly and given to pilfering. After school she held five places, each for less than a month. Follow-up shows that after leaving her training school she became a prostitute.

In an attempt to arrive at a common meaning underlying the facts which get tabulated as dry statistical data, we made an attempt during the reading of each of the individual case-records, to come to some conclusion about the relative contributions of constitutional predisposition on one side and environmental factors on the other. In about two thirds of the cases (62 per cent) we could not put a finger on any constitutional predisposing factors (if hypothetical deviations of personality and hypothetical genetical contributions were disregarded); but in only 8 per cent of cases were we unable to say that some definite and obvious environmental factor had been involved. In only 5 per cent of cases were we left unable to give ourselves what we would accept as a plausible explanation of the drift into delinquency.

Among constitutional predisposing factors, defective intelligence ranked high, and we thought it had played a significant part in 13 per cent. In the same proportion there was evidence of other forms of abnormal central nervous function or delayed maturation, such as enuresis, EEG abnormalities or even epilepsy, etc. Hardly less important was one or other form of impaired physical health (10 per cent); generally poor physical condition was commonly noted, as also a history of skin conditions, defective sight or hearing, chronic respiratory disorder, migraine. Physical defects, such as congenital dislocation of the hip, squint, extreme myopia, scaly skin, appeared in individual cases; and it seemed to us that in a number of cases physical blemishes, such as a bad skin, obesity, etc., had had their effect by impairing the girl's happiness or confidence.

On the environmental side, the overwhelming factor, dominating in more than two thirds of the cases, was the unhappy home. In about 50 per cent of cases there was a deprived child, lacking ordinary love and care from one or other or both parents, usually the mother; but sometimes (about 7 per cent) the lack of a father's support and guidance seemed to be the main feature. In about 10 per cent there were the worst degrees of marital discord, and also in about 10 per cent cruelty, ill-treatment or gross neglect (including in some cases incestuous attempts from the side of the father or step-father). Actual physical illness in father or mother played a part in 10 per cent, and neurotic nagging was even more common. In about 7 per cent of cases it seemed that the child was living in an almost totally affectionless environment. More often the deficiency was in over-restrictiveness, over-indulgence, and inconsistency.

The personalities of both parents were clearly involved, that of the mother much more closely than that of the father. On the father's side we found as the most maleficent feature, emotional disturbance, violence, aggression, ill temper; less commonly harshness and over-restrictiveness and lack of kindness. The main factors on the mother's side were in the nature of inadequacies, nagging, complaining, hypochondriacal worrying, unreliability and ineffectiveness; much less common were the gross personality deviations, loveless egoism, promiscuity, periodic depression, paranoid traits, overbearing dominance.

It is a contemporary cliché to speak of the need of family psychiatry. In studying these families the observer is struck by the justice of this term. When all allowance has been made for the abnormalities and the deficiencies of each of the individuals significant in the child's life (unfortunately our information does not extend beyond the parents to cover the nearly equally important brothers and sisters), one has the clearest impression that what has gone wrong is the family and home as a unity. In one considerable group home life is unhappy and distorted by intolerable conflicts, the parents estranged, or governed by rigidity and restrictions, or isolating the girl in an affectionless world. In another equally important group one sees disintegration, all the children going their own way, no contact with the parents, who can give no supervision or support, chronic insecurities caused by many moves, many schools, no roots, the home comfortless, overcrowded, squalid, or simply chaotic. Children from such homes are brought before the magistrates again and again, with equal punctuality being sent back to them again, for further neglect, or further harm.

Sex differences in delinquency

In his well-informed and scholarly, but one-sided work on the criminality of women, *Otto Pollak* (1950) takes the view that the human female is no less criminal than the male; the differences in overtly criminal behaviour which are observed between the sexes are to a large extent due to the fact that the criminality of women remains hidden. The thesis can be sustained only by making as much as possible of data relating to sexual misbehaviour, especially prostitution and the procuring of illegal abortion.

The position taken by this writer is, as far as we know, unique. There is universal agreement among criminologists that girls and women fall foul of the law much less frequently than men and boys; and that when they do so, by and large their delinquencies do not take on the aggressive and socially destructive qualities of much of the criminal behaviour of the male, and can in fact be regarded in a much less serious light. If one were to conclude from this that 'criminal' tendencies in the female were less than in the male, one would not be deterred by the consideration that there is a great deal of petty pilfering and sexual and other misbehaviour by women which never gets into official statistics. The official statistics would seem to reflect the extent to which criminal behaviour constitutes a problem for society; and in this sense women clearly cause much less wilful damage to society than men do. It would seem fair to say that women are more law-abiding than men; and this broad generalization would be very widely if not universally subscribed to by sociologists and psychiatrists.

The work which is reported in this book is essentially a psychiatric study of a year's intake of adolescent girls into a classifying approved school. For such an administrative measure to be taken by the juvenile courts the cases must have been extreme ones. Not only were these badly behaved girls, but many of them had been found incorrigibly so. One might say that in southern England these were the most criminal girls of the year. And yet, if one looks at their delinquent acts, they are of a very petty and trivial kind. These girls had to be removed from society into the security of a residential school much more for their own sakes than to protect society. The problems created by delinquent boys are of an entirely different order.

Though the behaviour of delinquent girls is much less obnoxious than that of delinquent boys, and deviates less from standards of legality and of acceptable social behaviour, yet the girls themselves constitute a more abnormal sample. The results of our investigation support the very wide consensus that girl delinquents deviate from sociological and psychological norms much more than boy delinquents. This sex difference must lie close to the aetiological factors that go to the causation of delinquency, and an effort must be made to understand it. The evidence of those who have made comparative studies runs consistently in one direction (*Fernald, Bingham, Healy and Bronner, Sheldon and Eleanor Glueck, Bagot, Otterström, Atcheson and Williams, Wattenberg and Saunders, Monahan, Morris, Schofield, Walker*). Comparing delinquent girls with delinquent boys, the girls are found to come from economically poorer homes, with more mental abnormality in the family, with poorer moral standards, worse discipline, more often a broken home, more frequent change of home, more conflict at home and more disturbed intrafamilial relations. If there is a shift of intelligence to the left, it is more marked in girls than boys; the girls have a worse school record, and more often have developed a hostile reaction towards schooling; they show a larger degree of rejection of family influence; their working careers are worse.

Pathological psychiatric deviations are much more common in delinquent girls than boys. We are unable to estimate the contribution of minimal brain damage, i.e. the minor degrees of cerebral dysfunction for which a brain lesion seems probable even if it cannot be proved; this is a field in which further work is required. However in delinquent boys gross brain lesions are very uncommon, more so than in girls; and in boys epilepsy, schizophrenia and manic-depressive illness play an almost negligible role. In our sample 8 per cent of the girls required in-patient treatment in a psychiatric hospital. Delinquent girls more often than boys have other forms of impaired physical health; they are noticed to be oversized, lumpish, uncouth and graceless, with a raised incidence of minor physical defects. Yet with all this greater amount of abnormality, the peak age for delinquency comes about one year later in adolescent girls than in boys, and the ultimate outlook for social adjustment is better for girls than boys.

Three of our authors have attempted to interpret these differences. Otterström suggests that (1) girls are less hereditarily prone to delinquency than boys, and so (2) require greater influence from their environment to fall into bad ways. Differences between the sexes in hereditary predisposition could be explained by sex-linked genes. Furthermore the female mode of personality, more prudent, more timid, more lacking in enterprise, may guard her against delinquency. The behaviour of boys may be more sensitive to environmental influences, and may need relatively small stresses to become delinquent, compared with the large stresses needed in the case of the girl. In the simplest form of this theory, behaviour is regarded in the form of an interaction between predisposing forces personal to the individual and those derived from the milieu; and the theory hypothesizes that the milieu forces are much the same for the boy and the girl, but that the female psychosomatic constitution is more resistive to pressure from those of the milieu forces which push the individual towards delinquent behaviour. The greater immunity enjoyed by the female can be impaired by physical and psychological disadvantages of very many kinds, and it can be overwhelmed if the environmental forces are of unusual strength. A large part of the observed data are explained by such a theory; but the fact that, once delinquency has occurred, it takes such a different form in the female and the male, requires explanation also.

Wattenberg and Saunders do not formulate any general theory, though they would probably find the above statement acceptable. They emphasize that delinquency in the two sexes is most alike in form and frequency in prepubertal ages, before the rapid sexual differentiation of adolescence has begun. Defects of interpersonal relations, expecially conflicts within the family, play a larger role in causing delinquency in girls than boys; and much male delinquency results from the kind of social life (e.g. gang life) which the adolescent enters into.

Nye's view is that delinquent behaviour is the norm, from which socially adjusted behaviour constitutes an artificially induced deviation. Behaviour reverts to delinquent patterns if the controls which should prevent it break down. These controls are of two kinds, the internal controls which are built up within the individual by upbringing and education, and the direct controls which are the prohibitions and the punishments attaching to their infringement which are imposed from without. It is Nye's thesis that the big difference between the sexes is in the incidence of direct controls. Particularly at the time of adolescence girls are subjected to a much more restricted life than boys. These controls are exercised more by the family than by the wider environment. Putting Nye's argument into more concrete shape, one might say that girls are less frequently delinquent than boys because they are kept under better control by their families, and this close family control constitutes a kind of bottleneck, holding them back from their natural path towards delinquency. Any slackening of control will be most effective if it takes place at the bottleneck, and so it is that one finds more often in girls than boys some breakdown in family control. One might perhaps go further than this and say that the sort of delinquency into which a girl is likely to enter is one which is normally detected and prevented by family members (e.g. promiscuity), rather than behaviour offensive to society at large and prevented by the police (such as serious property crimes). There are some difficulties with Nye's theory. It is for instance not easy to understand how it is that with generally higher standards of behaviour the girl should contravene them less frequently than the boy does with his more permissive ones. One would seem to need some supplementary hypothesis; for instance conditions would be met if it were found that the wider the limits of behaviour which the child was allowed, the more likely he was to exceed them (!).

The view that the growing girl spends her life within narrower social limits than her brother, so that disruptive events within the family circle are more critical to her than to him, may have once been a very plausible one, but is much less so today. If she feels more affectionately towards her family, more dependent on it and less willing to rebel against it, this has the appearance of a sex difference more likely to be related to the biological than to the socio-psychological background. Other aspects of delinquency are also likely to be related to developmental sex differences. The fact that girls mature earlier than boys, but have their peak age for delinquency one year later, is not so paradoxical as it appears. The girl's delinquency is predominantly in the form of sexual behaviour (e.g. promiscuity) requiring a more advanced degree of maturation than the (mainly non-sexual) delinquencies of the boys. Furthermore the attitude taken by society differs in the two cases. At equivalent biological ages the sort of thing that gets the girl of 16 into trouble passes without official disapproval in the boy of 18. In fact sexual maturation in the girl predisposes her to a form of behaviour to which society is much more allergic in her case than in the case of the male, and her earlier maturation is likely to bring it out before the critical age at which official prohibitions are relaxed.

The liability to delinquency

We can consider the liability to delinquency as a graded characteristic, with a normal distribution of the same kind as is seen in other graded characteristics such as stature or intelligence. With increasing liability, there is an increasing risk for the individual of being ascertained as delinquent. The threshold at which deviant behaviour becomes delinquent behaviour is set by rules drawn up by society, which vary from society to society, but in all societies are not the same for the two sexes. In England the standard of what is acceptable in the way of sexual behaviour is stricter for girls than for boys; and the liability of girls to unacceptable sexual behaviour is greater than that of boys of the same age because of their earlier maturation. It is therefore no matter for wonder that girls charged with sexual delinquencies are more numerous than boys so charged. However, in respect of indictable offences such as housebreaking and larceny, society's standards are the same for both sexes. In this field the liability of the female is very much less, and the increase in delinquency rates starts later than in boys and has a lower gradient. When all forms of misbehaviour are taken together, delinquent girls make up a much smaller proportion of their generation than delinquent boys; and they represent accordingly a more extreme selection.

We can regard the relative immunity of the female to delinquent behaviour as the result either of a lower liability, or of relatively better protection against the stresses that provoke delinquent behaviour, or both. It seems probable that the former factor is the more important. Sex differences in delinquency rates have remained fairly steady for many decades, despite a progressive approximation of the liberties allowed to growing girls to those permitted to boys. Moreover in economically depressed classes, in over-large and problem families, where the upbringing of girls and boys is equally haphazard and undisciplined, the large male preponderance of delinquents is still maintained. The level of psychiatric abnormality, so much higher among delinquent girls than delinquent boys, also points to a greater constitutional resistance of the female to delinquent manifestations, and not to a lower incidence of stress.

When we come, as we shall shortly, to review our information on the subject of environmental background factors, we shall find that, with one suggested exception, they affect both boys and girls in approximately equal measure. Nye has drawn attention to one differential factor, the greater degree of direct control to which girls are subjected, both within the home and outside it; but it is hardly plausible to suppose that a relatively small difference in this field could account for a male preponderance in delinquency running up to 14:1. It is more natural to suppose that the male-female difference, both in delinquency rates and in the forms that delinquency takes, would be closely connected with the masculine or feminine pattern of development of personality. This again would be related to biological and somatic differences, including differences in hormonal balance; and these would at the ultimate remove be derived from chromosomal differences between the sexes.

Chromosomal and genetical factors

In this field there has recently been a very remarkable addition to our knowledge. The sex development of the individual is directly determined by whether or not he possesses a Y-chromosome; the normal female has two X-chromosomes, and is in fact of XX constitution, while the male is of XY constitution. Aberrant types such as XXY and XXXY individuals are phenotypically male, though sterile; and the individual with a single X-chromosome (written as having XO constitution) is phenotypically female. What has been discovered is that among male criminals there can be found individuals of XYY and XXYY constitution, in sufficient numbers to suggest that there may be some link between multiple

Y-chromosome constitution and criminality. Men with two Y-chromosomes, so far as they have yet been discovered, are mentally retarded and taller than the average male, and have begun their delinquencies at an earlier age. It is therefore not impossible that Y-borne genes, as suggested by Otterström, may predispose to delinquent modes of behaviour. But there is no need to postulate any specificity about the relationship between chromosomal constitution and delinquency. A simple and obvious hypothesis is that the Y chromosome merely determines the development of a masculine pattern of psychosomatic constitution, and that it is this masculinity as such that predisposes to delinquency, and predisposes to masculine types of delinquency. On this view all that the behaviour of the male with an extra Y chromosome demonstrates is that the greater the degree of masculinity, the greater the delinquent predisposition.*

We assume then that the chromosomal difference between the sexes starts the individual on a divergent path, leading either in a masculine or a feminine direction. The developing male and female then enter environments subtly different from one another. It is possible that the methods of upbringing, differing somewhat for the two sexes, may play some part in increasing the angle of divergence. We know of no evidence with a direct bearing on this point. Common sense suggests that the main factors are somatic ones, especially hormonal ones, since it is at puberty that the psychological and bodily differences between male and female become so broad and so deep as to dominate further development.

Is there any evidence that masculinity or feminity of bodily constitution plays any part predisposing to delinquency and in determining the form it takes? There is at least enough evidence for this to suggest the desirability of further research. Delinquents of both sexes tend to be larger than controls, and overgrown by population standards. The Gluecks found that boy delinquents were better developed and muscularly stronger than matched controls. Healy and Bronner showed that both delinquent boys

---

* For a description of a prepubertal boy with an XYY karotype see Cowie, J. and Kahn, J. 'XYY Constitution in Prepubertal Child.', *Brit. Med. J.*, 1968, *1*, 748.
From provisional findings still unpublished, it seems quite likely that sex chromosomal anomalies may be more than normally frequent in delinquent girls also.

and delinquent girls were overgrown for their age. Markedly masculine traits in girl delinquents have been commented on by psychoanalytical observers (*Galvin* 1956, *Lander* 1963). Gibbens (1957) has noted the frequency of homosexual tendencies among girls under care for prostitution. Energy, aggressiveness, enterprise and the rebelliousness that drives the individual to break through conformist habits are thought of as being masculine more than feminine traits; they certainly have some connection with the occurrence of delinquent behaviour; and in both sexes, though more in males than females, they take on an upsurge at the time of puberty. We can be sure that they have some physical basis. Valid ways of testing the hypothesis that male-female constitutional differences lie at the root of the sex difference in delinquency, would be to enquire whether delinquents deviate from age-sex norms in hormonal balance and in their androgyny index.

While it seems very probable that the sex chromosome constitution is one of the basic factors determining the liability to delinquency, the evidence that specific genes play a significant role is not so strong. One of the findings we made in studying the family history of our girls is worth stressing in this connection: psychiatric abnormality in the mother was associated not with abnormality of personality in the daughter but with the presence of overt symptoms, i.e. some form of emotional disturbance or temporary reactive state. In other words the mother's abnormality was operating as a precipitating factor in the home environment, rather than as a manifestation of a deviant genetical make-up, common to mother and daughter.

The most important evidence which implicates the genetical constitution has been derived from the study of twin pairs. In Table A27 is shown a tabulated summary of the relevant twin findings from the literature.

If a condition is preponderantly caused by genetical factors, with environmental factors playing a minor role, we would expect a high degree of resemblance in monozygotic (MZ, one-egg or 'similar') twin pairs, and a considerable but much lower degree of resemblance between the two members of dizygotic (DZ, two-egg or 'dissimilar') twin pairs. If genetical factors play a minor role, and the environmental factors involved are those which affect the individual when he is adult or has begun to separate himself from his original family, we would expect twin pairs of neither type to show much intra-pair resemblance. If, finally, the condition is mainly determined by environmental factors which have their main incidence early in childhood, then we would expect to find high levels of resemblance within twin pairs, both of the MZ and the DZ kind. The only workers to have studied a large series of twin juvenile delinquents are *Rosanoff, Handy and Plessett* (1941), and their findings are shown below:

	Monozygotic twins		Same-sexed dizygotic twins	
	both delinquent	*one delinquent*	*both delinquent*	*one delinquent*
Boys	29	0	12	5
Girls	11	1	9	0

Comparable findings have been made by *Shields* (1963) at the Maudsley Hospital: resemblance in respect of juvenile delinquency and aggressive behaviour disorders was shown in four out of five male MZ pairs, but also in seven out of nine male DZ pairs. In Rosanoff's material, taking the two sexes together, there is a 'concordance' rate of 98 per cent in the MZ pairs, but also one of 86 per cent in the DZ pairs. These findings suggest that family resemblances in respect of delinquency are likely to be traceable to environmental factors operating in the home background, with individual gene differences playing a relatively modest role.

In the adult twin series there are bigger differences between monozygotic and dizygotic twin pairs, with substantially higher concordance rates in the former. Some of the adult investigations have involved very detailed and penetrating studies of the individuals involved; and what then emerges is the extent to which the main lines of the personality have been determined by hereditary factors. However, whether or not a predisposed personality actually engages in criminal behaviour often proves to be something into which fortuitous circumstances enter. The crimes committed by members of MZ pairs often resemble one another closely, whether they are, say, ones of fraud, or petty larceny, sexual misdemeanours or robbery with violence; among DZ pairs, even when both members of the pair are both criminals, such resemblances are much less close.

Yoshimasu (1965) has shown that the careers of criminals can

be classified by criteria which extend into a number of dimen-
sions:– (1) by the time of starting, early or late; (2) by the
direction taken in criminal behaviour, whether into offences
for profit, offences of violence, sexual offences, offences of secret
destruction, or offences of escape; furthermore whether these
directions are monotropic (always into the same crime), homo-
tropic (into crimes of the same group), ditropic or polytropic; (3)
by the form of alternation between actively criminal and non-
criminal life phases, which can be classified as successive, remittent,
intermittent, or suspensive. In all these respects individual
criminals show their own personal characteristics; and in all these
respects there is a marked degree of resemblance within monozygotic pairs. One can summarize the whole of a lifetime in the form
of a curve, and the shapes of these curves are much alike from
twin to twin.

The relative contribution of hereditary and environmental
factors to the causation of adult criminality remains an open
question. The preponderance of opinion favours the greater
importance of social and environmental factors in determining
whether an individual falls into criminality or does not; but the
type of crime into which he may drift, and the extent to which his
life is governed by his criminal tendencies, would seem to be largely
a reflection of his personality, with genetical factors lending much
that is most characteristic.

Background factors increasing liability

We may use the general principle that the female is better
protected than the male against the appearance of delinquent
behaviour, and therefore requires a higher level of stress to react
in this way, to sort out the background factors which may lead to
delinquency. If we find some feature of the environment is more
prominent in the history of delinquents than in the history of
control groups, we may suspect that it plays some part in the
causation of delinquency. If in addition we find that it is more
frequent and more marked in the background of delinquent girls
than delinquent boys, we shall be the more disposed to think that
it has significance in its own right, rather than as a correlate of
some more basic operative factor. The incidence in females can,
in fact, be looked on as a kind of touchstone. It is, however, not so
easy to say how on first principles one should interpret a finding

that some observation is commoner in boys than girls. A sex difference in this direction is most likely to emerge where the ways of life of boys and girls differ sharply, and to be shown in a trait which belongs in the field of normal rather than abnormal psychology.

An example of such a factor is the social influences which go to determine delinquency. This has hardly emerged from statistical examination of the records of the Magdalen girls, though its effects were clearly apparent to the clinical psychiatrist (J.C.) in his interviews with many of the girls, especially the psychiatrically normal ones. However the operation of social factors is much more strikingly obvious in the case of boys. *Scott* (1965) quotes the vivid description by *J. B. Mays* of delinquency in Merseyside, which

> seems to be part and parcel of that established way of living or subculture, to which the majority are obliged to conform. Petty larceny, shop-lifting, lorry-skipping, bunking into cinemas without paying, rowdiness and occasional outbursts of physical violence flourish amongst the children of ill-regulated homes and have become almost acceptable modes of behaviour. The deviant boy in such a neighbourhood is the one who abstains from any form of delinquent act and he is likely to be penalized by ostracism and ridicule.

The sisters of these boys are living in the same neighbourhood, but appear to be much more immune to the neighbourhood influence. It is a phenomenon of extreme rarity for girls to make up gangs of their own. As individuals they may adhere for a time to a boys' gang, but soon drift off again, perhaps after detaching one of the boys. It is in fact the girl-friends who are largely responsible for the gradual erosion of delinquent gangs of boys. Girls are less bound to their local environment and are more socially mobile. They are likely to be less influenced by their class-mates than by what they read in the women's magazines. For them everything is going to depend on the man they marry, and he may easily come from a world far different from that of their brothers and their friends.

The same background factors are there with both boys and girls, but the girls seem to be less influenced by them. 'Broken homes', for instance, must be just as common an experience for persons of either sex; but the two sexes react differently. The pattern of development in personality and behaviour is more stable and more constant in the female than in the male, and can take a larger stress before being disrupted. In Chapter 5, we noted that the broken home passes our test of differential incidence in the sexes. Whether we give this somewhat ambiguous term a subjective clinical meaning or a precisely defined concrete meaning, delinquent girls have been found to come from broken homes with a much higher frequency than could have been expected from a random sample of the population. In our material orphanhood as such did not appear to be excessively frequent; but anomalies of family structure, and still more histories of unhappiness, instability, and discord and conflict in the home were so frequent that less than 20 per cent of our sample could be regarded as having come from a 'normal' home, such as is enjoyed by the majority of children.

Such findings are universally made. The difficulty lies in the interpretation, for it is possible to suggest that what is observed is a consequence of administrative action. It seems certain that the existence of a broken home supplies a motivation for magistrates and others in deciding to commit a delinquent girl to an approved school. However in some of the samples investigated this selective bias can only have entered in an attenuated form, and in others not at all; while the results obtained by all workers run in the same direction. The work of *Bagot*, of *Healy and Bronner*, and of *Monahan* was carried out on convicted offenders, regardless of the administrative action taken, and so was not related to committal. The samples taken by *Atcheson and Williams*, and by *Burt*, were from children who so far had only been charged with offences. *Merrill* selected children who had been referred to a juvenile court, whether or not they were later charged; and *Morris* took those who had had two or more police contacts, whether or not they were ever subsequently brought before the court. The series studied by *Wattenberg and Saunders* was still closer to the source, including all children against whom a complaint had been made. And finally the samples of both *Nye* and *Schofield* do not involve any form of administrative selection at all. Yet in all these studies evidence of the operative influence of broken or distorted home relationships clearly emerges. Similar observations are made in both sexes, but always with higher levels of home disruption in girls than in boys.

The evidence seems quite overwhelming that disturbance of home life is one of the main causes, if not the main cause, of juvenile delinquency. It is a much more difficult matter to decide whether there is a critical stage in which abnormalities of home life have a deeper or more lasting effect than at any other. It is the essential feature of the 'maternal deprivation' hypothesis that the deficiencies suffered at an early age may so slant the development of the personality that difficulties in forming social relationships emerge at a later age, even though at that later age maternal relationships have long been normal. What we found was, of course, that home life was unsatisfactory, and the children frequently deprived of normal maternal love and care, *at the time they were ascertained as delinquent*. The disturbed home was an immediate cause of the disturbed behaviour, there and then. But with many of these girls the disturbance of home life went back many years. It seems likely enough that it had begun to have its evil effects much earlier than the present crisis of adolescence, critical only for the open manifestation of what had long been—latent?, or perhaps easily noticed if only someone had troubled to look?

If we look at the official record of our girls, we find that they go back a few months only in two fifths of the cases, in a further two fifths for about one to three years, but in one fifth from three years to twelve years, i.e. into early childhood. Thirty-three girls were the subjects of enquiries by child guidance clinics, psychiatrists and social workers between the ages of 5 and 9, for problems of maladjustment and behaviour disorders. However, this is no reason to think, even in these cases, that irreparable damage was then done. These may have been only the temporary manifestations of a chronically unhappy situation which went grumbling on from year to year.

Although the evidence is inconclusive, it suggests rather that the damage done at an early stage may be repaired or recovered from later on. We found that the repetition of delinquency was associated with stresses occurring at the time of repetition. The girls showed themselves as school trainees to have a great deal of malleability. Training schools varied very much, but even in the least successful of them the behaviour of the girls was much better under supervision than after discharge, and a good deal better after discharge than it had been before admission.

Practical consequences

In most western countries, with some notable exceptions such as Portugal and Spain, there has been a steady increase in crime, especially in juvenile delinquency. *Melitta Schmideberg* (1962) has drawn attention to the apparent paradox that this has occurred despite evident improvement in living conditions, the acceptance and implementation of medical-psychological theories, the use of growing systems of social services, the increased use of probation, suspended sentence and related measures, improvements in the treatment of prisoners and a greater amount of after-care. There are wide national variations, increased lawlessness tending to show itself most where morality and discipline are most relaxed. There is perhaps twenty times as much criminality in the USA as in the UK.

Melitta Schmideberg is a psychoanalyst who has specialized in offender therapy. She says that it is fallacious to give the impression that all that is needed is more psychiatrists providing more treatment. Treatment does not necessarily get good results. Calling the offender 'sick' glosses over a fundamental issue. His maladjustment is radically different from that of the neurotic or psychotic. They are socially oriented and try hard to adjust; they suffer, while the offenders cause suffering to others. 'The suffering of offenders is not primary, but the consequence of their antisocial behaviour. The neurotic is oversensitive and overconscientious, acts too slowly, thinks and worries too much; the offender is underconscientious, unconcerned about others, insensitive, acts too quickly, and fails to think of consequences. It follows therefore that he requires a different therapeutic approach and treatment aim.'

The problems of delinquency should be tackled, if possible, in the first place by prophylaxis. Even more in the case of girls than boys, the facts are sufficiently well established for some efforts to be made in this direction. We need to prevent the child from entering an environment in which she is unwanted, unloved or unlikely to be well brought up. Effective family planning as a national policy would probably make a considerable contribution to the reduction of delinquency. If parents had no more children than they wished and planned to have, the problems of the over-stressed mother would be less. It is especially the unwanted children, and children coming from large sibships who are at risk for delinquency.

Over-burdening of the mother was a frequent cause of unsatisfactory upbringing in our series of girls. If maternity and child-welfare clinics were alive to this issue, more might be done about it. If the mother is not able to look after her children properly, she should if possible be helped to do so. If they are so many that she just can't cope, other homes should be found for some of them. If, as is sometimes the case, by reason of weakness of mind or unsuitability of temperament she is simply incapable of giving a child a secure and happy home, she should be encouraged to guard herself against all further pregnancies, e.g. by being sterilized. Parents who are demonstrably incapable of bringing up their children to an adequate standard should be relieved of their care; they will usually be happy enough to see them go. Parents who are full of good will and good intentions and still cannot manage may be helped by education and training as well as by practical assistance. The right time for basic training in home-making and parenthood is, of course, during school years, before the parent-to-be has yet undertaken these serious responsibilities. There is so much know-how needed, in budgeting, dietetics, simple cookery, practical house-management, infant and child care, that one might well be amazed that all adolescent girls are not given systematic instruction. As our standards get higher and higher, and as the distance between the generations gets greater in terms of social change, up-to-date teaching becomes more necessary.

Another place where some change in contemporary attitudes seems to be called for is in our appreciation of the balance between tolerance, permissiveness and encouragement on one side, and regulation and control on the other. There is growing recognition that the child needs a system of rules which he can clearly understand, and that an unduly permissive upbringing does not lead to his health or happiness, or to his becoming a tolerable member of society. If there are no limits, he must press further and further, even in socially outrageous ways, until at last he can find something which is firmly forbidden. The younger the child, the more he needs in the way of a firmly structured world, where he knows exactly where he is, what he may do and what he may not. As he gets older he will himself try to push out his frontiers, to increase his liberty of action, and must be allowed gradually to do so. But he never faces a world without prohibitions, for when those of childhood are superseded, those of an adult society remain. There is a case to be made for the view that young people have been allowed to throw off the restraints that apply to immaturity, before they have accustomed themselves to those which hold for everyone.

In some liberal circles, 'discipline' has come to be almost a dirty word, signifying treatment of the child which is harsh and unloving. Discipline in its proper sense is training in self-discipline. For it there must be a method of habit-training which encourages socially amenable and considerate behaviour, and builds up standards to serve for guidance through the whole of one's life. Rewards and punishments together constitute the positive and negative reinforcement of conditioning processes. Those investigators of delinquency (e.g. *Bingham, Fernald,* the *Gluecks, Healy and Bronner, Merrill, Nye*) who have studied this aspect of the life of the delinquent child have been impressed with the extent and the degree by which it fell below the usual standards. They agree in concluding that strict discipline, even though taken to a point which today would be thought objectionable, is not associated with delinquency, as long as it is consistent. Undue laxity is more unfavourable. But most unfavourable of all is haphazard variation between one extreme and the other, leaving the child after any and every act unable to know what he has to expect. These findings are just what might have been predicted from our present knowledge of conditioning theory. It is a matter of ironic interest that a recent study by *Craft* (1966) has shown that, in the treatment of delinquent boys, a better future awaited the boys who had been handled in a somewhat authoritarian regime in the hospital, than the boys who had been treated in the same hospital by psychotherapeutic methods in the ambit of a permissive regime.

The next point of practical importance is that interest should be shown in the early diagnosis of the unhappy or mismanaged child and the hostile or the disorganized home. The country is sufficiently well supplied with psychiatric clinics for children for this to be a matter of no great difficulty. Unhappy children, neurotic children and children with behaviour disorders do get brought, perhaps in a majority of cases, to these clinics for advice. It may be the case, such is the emphasis on permissiveness, insight therapy for mothers and play therapy for children, that they have not been handled as effectively as they might have been, if the practical aim of prevention of delinquency had been in the centre of the picture. However, there are thoroughly bad homes where unhappy and misbehaved children are given no help and are left to fend for themselves. Here the school might play a part. The rejected child, the child under stress, the child who is misbehaving, who is not absorbed in the school community, who is under-attaining for his ability, who is neurotic or disturbed or autistically withdrawn, sticks out like a sore finger. There should be no difficulty in recognizing him (or her). Once the children who are in need of help are ascertained, their homes should automatically come under scrutiny; nearly always it is in the home where the pathology lies, and where effective treatment must be applied. School teachers should know their children, and there should be an effective relationship between teacher and child. *Hemming* (1960) has shown how much adolescent girls need guidance, and are aware of their need; and how relatively simple it would be to organize the work of the teacher so that each pupil had, throughout her school career, friendly understanding adult guidance.

When the delinquent child is eventually brought before the juvenile court, the court should recognize that what they now see is the end-result of a chain of cause and effect. It will only be in a small proportion of cases that the child herself is at fault, and then because she is, as it were, a faulty piece of mechanism, weak-minded or brain-damaged or constitutionally unstable, i.e. presenting a medical problem in which medical considerations should take precedence. In the overwhelming majority of cases the fault will lie in the environment, most often the home itself. Questions of guilt and punishment should not arise. What is then required is effective intervention to remedy the basic defect of the child's environment, or to remove her permanently to a better one. Too often we have seen from our records a girl brought repeatedly before the court, sent back again and again to a pathological home in which normal emotional and social development is impossible.

What we have to face in a number of cases, in a high proportion of those we investigated, is a thoroughly bad home, directly inimical to the growing girl. It would seem that in any community there must always be a proportion of families in which the emotional life is unfavourable to the immature, sensitive over-reacting adolescent. To us it seems more than doubtful whether children should be allowed to go on living in such a hostile environment, just because it is the parental home, once their neurotic or delinquent reaction has been shown. It is indeed a widespread view that children should not be removed from their natural home even when it is a bad one, and should not be removed from their natural mother even when it is plainly manifest that she cannot manage them, or is even doing them active harm. This opinion is based on no good evidence that we know. There is no evidence that institutional life as such *must* be detrimental; indeed, Aberlour Orphanage, the largest orphanage in Scotland, and Dr. Barnado's homes in England have excellent records for turning out healthy, happy and non-delinquent children. Admittedly, in the past institutions have lacked much that we now recognize as vital for the child's needs. There is no reliable evidence that adoptive parents are not as successful with their families as natural parents; nor evidence that foster-parents, given stability of guardianship, fail in providing the needed love and care. In fact, from the child's point of view, the intrinsic superiority of the natural mother over all mother-substitutes whatever would seem to be something of a myth: at least the presumption that she is the best guardian for the child should be regarded as suspect once matters go seriously wrong. The time is obviously coming when the citizen's right to unlimited parenthood will have to be restricted. In the same way, for the health of the succeeding generation, the right of parents to look after their child will have to yield in priority to the child's right to be properly looked after.

Bibliography

AHNSJÖ, SVEN (1941). 'Delinquency in Girls and its Prognosis.' *Acta pædiat., 28,* Suppl. III.

AICHHORN, AUGUST (1949). 'Some remarks on the psychic structure and social care of a certain type of female juvenile delinquents.' *The Psychoanalytic Study of the Child,* vols. III/IV. London, Imago Publishing Co., 439–448.

AINSWORTH, M. D., ANDRY, R. G., HARLOW, R. G., LEBOVICI, S., MEAD, M., PRUGH, D. C., WOOTTON, B. (1962). 'Deprivation of Maternal Care. A Reassessment of its Effects.' Geneva (WHO).

ASSOCIATION OF HEADMASTERS, HEADMISTRESSES AND MATRONS OF APPROVED SCHOOLS TECHNICAL SUB-COMMITTEE (1954). 'Girls in Approved Schools.' Monograph No. 6. Issued as supplement to Approved Schools Gazette, vol. 48.

ATCHESON, J. D. and WILLIAMS, D. C. (1954). 'A study of juvenile sex offenders.' *Amer. J. Psychiat., 111,* 366–370.

BAGOT, J. H. (1941). *Juvenile Delinquency. A comparative study of the position in Liverpool and in England and Wales.* London (Jonathan Cape).

BARNETT, C. D. and TARVER, W. N. (1959). 'Self-rated problems of institutionalized delinquent *vs.* non-delinquent girls.' *Psychological Reports, 5,* 333–336.

BEANE, J. C. (1931). 'A study of three hundred delinquent girls.' *J. juv. Res., 15,* 198–208.

BERGSTRAND, C. G. and OTTO, U. (1962). 'Suicidal attempts in adolescence and childhood.' *Acta pædiat. (Uppsala) 51,* 17–26.

BINGHAM, ANNE T. (1923). 'Determinants of sex delinquency in adolescent girls based on intensive study of 500 cases.' *J. crim. Law and Criminol., 13,* 494–586.

BLANK, L. (1958). 'The intellectual functioning of delinquents.' *J. soc. Psychol., 47,* 9–14.

BOVET, L. (1951). *Psychiatric Aspects of Delinquency.* Geneva (WHO).

BOWLBY, J. (1946). *Forty-four juvenile thieves, their characters and homelife.* London (Baillière Tindall & Cox).

BOWLBY, J., AINSWORTH, M., BOSTON, M. and ROSENBLUTH, D. (1956). 'The effects of mother-child separation: a follow-up study.' *Brit. J. med. Psychol., 29,* 211–247.

BURT, C. (1948). *The Young Delinquent.* 4th ed., London (Univ. London Press).

CAPWELL, D. F. (1945). 'Personality patterns of adolescent girls. II Delinquents and non-delinquents.' *J. appl. Psychol.*, *29*, 289–297.

CARR-SAUNDERS, A. M., MANNHEIM, H. and RHODES, E. C. (1942). *Young Offenders. An Enquiry into Juvenile Delinquency.* Cambridge (Cambridge University Press).

CHIEF EDUCATION OFFICER OF BIRMINGHAM. (1937). Report on the Present Problem of Juvenile Delinquency. Unpublished, discussed by Carr-Saunders et al. (No. 18).

CHINN, W. L. (1938). 'A brief survey of nearly one thousand juvenile delinquents.' *Brit. J. educ. Psychol.*, *8*, 78–85.

CLARKE, J. (1962). 'Delinquent personalities.' *Brit. J. Crim.*, *3*, 147–161.

CLOWARD, R. A. and OHLIN, L. E. (1961). *Delinquency and Opportunity: A Theory of Delinquent Gangs.* London (Routledge and Kegan Paul).

COWIE, J. (1966). 'Psychiatry in an Approved School.' *Approved Schools Gazette*, *59*, 495–505.

COWIE, V. (1961). 'The incidence of neurosis in the children of psychotics.' *Acta psychiat. scand.*, *37*, 37–87.

CRAFT, M. J. (1966). *Psychopathic Disorders and their Assessment.* Oxford (Pergamon Press), Pp. 130–134.

CRAIKE, W. H. (1953). 'Psychiatric treatment of adolescent delinquent girls.' *Howard Journal*, *8*, 258–262.

CORMIER, B. M., KENNEDY, M. and SANGOWICZ, J. (1962). 'Psychodynamics of father daughter incest.' *Canad. psychiat. Assoc. J.*, *7*, 203–217.

DALTON, K. (1961). 'Menstruation and crime.' *Brit. med. J.*, *ii*, 1752–3.

DAVIS, D. R. (1962). 'Birth order and maternal age of homosexuals.' *Lancet*, *i*, 540.

DESPERT, J. L. (1947). 'Is juvenile delinquency a psychiatric problem?' *The Nervous Child*, *6*, 371–391.

DILLER, JULIET C. (1955). 'A comparison of the test performances of male and female juvenile delinquents.' *J. genetic Psychol.*, *86*, 217–236.

DILLER, L. (1952). 'A comparison of the test performances of delinquent and non-delinquent girls.' *J. genetic Psychol.*, *81*, 167–183.

DOUGLAS, J. W. B. (1966). 'The school progress of nervous and troublesome children.' *Brit. J. Psychiat.*, *112*, 1115–1116.

DOWNES, D. M. (1966). *The Delinquent Solution: a study in subcultural theory.* London (Routledge and Kegan Paul).

DUREA, M. A. and ASSUM, A. L. (1948). 'The reliability of personality traits differentiating delinquent and non-delinquent girls.' *J. genetic Psychol.*, *72*, 307–311.

EAST, N., STOCKS, P. and YOUNG, H. T. P. (1942). *The Adolescent Criminal: A Medico-Sociological Study of 4,000 Male Adolescents.* London (Churchill).

EILENBERG, M. D. (1961). 'Remand Home Boys, 1930–1955.' *Brit. J. Criminol.*, *2*, 111–131.

ELLIOTT, Mabel A. (1952). *Crime in Modern Society*. New York (Harper and Bros.).

EPPS, P. (1951). 'A preliminary survey of 300 female delinquents in borstal institutions.' *Brit., J. Delinq.*, *1*, 187–197.

——(1954). 'A further survey of female delinquents undergoing borstal training.' *Brit. J. Delinq.*, *4*, 265–271.

FERGUSON, T. (1952). *The Young Delinquent in his Social Setting*. London (Oxford University Press).

FERNALD, Mabel Ruth, HAYES, Mary H. S., DAWLEY, Almena, RUML, B. (1920). *A Study of Women Delinquents in New York State*. New York: (Century Co.). Publications of the Bureau of Social Hygiene.

FORTES, M. (1933). 'The influence of position in sibship on juvenile delinquency., *Economica*, Aug., 301–328.

GALVIN, J. (1956). 'Some dynamics of delinquent girls.' *J. nerv. ment. Dis. 123*, 292–295.

GIBBENS, T. C. N. (1957). 'Juvenile prostitution.' *Brit. J. Delinq.*, *8*, 3–12.

——(1959). 'Supervision and probation of adolescent girls.' *Brit. J. Delinq.*, *10*, 84–103.

——(1961) *Trends in Juvenile Delinquency*. Geneva (WHO).

——(1963). *Psychiatric Studies of Borstal Lads*. London (Oxford University Press).

GITTINS, J. (1952). *Approved School Boys*. London (HMSO).

GLUECK, S. and GLUECK, E. T. (1930). *500 Criminal Careers*. New York (Knopf).

——(1934a). *One Thousand Juvenile Delinquents*. Cambridge, Mass. (Harvard University Press).

——(1934b). *Five Hundred Delinquent Women*. New York (Knopf).

——(1950). *Unraveling juvenile delinquency*. New York (The Commonwealth Fund).

——(1959). *Predicting Delinquency and Crime*. Cambridge, Mass. (Harvard University Press).

——(1962). *Family Environment and Delinquency*. London (Routledge & Kegan Paul).

GORING, C. (1913). *The English Convict. A Statistical Study*. London (HMSO).

GREENWOOD, M. and YULE, G. U. (1914). 'On the determination of size of family and of the distribution of characters in order of birth from samples taken through members of sibship.' *J. roy. statist. Soc.*, *1914*, 179–197.

GREGORY, I. (1958). 'Studies of parental deprivation in psychiatric patients.' *Am. J. Psychiat.*, *115*, 432–442.

HEALY, W. and BRONNER, Augusta F. (1926). *Delinquents and Criminals: Their Making and Unmaking.* New York (Macmillan Co.).

—(1936). *New Light on Delinquency and its Treatment.* London (Oxford University Press).

HEMMING, J. (1960). *Problems of Adolescent Girls.* London (Heinemann).

HESTON, L. L. (1966). 'The adult adjustment of persons institutionalized as children.' (Privately communicated.)

HOOPER, P. M. F. (1963). 'Group work with borstal girls.' *Howard Journal, 11,* 119–133.

JOHNSON, Adelaide M. (1959). 'Juvenile delinquency.' *American Handbook of Psychiatry,* (ed. Arieti). New York (Basic Books).

JONSSON, G. (1967). 'Delinquent Boys, their Parents and Grandparents.' *(Acta psychiat. scand. Suppl.* 195, ad vol. 43.) Copenhagen (Munksgaard).

KAUFMAN, I., MAKKAY, Elizabeth S. and ZILBACH, Joan. (1959). 'The impact of adolescence on girls with delinquent character formation.' *Amer. J. Orthopsychiat., 29,* 130–143.

LABAR, Mlle. (1963). 'La délinquance chez les filles mineures.' *Ann. med.-psychol., 121,* 807–8.

LACK, C. (1952). 'Observations on the classifying of delinquent adolescent girls.' *Brit. J. Delinq., 3,* 46–51.

LANDER, J. (1963). 'Some aspects of female delinquency.' *J. Amer. Acad. Child Psychiat., 2,* 549–560.

LASKO, A. (1954). 'Parent behaviour toward first and second children.' *Genet. Psychol. Monogr., 49,* 97–137.

LEES, J. P. and NEWSON, L. J. (1954). 'Family or sibship position and some aspects of juvenile delinquency.' *Brit. J. Delinq., 5,* 46–65.

LESHAN, L. L. (1952). 'Time orientation and social class.' *J. abnorm. soc. Psychol., 47,* 589–592.

LEWIS, Hilda (1954). *Deprived Children.* London (Oxford University Press).

LITAUER, W. (1957). *Juvenile Delinquents in a Psychiatric Clinic.* Publ. London: I.S.T.D.

LUMPKIN, Katharine du P. (1931). 'Factors in the commitment of correctional schoolgirls in Wisconsin.' *Amer. J. Sociol., 37,* 222–230.

MANNHEIM, H. (1948). *Juvenile Delinquency in an English Middletown.* London (Kegan Paul, Trench, Trubner).

MATHEWS, Julia (1923). 'A survey of 341 delinquent girls in California.' *J. Delinq., 8,* 196–231.

McCORD, W. and McCORD, Joan (1959). *Origins of Crime: A New Evaluation of the Cambridge-Somerville Youth Study.* New York (Columbia University Press).

MERRILL, Maud A. (1947a). *Problems of Child Delinquency.* London (George G. Harrap).

—(1947b). *Problems of child delinquency.* Boston (Houghton Mifflin).

MILLER, E. (1944). 'The problem of birth order and delinquency.' *Mental Abnormality and Crime*, ed. L. Radzinowicz and J. W. C. Turner. London (Macmillan).

MINISTRY OF EDUCATION (1950). *Reading Ability: Some Suggestions for Helping the Backward.* Pamphlet No. 18. London (HMSO).

——(1957). *Standards of Reading 1948–1956.* Pamphlet No. 32, London: (HMSO).

MONAHAN, T. P. (1957). 'Family status and the delinquent child: a reappraisal and some new findings.' *Social Forces*, *35*, 250–258.

MORRIS, Ruth R. (1964). 'Female delinquency and relational problems.' *Social Forces*, *43*, 82–89.

MUNRO, A. (1965). 'Childhood parent-loss in a psychiatrically normal population.' *Brit. J. prev. soc. Med.*, *19*, 69–79.

NISBET, J. (1953). 'Family environment and intelligence.' *Eugen. Rev.*, *45*, 31–40.

NYE, F. I. (1957). 'Childhood adjustment in broken and in unhappy unbroken homes.' *Marriage and Family Living*, *19*, 356–361.

——(1958). *Family Relationships and Delinquent Behavior.* New York (John Wiley & Sons).

O'KELLY, Elizabeth (1955). 'Some observations on relationships between delinquent girls and their parents.' *Brit. J. med. Psychol.*, *28*, 59–66.

OSWALD, I. (1958). 'Deprivation of parents during childhood. Its frequency in some contemporary young servicemen.' *Brit. med. J.*, *i*, 1515–1516.

OTTERSTRÖM, Edith (1946). 'Delinquency and Children from Bad Homes.' A study of their prognosis from a social point of view, *Acta pædiat.*, *33*, Suppl. 5.

PATHAK, A. M. (1964). 'The remand home and the Government certified school for girls in Nagpur.' A work study. *Excerpta criminol.*, *4*, 791–2.

PEARCE, S. B. P. (1958). *An Ideal in the Working.* London (The Magdalen Hospital).

PENROSE, L. S. (1963). *Biology of Mental Defect.* 3rd ed. London (Sidgwick & Jackson).

——(1955). 'Genetics and the criminal.' *Brit. J. Delinq.*, *6*, 15–25.

POLLAK, O. (1950). *The Criminality of Women.* New York (University of Pennsylvania Press).

PRICE, W. H., STRONG, J. A., WHATMORE, P. B., and McCLEMONT, W. F. (1966). 'Criminal patients with XYY sex-chromosome complement.' *Lancet*, *i*, 565–566.

PRINGLE, M. L. K. (1961). 'The incidence of some supposedly adverse family conditions and of left-handedness in schools for maladjusted children.' *Brit. J. Educ. Psychol.*, *31*, 183–193.

PRINGLE, M. L. K. and BOSSIO, V. (1958). 'A study of deprived children, Pt. II: Language development and reading attainment.' *Vita Humana*, *1*, 142–170.

RAVENETTE, A. T. and KAHN, H. J. (1962). 'Intellectual ability of disturbed children in a working-class area.' *Brit. J. soc. clin. Psychol.*, *1*, 208–212.

RHODES, E. C. (1942). See CARR-SAUNDERS, A. M., MANNHEIM, H. and RHODES, E. C. (1942).

ROBEY, A., SNELL, J. E., ROSENWALD, R. and LEE, R. E. (1963). 'The delinquent girl.' I: The runaway girl. A reaction to family stress. *Excerpta criminol.*, *3*, 415–16.

ROBINS, LEE N. (1966). *Deviant Children Grown Up: A Sociological and Psychiatric Study of Sociopathic Personality*. Baltimore (Williams and Wilkins).

ROBINS, L. N. and O'NEAL, P. (1959). 'The adult prognosis for runaway children.' *Am. J. Orthopsychiat.*, *29*, 752–761.

ROSANOFF, A. J., HANDY, L. M. and PLESSETT, I. R. (1941). *The Etiology of Child Behavior Difficulties, Juvenile Delinquency and Adult Criminality, with Special Reference to their Occurrence in Twins*. Psychiatric Monographs No. 1 (Sacramento Department of Institutions).

SCHMIDEBERG, Melitta (1962). 'The promise of psychiatry: hopes and disillusionment.' *Northwestern University Law Review*, *57*, 19–28.

SCHOFIELD, M. (1965). *The Sexual Behaviour of Young People*. London (Longmans).

SCOTT, P. D. (1965). Delinquency. Chapter in *Modern Perspectives in Child Psychiatry* (ed. Howells). Edinburgh (Oliver and Boyd).

SEAGRAVE, Mabel (1926). 'Causes underlying sex delinquency in young girls.' *J. soc. Hygiene*, *12*, 523–529.

SHAW, C. R. and MCKAY, H. D. (1931). 'Social Factors in Juvenile Delinquency.' Washington: National Commission of Law Observance and Enforcement, Report No. 13.

SHIELDS, J. (1963). 'Some delinquent twins.' Talk given to the British Society of Criminology on 6.12.1963.

SLATER, E. (1962). 'Birth order and maternal age of homosexuals.' *Lancet*, *i*, 69–71.

SLETTO, R. F. (1934). 'Sibling position and juvenile delinquency.' *Am. J. Sociol.*, *39*, 657–669.

SMITH, P. M. (1955). 'Broken homes and juvenile delinquency.' *Sociology and Social Research*, *39*, 307–311.

STOTT, D. H. (1962). 'Evidence for a congenital factor in maladjustment and delinquency.' *Amer. J. Psychiat.*, *118/9*, 781–794.

THOMAS, W. I. (1923). *The Unadjusted Girl*. Boston (Little, Brown and Co.).

Toby, J. (1957). 'The differential impact of family disorganization.' *Am. Soc. Rev.*, *22*, 505–512.

Walker, Anneliese (1961). 'Special problems of delinquent and maladjusted girls.' *Approved Schools Gazette*, *55*, 270–278.

Walker, L. (1962). 'Behaviour problems of delinquent girls.' *Approved Schools Gazette*, *55*, 467–473.

Walters, A. A. (1963). 'Delinquent generations.' *Brit. J. Criminol.*, *3*, 391–395.

Warren, W. (1961). 'Behaviour disorders in girls.' *Approved Schools Gazette*, *55*, 237–243.

Wattenberg, W. W. and Saunders, F. (1954). 'Sex differences among juvenile offenders.' *Sociology and Social Research*, *39*, 24–31.

——(1955). 'Recidivism among girls.' *J. abn. soc. Psychol.*, *50*, 405–406.

Wilkins, L. T. (1960). *Delinquent Generations*. Home Office Research Unit Report No. 3. London (HMSO).

Williams, J. M. (1961). 'Children who break down in foster-homes: a psychological study of patterns of personality growth in grossly deprived children.' *J. Child Psychol. Psychiat.*, *2*, 5–20.

Williams, Prys (1962). *Patterns of Teenage Delinquency*. London (Christian Economic and Social Research Foundation).

Wilson, Harriett (1962). *Delinquency and Child Neglect*. London (Allen and Unwin).

Wiseman, S. (1964). *Education and Environment*. Manchester University Press.

Wolfgang, M. E. et al. (Eds.) (1962). *The Sociology of Crime and Delinquency*. New York (Wiley).

Woodward, Mary (1955). *Low Intelligence and Delinquency*. London (ISTD).

Wootton, Barbara (1959). *Social Science and Social Pathology*. London (Allen and Unwin).

Yoshimasu, Shufu (1965). 'Criminal life curves of monozygotic twin-pairs.' *Acta Crim. Med. leg. jap. 31*, 144–153 and 190–197.

Appendix A

Statistical Tables

Delinquencies	Youngest sixth	Older girls	Total
Sexual	24	167	191
Other	29	98	127
Totals	53	265	318

TABLE A1. Of the older girls 63 per cent are charged with a sexual offence, of the youngest 53 only 45 per cent. For this distribution $\chi^2 = 5\cdot79$, $0\cdot02 > p > 0\cdot01$.

	Youngest sixth	Older girls	Total
Home 'Poor' or institutional	26	80	106
Home otherwise	27	185	212
Totals	53	265	318

TABLE A2. The youngest children are more than normally likely to come from poor or institutional homes. For this distribution $\chi^2 = 7\cdot07$, $0\cdot01 > p > 0\cdot001$.

Age limits	N	Σx	$\bar{x}$
13·2 – 13·5	2	188	—
13·11 – 14·1	13	1085	90·4
14·2 – 14·4	17	1620	91·8
14·5 – 14·7	17	1609	98·2
14·8 – 14·10	23	2369	97·7
14·11 – 15·1	13	1202	100·8
15·2 – 15·4	16	1673	97·8
15·5 – 15·7	33	3189	99·0
15·8 – 15·10	31	3058	95·9
15·11 – 16·1	33	3059	95·6
16·2 – 16·4	27	2579	95·1
16·5 – 16·7	28	2727	97·0
16·8 – 16·10	41	4005	97·0
16·11 – 17·0	24	2285	—

TABLE A3. Numbers of observations and sums of IQs are shown in all age classes. The fourth column shows means, partially smoothed by combining class shown with the two adjacent classes. These figures are also shown in Figure 2. Variance analysis of above data shows sum of squares 104,405; variance between age groups (13 d.f.) 14,345; variance within groups (304 d.f.) 90,060; variance ratio 3·72, p <0·001.

Retardation in Reading	Retardation in Arithmetic, by proportion of age			
	less than 15%	15%–29%	30% and over	Total %
less than 15%	57	69	31	157 (49·5)
15%–29%	13	38	47	98 (30·9)
30% and over	—	12	50	62 (19·6)
TOTALS AND PER CENT	70 (22·1)	119 (37·5)	128 (40·4)	317

TABLE A4. Correlation of degree of retardation in reading and arithmetic, as proportions of chronological age (maxima, reading 15 years, arithmetic 14½ years). In the case of one girl out of the 318, no estimate was made of reading age.

	Standard in years		Samples			
	Watts-Vernon	Schonell	15-year old girls per cent		Magdalen 1958	
			1948	1956	N	%
Superior	17·0+	14·5+	8·6	7	19	7·9
Average plus	13·8+	13·2+	30·4	38	75	31·4
Average minus	12·0+	12·0+	28·7	26	59	24·7
Backward	9·0+	9·0+	27·1	25	66	27·6
Semi-literate	7·0+	7·0+	4·1	4	16	6·7
Illiterate			1·1	0	4	1·7

TABLE A5. Reading age of Magdalen girls aged 15 and over, compared with sample of girls aged 15 in 1956 (Ministry of Education).

Years in Retardation	Intelligence Quotients																					
	51–59		60–69		70–79		80–89		90–99		100–109		110–119		120–129		130–138		141–149		Total	
	RA	AA	RA	AA	RA	AA	RA	AA	RA	AA	RA	AA	RA	AA	RA	AA	RA	AA	RA	AA	RA	AA
Ahead Level	—	—	—	—	—	—	—	—	1	—	—	1	1	1	1	—	—	—	—	1	3	2
0·1 – 0·11	—	—	—	—	—	—	—	—	—	—	—	3	—	3	—	4	—	2	1	2	1	12
1·0 – 1·11	—	—	—	—	2	1	5	2	7	8	15	9	9	3	13	5	4	3	4	1	54	13
2·0 – 2·11	—	—	2	—	6	1	11	11	23	11	18	9	17	7	7	5	4	1	—	1	76	33
3·0 – 3·11	—	—	—	—	8	10	12	16	25	21	15	7	5	10	1	5	—	2	—	—	63	38
4·0 – 4·11	1	1	3	1	2	14	14	17	13	23	1	10	4	5	—	5	—	—	—	—	38	53
5·0 – 5·11	1	1	2	6	9	7	7	9	8	15	1	16	—	5	—	1	—	—	—	—	29	75
6·0 – 6·11	1	2	4	2	9	7	6	17	3	4	1	5	—	7	—	—	—	—	—	—	22	58
7·0 – 7·11	1	2	3	3	3	3	3	9	1	1	—	—	—	—	—	—	—	—	—	—	15	24
8·0 – 8·11	1	—	—	—	3	—	2	1	2	—	—	—	—	—	—	—	—	—	—	—	11	10
9·0 – 9·11	1	—	—	—	—	—	1	—	1	—	—	—	—	—	—	—	—	—	—	—	3	—
10·0 – 10·10	1	—	—	—	—	—	—	—	—	—	—	—	—	—	—	—	—	—	—	—	1	—
Mean yrs. mo.	6	6	12	12	37	37	57	57	83	84	51	51	36	36	22	22	8	8	5	5	317	318
	7.9	6.1	6.10	5.10	4.8	5.3	3.10	4.9	2.8	3.11	1.8	3.1	1.7	2.3	0.10	1.9	0.11	1.1	0.6	0.5	2.10	3.8

TABLE A6. Correlation of intelligence with degree of retardation in reading age (Schonell: maximum 15 years) and arithmetic age (Burt: maximum 14½ years) behind the chronological age.

	Present material N %	Pringle's data %	National figures %
Parents divorced	33 10	20	1
Half-orphaned	58 18	8	?
Step-parent	64 20	18	?
Illegitimate	74 23	18	5
Adopted	28 9	11	2
Left-handed	? ?	14	7

TABLE A7. Comparison of present findings with those of Pringle on 537 girls in schools for the maladjusted. National figures given for comparison are quoted from Pringle.

Type of Delinquency	Maternal Deprivation		Total
	Present	Absent	
Sex	67	124	191
Larceny	31	43	74
Other	22	31	53
TOTALS	120	198	318

TABLE A8. Relationship between maternal deprivation and type of delinquency. The expected number of maternally deprived among the girls in the larceny class 27·9, and among the sex offenders 72·1. Differences between observation and expectation are not significant, $\chi^2 = 1·44$, $0·50 > p > 0·30$.

Last Birthday	Number	%
0	57	18
1	66	21
2	70	22
3	78	25
4	81	25
5	87	27
6	97	31
7	97	31
8	95	30
9	94	30
10	98	31
11	97	31
12	100	31
13	104	33
14	105	33
Later	84	26
Present time	104	33

TABLE A9. Numbers of children not with their own mothers at given year of age. Both first and last years of separation are included, e.g. a girl separated from her mother from the age of 6 to 13 will be included in both the years 6 and 13. The last line of the table shows the number of girls separated from their mothers at the time of admission to the School.

Size of Sibship

| | | | Mean size of sibship | | |
| | | | Uncorrected | | Corrected |
Date	Author	Probands	Probands	Controls	Probands
1913	Goring	men	7·00	—	4·64
1920	Fernald	women	5·76	—	3·34
1926	Healy and Bronner	boys and girls	4·44	—	3·01
1930	Gluecks	men	5·30	—	—
1933	Fortes	boys and girls	5·22	—	4·01
1934	Bagot	boys	5·18	—	—
1934	Bagot	girls	5·37	—	—
1934	Gluecks	boys	4·98	—	—
1934	Gluecks	women	6·43	—	4·71
1936	Bagot	girls	5·28	—	—
1937	Bagot (Birmingham)	boys and girls	6·9	—	—
1938	Chinn	boys	5·07	—	3·93
1938	Chinn	boys (youngest)	5·16	—	—
1938	Chinn	boys (oldest)	4·89	—	—
1942	Rhodes	boys (maxima)	5·3	4·4	—
1942	Rhodes	boys (minima)	3·6	3·0	—
1950	Gluecks	boys	6·85	5·90	4·09
1952	Ferguson	boys	5·4	4·7	—
1954	Lewis	deprived boys and girls	3·9(?)	—	—
1962	Wilson	neglected boys and girls	7·4	—	—
1966	(present)	girls (total)	4·27	—	2·64
1966	(present)	girls (from intact families)	5·08	—	3·49

TABLE A10. Sizes of sibships from which delinquents and criminals are drawn: data from the literature.

	Delinquents	Controls	Diff:
London A	5·3	4·4	0·9
B	3·6	3·6	0·0
C	5·1	3·6	1·5
D	4·1	3·7	0·4
E	4·1	3·0	1·1
F	4·3	4·0	0·3
G	4·3	3·4	0·9
Manchester	4·4	3·2	1·2
Leeds	4·0	3·8	0·2
Sheffield	4·0	3·7	0·3
Hull	4·9	4·0	0·9
Nottingham	4·2	3·9	0·3
Cardiff	5·2	3·9	1·3

TABLE A11. Mean size of sibship for delinquent boys from seven London Courts and six provincial cities, together with matched controls (from Rhodes 1942).

Sibship Size	Population sample	Present material
Only child	13	15
Sibship of two	29	14
Sibship of three	21	16
Sibship of four or more	30	55
Sibship not known	8	—
TOTAL	101	100

TABLE A12. Distribution of sibships compared with those of 2,190 girls born in 1947 (National Survey of Health and Development).

	Common sibships	Born sibships	Home sibships
Number of sibships for which data available .	238	72	77
Total number of sibs excluding proposita . .	738	277	182
Mean number of sibs .	3·10	3·85	2·36
Sibships of two or more for which data available on birth order . .	202	54	49
Mean birth order . .	0·4145	0·5373	0·4068

TABLE A13. Birth order in different types of sibships. Common sibships are those of full sibs with or without maternal half-sibs, into which the proposita was born and in which she grew up. Born sibships are sibships into which she was born, but from which she was later separated. Home sibships are sibships not related by blood, into which the proposita came by adoption or by fostering and in which she grew up.

Sibship Size	Other sibs with a record of delinquency								Totals		All
	No.	0	1	2	3	4	5	6	del.	non-del.	
?	8	7	1						1	?	?
1	47										
2	43	41	2						2	41	43
3	51	43	5	3					11	91	102
4	45	41	1	2	1				8	127	135
5	53	37	10	4	1	1			25	187	212
6	23	18	3	2	—	—	—		7	108	115
7	16	11	2	—	2	1	—	—	12	84	96
8	13	6	4	2	1	—	—	—	11	80	91
9	7	2	2	2	1	—	—	—	9	47	56
10	3	1	—	1	—	1	—	—	6	21	27
11	4	1	1	—	1	1	—	—	8	32	40
12	1	1	—	—	—	—	—	—	—	11	11
15	1	—	1	—	—	—	—	—	1	13	14
16	1	—	—	—	—	—	1	—	5	10	15
18	1	—	—	—	—	—	—	1	6	11	17
23	1	—	—	—	—	—	1	—	5	17	22

TOTAL 318   209   32   16   7   4   2   1

(excluding sibships size ? and 1) :—

              263   202   31   16   7   4   2   1   116   880   996

TABLE A14. Further delinquencies in sibship by sibship size.

Sibships with other sibs delinquent	Number Observed	Number Expected
0	202	182·52
1	31	57·91
2	16	14·63
3	7	4·76
4	4	1·87
5	2	0·78
6	1	0·53
Total sibships	263	263·00
Total delinquents	116	116·01

TABLE A15. *Clustering of delinquents in sibships.

*For the preparation of this Table, the expectancies of Table A14 have been used to calculate, within each sibship size, the expected proportions of sibships with 0, 1, 2 ... delinquent sibs; within sibships of stated size n, these proportions are obtained from the binomial expansion of $(1-p+p)^n$, where p is the expectation of delinquency for that size of sibship.

Age	Non-del.	Del.	Proportion
0 – 4	26	—	0·00
5 – 9	43	6	0·12
10 – 14	39	23	0·37
15 – 19	34	42	0·55
20 – 24	30	29	0·49
25 – 29	20	9	0·31
30 +	5	1	0·17
TOTALS	197	110	

TABLE A16. Age distribution of sibs in families with secondary cases of delinquency. The third column shows the proportion of all sibs in each age-class who are reported to have a record of delinquency.

Birth order	Non-del.	Del.	Proportion
+ 8 to + 4	37	—	0·00
+ 3	17	4	0·19
+ 2	24	10	0·29
+ 1	30	18	0·38
− 1	16	36	0·69
− 2	22	19	0·46
− 3	18	10	0·36
− 4 to − 7	33	13	0·28

TABLE A17. Distribution of sibs, delinquent and non-delinquent, in birth order in relation to index case. Eldest are at the head and youngest at the foot of the table.

Order in sibship		Non-del.	Del.	Total
+ 3 to + 8	Obsd.	54	4	58
	Expd.	52·59	5·41	
+ 2 to − 1	Obsd.	70	64	134
	Expd.	80·38	53·62	
− 2 to − 7	Obsd.	73	42	115
	Expd.	64·03	50·97	
TOTALS	Obsd.	197	110	307
	Expd.	197·00	110·00	

TABLE A18. Distribution of sibs, delinquent and non-delinquent, in birth order in relation to index case, compared with expectations on basis of age of sib. (χ^2 6·76, 2 d.f., $p <$ ·05.)

Psychiatric classification	N	mean IQ
'Abnormal'	101	100·70
'Symptoms'	64	96·14
'Normal'	153	93·31

TABLE A19. Mean IQ by psychiatric classification. Total variance = 104,405; variance between groups 3,382; variance within groups 101,023; variance ratio = 5·27, 0·01 > p > 0·001.

Psychiatric classification	Estimates of birth order	
	N	mean birth order
'Abnormal'	81	0·4689
'Symptoms'	50	0·2888
'Normal'	120	0·4271

TABLE A20. Mean birth order by psychiatric classification. Total variance = 38·856018; variance between groups = 1·048472; variance within groups = 37·807546; variance ratio = 3·44, 0·05 > p > 0·01.

Psychiatric classification	Home Background						Totals
	'Good'		'Fair'		Other		
	Obs	Exp	Obs	Exp	Obs	Exp	
'Abnormal'	46	36·53	25	25·41	30	39·06	101
'Symptoms'	18	23·14	13	16·10	33	24·76	64
'Normal'	51	55·33	42	38·49	60	59·18	153
TOTALS	115		80		123		318

TABLE A21. Association of home background with psychiatric classification; marked excess of 'abnormal' girls coming from 'good' homes, and of girls with 'symptoms' coming from poor or institutional homes. χ^2 for 4 d.f. = 9·71, 0·05 > p > 0·02.

Index case	Mother			
	'Abnormal'		'Normal'	
	Obs	Exp	Obs	Exp
'Abnormal'	30	26·16	45	48·84
'Symptoms'	25	17·09	24	31·91
'Normal'	28	39·76	86	74·24

TABLE A22. Association of psychiatric status of mother with psychiatric classification of the girl ($\chi^2 = 11\cdot87$, $\cdot01 > p > \cdot001$).

Psychiatrist's Assessment of Personality	N	Headmistresses' Rating of Response to Training					Mean Score	Number of repeatedly delinquent
		'very good'	'good'	'fair'	'poor'	'hopeless'		
'Normal'	145	36	33	35	32	9	2·62	44
'Symptoms'	62	16	13	9	16	8	2·79	25
'Abnormal'	98	31	13	25	21	8	2·61	33
TOTAL	305	83	59	69	69	25		102

TABLE A23. Two measures of success of training set against the psychiatrist's personality classification. No significant correlation is shown.

	N	1 Mean Age Yr. Mo.	2 Mean I.Q.	3 % Psych. deviant	4 Mean Score	5 Per cent F or B	6 Per cent Rpt.
Intermediate Schools							
P	17	14 9	96	59	2·41	18	12
I	14	15 1	121	38	2·50	37	31
Misc	20	14 7	84	55	2·55	25	25
G	18	15 2	92	68	3·28	21	42
L	13	14 9	76	43	3·46	7	21
All	82	14 10	96	56	2·82	22	37
Senior Schools							
C[1]	26	16 5	103	58	1·96	8	27
Misc	17	16 3	93	41	2·06	11	39
A[2]	26	16 5	104	38	2·23	23	19
E	13	16 4	97	54	2·23	8	23
D[3]	21	15 11	118	86	2·24	24	29
T	22	16 4	99	52	2·45	17	39
B	21	16 2	94	39	2·76	9	39
F	23	16 5	94	48	2·96	26	39
W	16	16 0	76	41	3·06	0	23
S	19	16 4	80	42	3·37	16	42
K	19	15 11	103	70	3·42	15	55
All	223	16 3	96	53	2·60	14	34

TABLE A24. Differences between schools, in type of girls admitted for training, and in mean score on follow-up rating. A high score indicates poor result. Schools are arranged in order of mean result obtained. Variance analysis of the raw scores shows highly significant differences between the schools. Some schools distinguished themselves by having a special type of intake psychiatrically:—

1 significant excess of girls of abnormal personality,
2 significant deficiency of girls of abnormal personality,
3 significant deficiency of girls of normal personality.

The sixth column shows the proportion of girls made subject to a 'fit person' order, or 'brought back' from absconding. The seventh column shows the proportion of girls with repeat delinquencies.

Correlations: $r_{23} + \cdot37$; $r_{24} - \cdot53$; $r_{25} + \cdot59$; $r_{26} + \cdot08$; $r_{34} - \cdot13$; $r_{35} + \cdot15$; $r_{36} + \cdot16$.

Home background rating.	Psychiatric after-history in:		
	Number:	Per cent:	Expected Number:
Good (115) . . .	24	20·8	17·52
Fair & Poor (150) . . .	9	6·0	22·85
Institutional (37) . . .	13	35·1	5·63

TABLE A25. Girls with psychiatric after-history, classified by home background. ($\chi^2 = 22\cdot39$, 2 d.f.)

	Psychiatric rating at Magdalen Hospital:			
	Normal (155)	Symptoms (64)	Abnormal (99)	Total: (318)
Hospital diagnosis:				
Epilepsy or EEG abnormality suggestive of epilepsy. .	2	—	4	6
Depressive illness (one also included under personality disorder). .	1	1	2	4
Schizophrenia (one not agreed by present authors).	2	—	1	3
Hysteria	—	—	1	1
Personality disorder (one also included under depression) . . .	—	1	11	12
No diagnosis given . .	—	—	1	1
TOTAL (No. not counted twice).	5	2	19	26

TABLE A26. Girls admitted to hospital for psychiatric reasons during the follow-up period; hospital diagnosis against psychiatric rating at the classifying school.

	monozygotic pairs		dizygotic pairs		concordance rate as %	
	conc.	disc.	conc.	disc.	MZ	DZ
Rosanoff, Handy and Plessett (1941)						
child behaviour difficulties:						
preneurotic and prepsy- chotic types males	14	5	10	9	77	12
females	8	2	11	21	80	34
child behaviour difficulties:						
predelinquent types males	8	—	5	4	100	56
females	14	—	8	11	100	42
juvenile delinquency males	29	—	12	5	100	71
females	11	1	9	—	92	100
adult criminality males	29	9	5	18	76	22
females	6	1	1	3	86	25
all males	80	14	32	36	85	47
all females	39	4	29	35	91	45
Adult criminality, sexes undifferentiated						
Lange (1929)	10	3	2	15	77	12
Legras (1932)	4	—	—	5	100	0
Kranz (1936)	20	11	23	20	65	53
Stumpfl (1936)	11	7	7	12	61	37
Yoshimasu (1965)	14	14	—	26	50	0

TABLE A27. Concordance with regard to behaviour difficulties, delinquency and criminality in monozygotic and same-sexed dizygotic twin pairs (from the literature).

Appendix B

Statistical Note

Let us suppose we are sampling a population in which individuals are either A or Ā (not-A), B or B̄. The numbers of our sample are arranged in a 2×2 table for the calculation of χ^2, the four cells containing the numbers a, b, c and d, which are respectively the numbers of individuals found to be AB, ĀB, AB̄ and ĀB̄. If the sample is a representative one, and the distributions of A and B are independent, the cross-products ad and bc will be equal, with $\chi^2 = 0$; if A and B are positively correlated we shall find $ad > bc$, and χ^2 positive.

However, if we are taking A and B as criteria for selection of the sample, or if for any reason we select A and Ā, B and B̄ at different rates, the sample becomes unrepresentative and these relationships will not hold. Let us suppose the chances of being selected into our sample of individuals of the types A, Ā, B and B̄ are respectively α, α', β and β'. Then the cross-products ad and bc become $ad\,(\alpha + \beta - \alpha\beta)\,(\alpha' + \beta' - \alpha'\beta')$ and $bc\,(\alpha + \beta' - \alpha\beta')\,(\alpha' + \beta - \alpha'\beta)$. If $\alpha > \alpha'$ and $\beta > \beta'$, the factor by which bc is multiplied is greater than the factor by which ad is multiplied. So that if we select a higher proportion of A than of Ā and of B than of B̄ individuals, the evidence of positive correlation between A and B, if such correlation exists, may be diminished, annulled or reversed.

Appendix C

Statistical Note by Patrick Slater

For the Greenwood-Yule method of calculating mean sibship size in a sample obtained by ascertaining a member of a sibship, we write:

Family size: n	Number of cases found	Correction factor: $1/\binom{n}{1}$	Weighted sum	Product $\times n$
0	..	..	..	..
1	f_1	1	f_1	f_1
2	f_2	1/2	$f_2/2$	f_2
3	f_3	1/3	$f_3/3$	f_3
4	f_4	1/4	$f_4/4$	f_4
..	..	..	..	..
n	f_n	$1/n$	f_n/n	f_n
Sum			\$	S

mean sibship size = S / \$

The same principle extends to sibships of any larger size by generalizing the correction factor $1/\binom{n}{1}$ as $1/\binom{n}{m}$ where m is the number of members by which the sibship is ascertained. For m=2 we write:

0	..	..	..	..
1	..	..	..	..
2	f_2	1	f_2	$2f_2$
3	f_3	1/3	$f_3/3$	f_3
4	f_4	1/6	$f_4/6$	$2f_4/3$
..	..	..	..	..
n	f_n	$2/[n(n-1)]$	$2f_n/[n(n-1)]$	$2nf_n/[n(n-1)]$
Sum			\$	S

$$\$ = \overset{n}{\underset{2}{\Sigma}}(2f_n/[n(n-1)]) \qquad S = \overset{n}{\underset{2}{\Sigma}}(2f_n/[n-1])$$

mean sibship size for families of 2 and over = S / \$

Appendix D

Contents of the MS Volume

This is a MS volume deposited in the library of the Institute of Criminology at Cambridge.

Appendix E

Lady Wootton's Critical Survey

In the era covered by our review of the literature, the outstanding critical contribution was the important work *Social Science and Social Pathology* (1959) by Barbara Wootton, later Lady Wootton of Abinger. It is a pity that a book written with such scholarship and penetration, which must have had great influence among social scientists, at least those who are concerned with crime and delinquency, was informed by an attitude so generally and so severely critical. Under Lady Wootton's energetic hand a great deal of bathwater has gone down the drain; but we fear that a few babies have been lost as well. The comments on her work which are made in this appendix are intended to do only what we feel to be some of the more necessary rescue work.

Lady Wootton considers twelve criminological hypotheses, and discusses them on the basis of the evidence provided by 21 studies, selected on the basis that each deals with at least 200 subjects, contains data on nearly half the hypotheses under review, and contains an adequate account of the findings and the methods used. The presentation of the evidence will not be repeated here, but we will briefly outline the position Lady Wootton takes after her judicial summing up.

1. Size of Family. In England delinquents were found, with some consistency, to come from families that were larger than the average. The American evidence on the whole points the same way. The Swedish study showed two delinquent groups were drawn from families with more children than the general population average.

2. Criminality in the family. There is general agreement that the presence of one offender in the family increases the probability of the appearance of another. American and Swedish findings are consistent with the British ones. Attention is drawn to the very wide variation in the figures from one study to another.

3. Club Membership. Any effect of club membership in diminishing the risk of delinquency is so slight as to be insignificant.

4. Church Attendance. The evidence is scanty, but supports the view that regular church attendance or church membership is relatively uncommon among offenders.

5. Employment Record. All the investigators, British or American, who have gone into the matter, agree that delinquents tend to be characterized by poor work records.

6. Social Status. The 'unsurprising conclusion' is reached that delinquents are predominantly drawn from the lowest social classes; but we are not able to say whether there is any deviation from the similar predominance in the general population.

7. Poverty. British evidence does not wholly support the view (Bagot, 1941) that poverty is one of the strongest forces involved. American evidence is even less conclusive. On the whole the view is supported that poverty plays a part in delinquency, but the evidence is not satisfactory.

8. Mother's Employment outside the Home. The results here are diverse and inconclusive.

9. Truancy from School. There is fairly general agreement that truants are more than averagely likely to be also delinquents. There are, however, the widest variations in the closeness of the association; and if British educational authorities are right in their optimistic estimates of the extent of truancy, then the great majority of delinquents cannot also be truants.

10. The Broken Home. The belief that delinquency is associated with a 'broken home' is one of the most generally accepted; yet the evidence on which it is based is particularly difficult to assess. This depends on the lack of a precise definition of what constitutes a broken home, and by lack of information about the frequency with which homes have been broken, at any given age of the child, in the general population.

11. Physical Health. It is shown that in the more recent and better controlled studies, differences between the health records of delinquents and non-delinquents have not proved significant.

12. Educational Achievement. There is fairly general agreement that delinquents tend to have poor school records; but this is to be to some extent discounted by the consideration that the evidence is based on the assessments of school-masters, and therefore possibly biased. Delinquents are likely to be unpopular with their teachers.

Lady Wootton devotes a chapter to a discussion of theories of the effects of maternal separation or deprivation. Her criticism of the work that has been done in this field is penetrating and cogent. The more specifically such theories are formulated, the more inconclusive is the evidence for them. 'That the damage is life-long or irreversible, that maternal deprivation is a major factor in criminal behaviour, or that the younger the child the greater the risk, all these must be regarded as quite unproven hypotheses.' With this view the uncommitted reader is forced to agree. However, Lady Wootton accepts the truism that children deprived of affectionate care suffer according to their temperaments and circumstances. If they do suffer, the psychiatrist would say that they could hardly be expected to show the effects of suffering anywhere more prominently than in neurotic symptoms and behaviour disorders. One is, therefore, led to pursue enquiries in this direction, even if the information so far collected is no more than suggestive.

In the succeeding chapter there is an analysis of the evidence relating criminal behaviour with the age of the offender, and a critical examination of the concept of 'immaturity', as an explanatory hypothesis. The maturation theory is reduced to nothing more than a tautology, a restatement of the known facts, i.e. the sharp rise in the risk of delinquency at adolescence and its subsequent tailing off, and the fact that a minority of young criminals become recidivists while the majority do not. In this part of her work of demolition, Lady Wootton does not appear to be thinking along biological lines. Maturation is a phenomenon which shows itself in a number of different aspects of development, e.g. sexual, skeletal, psychological, electro-physiological, etc. The maturation hypothesis is really a working hypothesis, which calls for the investigation of individuals in the course of their development through the main period of risk of delinquency. The actual occurrence of delinquent behaviour might be found to be associated with some particular developmental age, independent of chronological age, or with disparities of development, or with relative retardation in some particular developmental aspect. However, it is natural to take up a sceptical attitude towards the maturation hypothesis, when little or none of its practical applications have been followed up.

When Lady Wootton comes to consider the practical conclusions that can be drawn from her review, she makes it clear that individualistic studies of delinquents have been rather overdone, and that social factors, e.g. faults and deficiencies in our social institutions, have been relatively neglected. It would seem to the present writers that there are good reasons why this should be so; and that Lady Wootton is to some extent insufficiently appreciative of the positive findings which have emerged from the individualistic approach. It is perhaps inappropriate for us, who are not sociologists, to comment on the progress of sociological research in this field; but it might be that sociological theories of the causation of delinquency are difficult to formulate in a way that leads to precise predictions which can then be tested. There are few who have any serious doubt of the reality of 'subcultural delinquency', of the perversion of standards of behaviour which may occur in delimited subgroups of the general population, and of the formation of delinquent gangs. If we are to put down such phenomena to deficiencies in our social institutions, it would be helpful to be provided with some hints about which of our institutions are at fault, and in what way. Thus it seems probable that among the children of certain occupational groups, among those living in certain areas of large towns, among those living in particular streets in a working-class neighbourhood, among those attending particular schools, the risk of delinquency is many times that which obtains for the generality of youngsters of the same age living in comparable circumstances. But no one seems to have elicited any common factor by which these endangered occupations, areas, streets and schools distinguish themselves. One might even say that the best known of all social institutions, whose deficiencies greatly increase the risk of delinquency, is that of the individual family; and that the importance of family life has been established mainly by work along individualistic lines.

In her discussion of twelve criminological theories, Lady Wootton concludes (p. 134) pessimistically that, despite the methodological merits of the works she has reviewed, only the most meagre and dubiously supported generalizations emerge.

> On the whole, it seems that offenders come from relatively large families. Not infrequently (according to some investigators very frequently) other members of the delinquents' (variously defined) families have also been in trouble with the law. Offenders are unlikely to be regular church-goers, but the evidence as to whether club membership discourages delinquency is 'wildly contradictory'. If they are of age to be employed, they are likely to be classified as 'poor' rather than 'good' workers. Most of them come from the lower social classes, but again the evidence as to the extent to which they can be described as exceptionally poor is conflicting; nor is there any clear indication that their delinquency is associated with the employment of their mothers outside the home. Their health is probably no worse than that of other people, but many of them have earned poor reputations at school, though these may well be prejudiced by their teachers' knowledge of their delinquencies. In their schooldays they are quite likely to have truanted from school, and perhaps an unusually large proportion of them come from homes in which at some (frequently unspecified) time both parents were not, for whatever reason, living together; yet even on these points, the findings of some enquiries are negative. And beyond this we cannot go.

One misses any synthetic approach to the findings which have been reasonably well established, taking account also of those which are not supported by recent work. Thus the significance of severe poverty, and of poor physical health, which were once allotted great importance, now looms very small; any up-to-date theory of the causation of delinquency cannot lay stress on these factors. On the other hand, from Lady Wootton's own analysis, the data on size of family and criminality in the family, both making use of 'hard' data, are well established, and can only be seen as contributing to the causes of delinquency, rather than as resulting from biases arising in the selection of the index cases subjected to investigation. Truancy from school and poor employment record, also found associated with delinquency, would appear more to be symptomatic of the disordered way of life of the delinquent or pre-delinquent, than causative of delinquency. It is not the place here to try to organize the evidence, which has been attempted elsewhere; but we consider that the final picture of the fruit of all individualistic investigations, which Lady Wootton presents, is altogether too cheerless.

Authors' Index

Subject Index

218

DUE